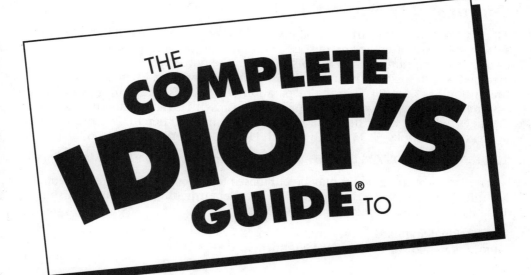

THE COMPLETE IDIOT'S GUIDE® TO

Managing People

by Arthur R. Pell, Ph.D.

alpha books

A Division of Macmillan General Reference
A Simon & Schuster Macmillan Company
1633 Broadway, New York, NY 10019-6785

Macmillan Publishing books may be purchased for business or sales promotional use. For information please write: Special Markets Department, Macmillan Publishing USA, 1633 Broadway, New York, NY 10019-6785.

International Standard Book Number: 0-02-862933-7
Library of Congress Catalog Card Number: 95-080490

01 00   8 7 6 5

Interpretation of the printing code: the rightmost number of the first series of numbers is the year of the book's printing; the rightmost number of the second series of numbers is the number of the book's printing. For example, a printing code of 99-1 shows that the first printing occurred in 1999.

Printed in the United States of America

Note: This publication contains the opinions and ideas of its author. It is intended to provide helpful and informative material on the subject matter covered. It is sold with the understanding that the author and publisher are not engaged in rendering professional services in the book. If the reader requires personal assistance or advice, a competent professional should be consulted.

Alpha Development Team

Publisher
Kathy Nebenhaus

Editorial Director
Gary M. Krebs

Managing Editor
Bob Shuman

Marketing Brand Manager
Felice Primeau

Editor
Jessica Faust

Development Editors
Phil Kitchel
Amy Zavatto

Production Team

Development Editor
Sora Song

Copy Editor
Sandy Doell

Production Editor
Kristi Hart

Cover Designer
Mike Freeland

Photo Editor
Richard H. Fox

Illustrator
Jody P. Schaeffer

Designer
Nathan Clement

Indexer
Cheryl Jackson

Layout/Proofreading
Angela Calvert
Mary Hunt
Julie Trippetti

Contents at a Glance

The Complete Idiot's Reference Card

tear here

Six Tricks for Better Listening

➤ **Eliminate distractions.** If you know that you'll be having a lengthy discussion at your desk, arrange for someone else to handle your calls or set your voice mail to pick up all calls. Or go to a conference room—the phone there won't distract you.

➤ **Get rid of excess paper.** If your desk is strewn with paper, you probably sit there and let your eyes skim your papers until you realize that you're reading a letter or memo instead of listening. Get rid of those papers.

➤ **Don't get too comfortable.** Rather than take a relaxed position when you're in a discussion, sit at the edge of your chair and lean forward rather than backward. This position not only brings you physically closer to the other person, but also enables you to be more attentive and to maintain eye contact.

➤ **Be an active listener.** Ask questions about what's being said. Paraphrase or ask specific questions about key points.

➤ **Be an empathetic listener.** Listen with your heart as well as with your head. Empathetic listeners not only listen to what other people say but also try to feel what other people are feeling when they say it. In other words, you put yourself in the speaker's shoes.

➤ **Take notes.** Jot down key words or phrases. Write down figures or important facts—just enough to remind you of the principal points that were made. Immediately after a meeting, while the information is still fresh in your mind, write a detailed summary. Dictate it into a recorder, type it into your computer, or enter it in your notebook—whichever is best for you.

Eight Tips for Making Training Meetings More Productive

➤ **Treat team members as knowledgeable people, not as schoolchildren.** Team members are adults who are willing to learn.

➤ **Avoid lecturing.** A lecture is deadly. Make the meeting a participatory experience for all who attend.

➤ **Don't just repeat what's in the training manual or handouts.** Team members can read it for themselves. You're there to expand, clarify, and elucidate.

➤ **Prepare for each session.** You should know 10 times more about the subject than you present at the meeting.

➤ **Keep the sessions short.** Keep them short, but not so short that the material can't be adequately covered.

➤ **Use drama and a sense of humor.** Use your imagination to keep attendees awake, alert, and excited about what they're learning.

➤ **Use visual aids.** Use appropriate materials to augment what is spoken.

➤ **Set aside the last five minutes of each session for a summary.** Be sure to clear up any misunderstandings made obvious by participants' questions and comments. If a class lasts more than a day, spend 10 or 15 minutes summarizing the preceding day's discussion.

Three Tips to Ensure that an Applicant Tells You What You Need to Know

➤ **Use silence.** After an applicant has answered your question, wait five seconds before asking your next question. You'll be amazed at how many people add new information—positive or negative—to their original response.

➤ **Make nondirective comments.** Ask open-ended questions, such as "Tell me about your computer background." An applicant will tell you whatever he or she feels is an appropriate response. Rather than comment on the answer, respond with "Uh-huh" or "Yes" or just nod. This technique encourages applicants to continue talking without giving any hints about what you are seeking to learn. This approach often results in obtaining information about problems, personality factors, attitudes, or weaknesses that might not have been uncovered by direct questions. On the other hand, it can also bring out additional positive factors and strengths.

➤ **Ask probing questions.** Sometimes applicants can be vague or evasive in answering questions. Probe for more detail.

alpha
books

Ten Keys to Really Motivating Team Members

1. Know each team member's abilities and give him or her assignments based on these abilities.
2. Give clear directions that are easily understood and accepted.
3. Allow team members to make decisions related to their jobs.
4. Be accessible. Listen actively and empathetically.
5. Give credit and praise for a job well done.
6. Treat team members fairly, and with respect and consideration.
7. Show interest and concern for each person as an individual.
8. Make each person an integral member of the team.
9. Keep team members challenged and excited by their work.
10. Support team members in their efforts to perform superbly.

Guidelines for Effective Reprimanding

➤ Reprimand as soon as possible after the offense was committed.

➤ Don't reprimand when you are angry. Calm down first.

➤ Emphasize the what—not the who.

➤ Begin by stating the problem—then ask a question about it.

➤ Listen! Be Attentive. Be open-minded. Get the whole story.
Ask questions to clarify issues.

➤ Encourage the team member to suggest solutions.

➤ If pertinent, suggest what you and the rest of the team can do to help solve the problem.

➤ Establish a plan of action as to what will be done to resolve the issue.

➤ End on a positive note. Reassure the team member that you consider him or her a valuable member of the team.

Five Elements of Good Delegation

➤ **Be sure that the person you choose for the assignment is capable of doing the work.** You know the abilities of each of your team members. When you plan assignments, take into consideration which person can do a job most effectively.

➤ **Make sure that your instructions are not only understood but also accepted.** Asking the question "Do you understand?" is meaningless. Instead, ask "What are you going to do?" If a team member's response indicates that one or more of your points isn't clear, you can correct it before he or she does something wrong.

➤ **Set control points.** A control point is a key area in a project where you stop, examine what has been completed, and, if errors have been made, correct them. In this way, you can catch errors before they blow up into catastrophes.

➤ **Give your associate the tools and authority to get the job done.** You can't do a job without the proper tools or the authority to do what needs to be done. Providing resources is obvious, but giving authority is another story. If you want a job to be done without having to micromanage it, you must give the person who is doing the job the power to make decisions.

➤ **When you delegate, don't abdicate.** Staff members have questions, seek advice, and need your help. Be there for them, but don't let them throw the entire project back at you. Let them know that you're available to help, to advise, and to support, but not to do their work.

Contents

9 Training Tools and Techniques **103**

10 When Do You Graduate? You Don't! **119**

Part 4: Choosing Team Members   165

13   Creating Realistic Job Specs   167

14   Choosing Your New Team Member   177

Foreword

Across the board, managers today are faced with an identity crisis! Whether they're new or have many years of experience, it makes no difference. Managers are having great difficulty keeping pace with the needs of today's workforce and at the same time remaining true to themselves. In an environment where the term "going postal" is part of the vernacular, there's great confusion as to what their role should be.

The question is this: What is the most effective role for managers today? Is it to enhance productivity and get the job done? Is it to serve as leader, coach, counselor, facilitator, supervisor, mentor, or team leader? Or, is it a combination of all of the above? And, if so, how do they execute this most difficult assignment with a workforce that's been weaned on self-expression and loose discipline? I believe the answers are right here in Dr. Arthur R. Pell's *The Complete Idiot's Guide to Managing People*, Second Edition.

The ever-changing workplace unfortunately has become a management minefield, baited with complex employment laws and issues. EEO, OSHA, ADA, The Family Leave Act, diversity, team management, and unions are just a few of the obstacles a manager must navigate around. New issues constantly appear on the horizon, and the media is filled with accounts of multi-million dollar settlements in discrimination and harassment suits. The underlying fear among managers is that they will lose their jobs because of false accusations.

In addition, managers are faced with the burden of handling workplace productivity. When productivity is hampered, everyone loses—managers, employees, and the company alike.

Managing people may seem overwhelming, but it's not hopeless. Never before has the phrase "knowledge is power" been truer than in the managing game. Needless to say, outdated dictatorial management techniques are obsolete. If you don't believe it, just try it. The new workforce is comprised of bright, energetic, "what-can-you-do-for-me" people. So, read this book and gain the knowledge you'll need to coach, lead, and/or mentor to get your people to be all they can be. Remember, their success is your success.

Sometimes egos need to be left behind in order to respect differences. Whether it's race, gender, nationality, ideas, or approaches, they need to meld in order for you to lead your team to success. You might need to subordinate your methodology for the higher purpose, or give credit to someone else when maybe you feel it should be yours. As Dr. Pell states in this book, "You can't do it all yourself."

Dr. Pell's commonsense approach makes everyone a winner.

In this book, he'll show you how to select people who complement your weaknesses, and he'll teach you to earn respect by your knowledge and your sense of fairness. In the process, you can still tread lightly and carry a big stick.

Managing today is a tall order, but it is made a great deal easier through this complete step-by-step *Complete Idiot's Guide*. Read this book ASAP and implement the techniques that Dr. Pell clearly describes. The results will be a first-string team of stars—and you'll even learn how to get your second-string players to perform to their full potential. Good luck and, above all, have fun!

—Rosemary Maniscalco

Rosemary Maniscalco is president and chief operating officer of COMFORCE/Uniforce Staffing Services. She is a nationally recognized expert on employment and workplace trends and issues, as well as co-author of *Workstyles to Fit Your Lifestyle* (Prentice Hall, 1993).

Introduction

You've read books about management. You've taken seminars, courses, and workshops in your own company and at colleges and universities. You've attended countless meetings at professional and trade associations—all providing tips and techniques for managing people. So why another book?

The world is changing, and management changes with it. Whether you're starting your first assignment as a team leader or have years of experience, you have to keep up with these changes. Ideas that weren't even dreams a few years ago are now part and parcel of the corporate culture. You pick up a business magazine and every other article mentions such terms as "project management," "self-directed teams," "empowerment," and "total quality management." Of course, you know what they mean, but how do they affect the way you manage?

In *The Complete Idiot's Guide to Managing People,* I'll talk about these concepts and much more. I'll not only describe them but also provide suggestions and examples of how you can apply them in the day-to-day situations you face on the job.

Part 1, "What's the Fun in Being a Boss if You Can't Boss Anybody Around?" explores how the team concept enables you to take advantage of the skills, brains, and creativity of every person on your team. This part looks at the myths and misconceptions that have often dictated management style. Then it gets right into the pragmatic approaches to setting goals and developing channels of communication so that you can make sure that your ideas and instructions are understood and accepted by your team members. You'll also learn equally important techniques to encourage team members to contribute ideas and suggestions about every aspect of the work they do.

In **Part 2, "The Supervisor As Coach,"** you'll learn how to develop your team for optimum performance. You'll learn about not only the techniques of training and development but also how to get the most from your training buck.

The ramifications of the equal employment opportunity (EEO) laws are discussed in **Part 3, "Understanding and Complying with the Equal Employment Laws."** It presents a list of pre-employment questions you can and cannot ask. This part of the book pays special attention to the latest developments in this area, including the Americans with Disabilities Act, how to avoid sexual harassment complaints, and the role of the team leader in affirmative action.

Part 4, "Putting Together a Winning Team," discusses the important issue of choosing team members who can not only do the job but also fit in as part of your team. Also covered is how to write realistic job specs, pricing the job, and locating hard-to-find personnel.

The focus in **Part 5, "Motivating Your Team for Peak Performance,"** is on methods of motivating your team members. Some of the issues covered in this part are money (does it really motivate?), incentive pay programs, recognition programs that work, how to motivate people when they have the opportunity for advancement, and what "empowerment" is all about.

Part 6, "Dealing with Employee Problems on the Job," covers the day-to-day problems that leaders face on the job, including dealing with poor performance, stress and burnout, overly sensitive people, and alcohol and drug addiction. You'll learn how to counsel employees and when and how to refer them to professionals for help. This part also discusses how to manage people who don't work on-site, such as telecommuters and subcontractors, and how to work with self-directed teams.

Traditional and nontraditional methods of discipline, up to and including termination, are explored in **Part 7, "Doling Out Discipline."** This part also explores voluntary quits and reducing turnover. This part pays special attention to layoffs and downsizing, including a discussion of the WARN law and the concept of "employment at will."

How to Make This Book Work for You

Reading a book like this one can be interesting, enlightening, and amusing. I hope that this book will be all these things to you. More important, it should provide you with ideas you can use on the job. You'll find lots of these ideas in the following pages.

But it will all be a waste of your money, time, and energy, however, if you don't take what you read and put it into effect in the way you perform your day-to-day managerial functions.

Following these five steps should ensure that this book isn't just a reading exercise but also a plan of action for you:

1. At the end of the first chapter is a section that explains how to create an action plan to implement what you've learned. Create this type of action plan after you read each chapter. Indicate what action you will take, with whom you will take the action, and when you will begin.

2. Share your plan of action with your associates. Get them involved.

3. Set a follow-up date to check whether you did what you planned to do.

4. If not, reread the chapter, rethink what you did or didn't do, and make a new plan of action.

5. Do it, review it, renew it.

Extras

To add to the material in the main text of the book, a series of shaded boxes throughout the book highlight specific items that can help you understand and implement the material in each chapter:.

Manager's Minute

These provide you with practical instructions for enhancing your management expertise.

Secret Weapons

These tips and techniques will help you implement some of the ideas you pick up in the book. Some of them come from the writings of management gurus, and others come from the experience of managers like you, who are happy to share them.

Meanings & Gleanings

You may have a good idea of what most of these new expressions mean, but you don't have to guess about their meanings and implications. These definitions will put you in the know so that you won't have to bluff your way through when your boss throws these terms at you.

Communication Breakdown

Learn from these common mistakes made by managers and save yourself time, money, energy, and embarrassment.

Special Thanks

The Complete Idiot's Guide to Managing People was reviewed by an expert in the field who not only checked the technical accuracy of what you'll learn here but also provided insight and guidance to help us ensure that this book gives you everything you need to know to make the most of your management role. The publisher's special thanks are extended to:

Ronald B. Smith, who has had three books published and who has more than 25 years' experience in developing business computer systems on mainframes and on client/server systems for major corporations. He is the president of the Greenspoint Area Toastmasters Club in Houston, Texas. In addition to writing, he enjoys reading, teaching, and racquetball.

Part 1

What's the Fun in Being a Boss If You Can't Boss Anybody Around?

The old boss, whose motto was "Do it my way or you're on the highway," has been supplanted by the facilitator who develops and coordinates an intelligent, motivated team to get things done. Being a manager still can be fun—even more fun! There's real joy in observing each member of your team growing, watching the synergy that develops between them, and sharing their accomplishments with them.

You can learn to mold a team and help your team members become creative, contributing, collaborative colleagues. To do this, stop thinking like a "boss." Bosses make decisions and give orders. Today's managers coordinate groups of thinking adults who together face and work out problems. Today's managers provide a climate in which their team members are encouraged to make their own analyses of problems, suggest solutions, and participate in decisions.

In this part of the book, you'll see how to begin making this concept work for you.

Managing Ain't What It Used to Be

In This Chapter

➤ Understanding the changing face of management

➤ Evaluating your management style

➤ Learning to be a leader, not a boss

➤ Overcoming the challenges of downsizing

➤ Working with Gen X'ers

➤ Developing productive teams

Management is changing. But management, like all other aspects of life, is *always* in a state of flux. Nothing stays the same. Then why is the changing of management so important now?

Speed! That's why. Things are changing so fast that it's easy to fall behind. This chapter looks at some of the changes that have taken place in the management of people and how they've affected the way leaders lead—and the way people follow. You'll see how these changes affect you and how you can integrate them into your own management style.

Sound daunting? It really isn't. I've done it, I've helped my clients do it, and during the past few years, progressive managers in many companies have done it.

Chapter 1

The first thing you have to do is examine your current management style (the quiz in this chapter will help you). Then I'll show you step-by-step how to make the changes that will enable you to excite and motivate your team more effectively.

Am I Ready to Face the 21st Century?

The world of work has changed radically during the past decade, and it continues to change faster than it has since the Industrial Revolution. Now, in the computer age, managers have immediate and continuous access to new information, revolutionizing their decision-making. New managers today are faced with a culture bearing little resemblance to that of generations past.

Secret Weapons

Don't be afraid to try new approaches. The management climate is changing. To keep up and to make progress, you have to take risks. Go out on a limb. That's where the fruit is.

Gone is the old hierarchical structure. It used to be that top management made all the decisions and filtered them down through a series of layers to the rank-and-file workers. Today things are more collaborative. People at all levels are expected to contribute to every aspect of their organization's activities.

Many of those intermediate organizational layers—or middle management—have also been eliminated. More and more, the responsibility to get things done is assumed by teams—teams that consist of team leaders and team members who plan, implement, and control the work together.

Hey! What's All This Change About?

Companies are rapidly retooling the processes by which they operate. Old philosophies are being replaced with approaches that take advantage of new technologies and modern managerial thinking. I've outlined some of these approaches below:

➤ **Flatten the organizational structure.** Eliminating superfluous layers of management unclogs the channels through which orders and information flow.

Meanings & Gleanings

A *team* is a group of people who collaborate and interact synergistically to reach a common goal.

➤ **Encourage participatory decision-making.** Employees at all levels now collaborate to plan the work—which includes scheduling production, ensuring quality, and establishing standards of performance—and get it done. When team members participate, they are more committed to its accomplishment.

➤ **Use teams to get the work done.** The team leader has replaced the "boss." The team is a collaborative group, not just people taking orders and carrying them out.

➤ **Implement total project management.** Under this concept, a manager supervises an entire project from start to finish. To do so, the manager coordinates with departments other than his own and over which he has no direct authority.

➤ **Outsource rather than employ.** To save money, a company will subcontract various phases of a job to other firms. This means that the company's own teams might have to coordinate their work with the work of several different outside firms.

➤ **Adopt just-in-time delivery.** Rather than store large inventories of supplies or finished products, companies today arrange to have them delivered as needed. A project manager or team leader coordinates with suppliers to schedule and ensure deliveries.

➤ **Re-engineer.** Re-engineering involves the radical restructuring of business processes, not just tinkering with isolated methods and procedures. When a company re-engineers, its managers have to rethink every aspect of their jobs in order to incorporate the changes.

Manager's Minute

The first management consultant in recorded history was Jethro, the father-in-law of Moses. When Jethro saw how overworked Moses was, he advised him to establish a management hierarchy: to choose leaders "to be rulers of thousands, and rulers of hundreds, rulers of fifties and rulers of tens." (Exodus: 18:21)

How Do These Organizational Changes Affect Me?

If you have management responsibilities or are preparing for a promotion, you have to meet the changing requirements of your job as the style and process of management evolve.

Now is the time to examine the way you currently manage people and the ways in which you'd like to be a better manager, and to learn what effective managers are doing to become even more effective.

As you read this book, you'll learn how to better deal with the day-to-day problems of managing people, and you'll learn that *you can't do it alone*. To achieve success, you must utilize the talents of all members of your group. Beyond that, you must also take advantage of the brainpower and expertise of everyone involved—your own team members as well as the other people (within your company and from different firms) with whom you're collaborating.

Taking an Eagle-Eye Look at Management Style

You've been managing people for years and you think you've got your department running like a well-oiled piece of machinery when your boss says you aren't meeting the company's goals. "Get up-to-date or get out," he warns. You think, "I'm doing okay—the *boss* is being unreasonable."

Or you've just been promoted to your first supervisory job. The boss congratulates you, shakes your hand, and says "Take over." No training, no advice—just "take over." What about some training?

Or maybe the people who report directly to you are giving you a hard time. No matter how you try to get them to work harder, meet deadlines, or comply with quality standards, they continue to do just enough to keep from getting fired.

Stop blaming others. Look to yourself. Are you managing like a 19th-century autocrat or like a 21st-century leader?

Sure, you're entitled to your opinions, but you should keep an open mind. You want to do a better job—that's why you're reading this book. Use the quiz later in this chapter to take inventory of how you manage now. Then take a look at how your approach to management compares to what management gurus consider the "right way."

Don't Dictate—Facilitate

In today's corporate environment, people don't respond well to authoritative styles. Most people work best with a manager who treats them as adults, encourages them to make suggestions about their work, and listens to their ideas even when those ideas may conflict with the manager's own. Truly successful managers are those who encourage people to contribute rather than take orders; they obtain the *willing cooperation* of all involved.

Team Members—Your Not-So-Secret Treasure

How do you get people to cooperate willingly? Use the team approach.

And what is a team? Most people would define a team as a group of people working to achieve a common goal. But that's only half the answer. A key word must be added to this definition: A team is a group of people working *synergistically* to achieve a common goal. When people work together collaboratively, as a team, each team member benefits from the knowledge, work, and support of the others. A synergistic effort is much more productive than a mass of isolated individual efforts.

Consider the rocket ship as a good example of synergistic working. In order for the ship to function, each of its stages, or components, must be in tip-top condition. But even if all the components are in A-1 shape, the rocket won't get off the launching pad until every component works together interactively, or synergistically.

You are the rocket engineer; your team members are the components. If you want your project to lift off and reach success, you must ensure that your team members work at optimum capacity individually and, then, that they all work together synergistically.

Meanings & Gleanings

When a team has *synergy*, its whole is greater than the sum of its parts. That is, two plus two may equal more than four.

Molding Your Ragtag Group into a Team

Molding a group of people into a team involves more than changing each person's title from "employee" to "associate" or "team member." Your own attitude is the key to success. Act as a facilitator (as a coordinator or leader) rather than a boss and your staff members will begin to feel like—then act like—team members.

Teams don't happen by magic. Building your team requires careful planning. Start by clearly explaining the following factors to your team members:

➤ How they are expected to work.

➤ How this new method of operation differs from what they are used to.

➤ Where they can go for help.

➤ How the new team approach works.

Be wary of giving mere lip service to the team approach. You must "walk the talk." For example, change your way of dealing with problems. Rather than making decisions arbitrarily, encourage your team members to come up with their own solutions and implement them. You should guide and facilitate, not direct, the work of your team. The participation of all team members is the key to success (see Chapter 14).

Secret Weapons

Although you may be accustomed to handling many day-to-day details yourself, you should start delegating as many tasks as you can. You can't do it all by yourself, and you shouldn't have to. Help your team members develop their skills, then give them the ball and let them run with it.

When the Company Downsizes

Over the past several years, downsizing—reducing the work force—has become a way of life for many large organizations. Often, the first round of downsizing is followed by subsequent rounds. It is reported that two-thirds of firms that cut jobs in a given year will do it again the next year.

This poses a big problem for managers who have to maintain the morale and productivity of the survivors.

How do these survivors feel?

Lucky that they still have a job? Sure, for the moment.

Guilty because their co-workers were cut and they weren't? Quite often.

Loyal to the company? Not a chance. Downsizing erodes any sense of loyalty.

Downsizing is usually accompanied by salary freezes for the survivors (the company figures they're lucky enough to still have their jobs). Many people who survive the downsizing are forced to accept lower-ranking positions, which, of course, reduces their salaries, their status, and their power. And for those who get to keep their positions, their opportunity for advancement is stifled.

And that's just the beginning. After the downsizing, employees have to work harder and pick up the slack for those who were laid-off. Not only that, the colleagues who once facilitated their work are no longer there to help. Worse, teams can fall apart—some of the team members, whose collaboration was key to success, are gone.

Challenges to Managers

What can you do as a manager when your company downsizes your department?

1. Once the downsized people have left the company, bring the rest of your team together and have an open discussion about the situation. Let them express their concerns. You may not be able to assure them that the worst is over or that their jobs are safe, but point out that everyone must work together to make the most of the situation.

2. Elicit ideas on how to restructure the work most effectively and have the team create a plan to re-delegate duties.

3. Meet with team members individually to deal with personal concerns.

4. Determine what additional training is needed to cover the work once done by the laid-off members. Arrange for such training internally or with tuition-reimbursed outside programs.

5. Encourage team members to learn skills that might be needed in the future (e.g., computer skills, foreign languages, and so forth).

6. Once the dust has settled, boost morale by attending to each person's concerns, rebuilding team spirit, and recognizing accomplishments.

Manager's Minute

"Companies that downsize through buyouts and attrition—that help the workers get new jobs—have a better chance of retaining the loyalty of the surviving workers."—Robert Reich

Working with Generation X'ers

Working with the so-called Generation X is a new challenge to managers. Many older people look upon 20- to 30-year-olds as the MTV generation: They were raised on Nintendo and rock videos, never did anything without being plugged into their Walkmans, and have short attention spans. They see the world differently than their parents, their school teachers, and, of course, their bosses on the job.

Sure, many of these "kids" jump from one interest to another, but there's an upside to this phenomenon. These young people have trained their minds—perhaps inadvertently—to operate on many tracks at once. That's a worthy skill on the job. A young computer artist creates fantastic graphics while simultaneously listening to music and chatting with co-workers. Or a young banker handles multiple phone conversations with clients while responding to e-mail or working out complex computer tasks.

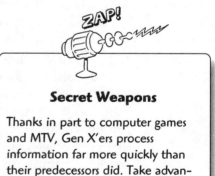

Managers should embrace these Gen X'ers. By taking advantage of their assets, managers will find them valuable employees.

Here are 10 suggestions on how to manage Gen X'ers.* These tips will help you become a better manager not only to Gen X'ers, but to all your employees.

Secret Weapons

Thanks in part to computer games and MTV, Gen X'ers process information far more quickly than their predecessors did. Take advantage of their agile minds when assigning them work.

1. Accept them. Learn to work with them rather than against them. As with any employee, a show of dislike creates only conflict and unnecessary turnover.

*Adapted with permission to use from "Generation X'ers—What They Think, What They Do" by Bob Loszyk, Public Management (PM), Dec. 1997, published by the International City/ County Management Association (ICMA), Washington, DC.

2. Use love and caring. Gen X'ers are smart, and they know that talk is cheap. A key in motivating them is to show your care and appreciation of them. But be sincere: They will immediately recognize and disdain anything that smacks of phoniness.

3. Support them outside work. In many ways, this is a trying time for young people. Show your support of them in difficult personal situations. Often, people don't have anyone who will listen, and they appreciate and reward those who do.

4. Don't baby them. Gen X'ers want guidance, but they, like all ambitious employees, also want to be independent self-starters. Still, encouragement and praise are important. Prove yourself to be a trusting, but caring and attentive manager.

5. Stay "hands off," but be there. Give them freedom and independence. Don't micro-manage. Empower them to make decisions, but let them know how far they can go before consulting you. Set goals with them and let them create a plan to attain the goals. X'ers enjoy creating, analyzing, and solving. They crave stimulation, so challenge them continuously to keep them from getting bored.

6. Ask. Ask. Ask. Manage by asking questions. Rule #1: Don't ask unless you have time to listen to their answers. Rule #2: Don't ask unless you are willing to implement the changes based on their answers.

   Asking X'ers lots of questions and implementing solutions based on their answers does three things: First, it shows you value and respect their opinions; second, it involves them in the decision-making; third, it builds loyalty and commitment.

7. Discuss your methods. Explain to them how you like to manage, communicate with, and evaluate people. By discussing your methods ahead of time, you can also gain a lot of insight about them. Find out exactly what they liked or disliked about the way they were treated by previous managers.

8. Train and orient. Meet with X'ers often—even daily. You must know if they are having problems and where they need help—and if they are happy with their jobs. Training is a key motivator. They see it as a way to learn new skills and behaviors that make them more marketable. X'ers have a strong desire to acquire cutting-edge technologies that will increase their worth. Probe the areas in which they need development and discuss their career plans. Target training and develop mentoring programs that relate to those areas. This will increase their loyalty.

9. Set specific standards. Write out the exact standards of behavior, responsibility, and policy you expect them to uphold. Contrary to popular opinion, this generation is not irresponsible. Rather, they're simply new to the workplace and to their particular responsibilities in it. They'll get things done, but must know the task at hand. Some X'ers might use this as a testing period to see what they can get away with. Don't overreact.

10. Make work fun. Make the workplace as much fun as possible. Have sales contests, games, or social events.

Test Your Managerial Skills

Okay, you agree that the role of the manager has changed. "Enough of this theory," you say—you want to learn the actual techniques that will help you meet your goals and the goals of your team. That's what this book is about. But before we get down to the tools of the trade, you'll have to take stock of your current style of management.

The following inventory will help you assess your managerial style. Read each statement, decide whether you agree or disagree with it, and check the appropriate box on the right. Then compare your responses to the answers that follow.

		Agree	Disagree
1.	It's unnecessary for a manager to discuss long-range goals with team-member subordinates. As long as team members are aware of the immediate objective, they can do their work effectively.	❏	❏
2.	The best way to make a reprimand effective is to belittle an offender in front of co-workers.	❏	❏
3.	Managers appear ignorant and risk losing face if they answer a question with, "I don't know, but I'll find out and let you know."	❏	❏
4.	It pays for managers to spend a great deal of time with a new employee to ensure that training has been effective.	❏	❏
5.	Managers should ask their associates for ideas about work methods.	❏	❏
6.	When disciplining is required, managers should avoid saying or doing anything that may cause resentment.	❏	❏
7.	People work best for tough managers.	❏	❏
8.	It's more important for a team to be composed of members who like their jobs than of people who do their jobs well.	❏	❏
9.	Work gets done most efficiently if managers lay out plans in great detail.	❏	❏
10.	To lead an effective team, managers should keep in mind the feelings, attitudes, and ideas of the team's members.	❏	❏

Okay, you've answered all the questions. Now look at the responses based on the advice of successful managers:

1. Disagree. People who know where they're going—who can see the big picture—are more committed and will work harder to reach those objectives than people who are aware only of immediate goals.

2. Disagree. Flaying a person doesn't solve the problem—it only makes the person feel small in front of co-workers. A good reprimand shouldn't be humiliating. It's best to reprimand in private—*never* in front of others.

3. Disagree. It's better to admit ignorance of a matter than to try to bluff. People respect leaders who accept that they don't know everything.

4. Agree. The most important step in developing the full capabilities of associates is good training on the part of managers. Managers who invest the time to lay a solid foundation in the beginning will reap huge returns: employees who are valuable assets to the organization.

5. Agree. People directly involved with the job can often contribute good ideas toward the solution of problems related to their work.

6. Agree. Resentment creates low morale and often leads to conscious or subconscious sabotage.

7. Disagree. Toughness is not as important as fairness or an inspiring attitude.

8. Disagree. The happiness and satisfaction of team members are important, but they are secondary to getting the job done.

9. Disagree. Psychologists have shown that most people work better when they are given broad project guidelines and can work out the details themselves. But there are some people who work better when tasks are given to them in detail. Good managers recognize the styles in which people work and then adapt to them.

10. Agree. Communication is a two-way street. To manage effectively, it's important to know what team members are thinking and how they feel about their jobs.

Secret Weapons

"By clinging to myths in the face of new realities, we close our minds to new ideas and viewpoints."

—Sen. William Fulbright

There is no passing or failing score for this inventory. Its purpose is to make you think about how you manage people. You may not agree with all the experts' answers, but do pay them some heed. Most of what you find here will be discussed in detail later in this book.

Creating Your Own Plans of Action

Based on what you learn in each of the following chapters, decide what new actions you will take. By the time you've finished reading this book, you should be able to identify two or three new techniques to incorporate into your managerial style. For each technique, spell out these details on paper:

1. Action (What will you do?)
2. Collaborators (With whom will you do it?)
3. Time (When will you start?)

Periodically review your progress toward completing these plans of action.

Do It, Review It, Renew It

As you begin to implement the ideas outlined later, use the phrase "do it, review it, renew it" to help you remember the key steps in planning a task:

> **Do it.** After you've decided what to do, coordinate with your team members and set a time for it to be done.

> **Review it.** Doing it is only the first step. Next, you must review what you've accomplished. What problems did you encounter, and how did you handle them? What did you and your team learn from this action?

> **Renew it.** Fine-tune new approaches and add them to the repertoire of methods and techniques your team will use in facing similar situations later.

Meanings & Gleanings

Members of an organization's *management team* must achieve specific results by effectively using the organization's resources. These include money, computers, materials, equipment, information, and employees.

The Least You Need to Know

➤ The job of the manager has changed. Bossing doesn't work. You have to lead.

➤ Team members respond better to participatory, rather than authoritarian, leadership.

➤ Give your associates the opportunity to use their talents, skills, and brainpower.

➤ A team is more than just a group of people—it's a synergistic, interactive, collaborative family.

➤ Think of yourself as a facilitator. Your job is to make it easy for team members to accomplish their jobs.

➤ If your company undergoes downsizing, work diligently with the survivors to restore morale and upgrade productivity.

➤ Gen X'ers have great talents. Take advantage of them to get the best from these youngsters.

➤ After you read each chapter of this book, develop a plan of action to implement the ideas you want. *Do it,* then *review it,* and, when appropriate, *renew it.*

Chapter 2

"Everything I Know I Learned From My Old Boss—And Boy, Was He Dumb!"

In This Chapter

➤ Dispelling myths and misconceptions about managing people

➤ Overcoming preconceptions

➤ Clearing your mind for positive action

Chapter 1 explored the changing practice of management and the importance of team leaders adapting to these new approaches. But managers' efforts to change are often frustrated by old-style bosses, colleagues, and associates who resist anything new.

What's the cause of this interference? Well, the field of management offers up loads of truisms that aren't true, "facts" that aren't factual, assumptions that aren't challenged, and attitudes based on generations-old folklore.

Myths and misconceptions that have governed people's thinking for years (for lifetimes, in many cases) are tough to overcome. But as a manager you must shatter them if you want to move ahead. This chapter examines some common myths, tells you how they impede progress, and explains how you can put them in perspective.

Managing Like a Professional

Some people are reluctant to take on leadership roles. To do so, they believe, they would have to display certain innate leadership traits—charisma, or that intangible *je ne sais quoi*—that would empower them to influence others.

It's true that some of the world's greatest leaders were born that way—they had that special charm, which enraptured the public. But they're the exception. The majority of successful leaders are ordinary people who have worked hard to get where they are.

People management is easier if you have natural talents, but you can certainly *acquire* the skills necessary to manage and lead people.

Unlike professionals in other industries—physicians, lawyers, psychologists, engineers—who are required to complete advanced study and pass exams for certification, managers learn primarily on the job. Some managers may have special education (for instance, degrees in business administration), but *most are promoted from the ranks and have little or no training in management.*

More successful managers are making an effort to acquire skills through structured courses of study, but most managers still pick up their techniques by observing those of their bosses. The model they follow may be good. Too often, however, new managers are exposed to their bosses' outdated and invalid philosophies.

Meanings & Gleanings

Leadership is an art that can be acquired. You can learn to guide people in a way that commands their respect, confidence, and whole-hearted cooperation. *Charisma* is usually inborn—it's the rare quality some people have that secures for them the devotion of others.

Debunking Myths and Misconceptions

Some of these ideas may have been valid in the past but are no longer; others were never true. Let's look at some of these myths and misconceptions about management.

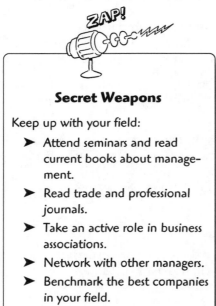

Secret Weapons

Keep up with your field:

➤ Attend seminars and read current books about management.

➤ Read trade and professional journals.

➤ Take an active role in business associations.

➤ Network with other managers.

➤ Benchmark the best companies in your field.

Management = Common Sense

One manager said, "When I was promoted to my first management job, I asked a long-time manager for some tips about how to deal with people who report to me. He told me, 'Just use common sense, and you'll have no trouble.'"

What is "common sense," exactly? What appears sensible to one person may be nonsense to another. Often the definition of common sense is culturally based. In Japan, for example, it's considered common sense to wait for a full consensus before making any decision; in the United States, this technique is often thought inefficient. Culture aside, different people also have their own ideas about what is good or bad, what is efficient or wasteful, what works and what doesn't.

We tend to use our own experiences to develop our particular brands of common sense. The problem is, a person's individual experience provides only limited perspective. To be a real leader, you must look beyond common sense. Books written by management experts abound. Make a practice of reading those books, subscribing to periodicals, and learning from the experiences of men and women who have been successful leaders.

You can learn a lot about the art and science of management by reading industry-related books and periodicals, attending courses and seminars, and actively participating in trade associations in your field.

Managers Know Everything

Managers don't know everything. Nobody does. Accept that you don't have all the answers. But know that you need the skills to get the answers. Get to know people in other companies who have faced similar situations, and you can learn a great deal. This *networking* process gives you access to new information and ideas, and provides you with a valuable source of assistance in solving problems.

Seeking organizations that have been successful in certain areas and learning their techniques is called *benchmarking*. Companies that participate in competitions such as the Malcolm Baldridge Awards (an annual recognition by the U.S. Department of Commerce of firms that demonstrate high quality in their work) must agree to share their techniques with any organization that requests this information. Benchmarking is one of the peripheral benefits of *total-quality management*.

Meanings & Gleanings

Networking means making contacts in other companies to whom you can turn for suggestions, ideas, and problem-solving strategies. Organizations that have achieved success in a certain area are often willing to share their techniques and methods. They provide *benchmarking* that other organizations can emulate.

"It's My Way or the Highway!"

Management by fear is still a common practice. And it works—sometimes. People will work if they fear that they might lose their jobs, but how much work will they do? Just enough to keep from getting fired. That's why this technique isn't considered effective management. Successful management involves getting the *willing* cooperation of your associates.

Moreover, it's not that easy to fire people. Considering the implications of the civil rights laws (see Part 3) and labor unions (see Chapter 25) and in many cases the difficulty and costs associated with

Meanings & Gleanings

One of the fastest-growing phenomena of the past decade is *total-quality management*. In this system, a company focuses entirely on producing high-quality products or services. It involves statistical processes, training in all aspects of quality management, and a commitment from every employee to work continuously toward improvement.

hiring competent replacements, firing people may cause more problems than keeping employees with whom you're not satisfied.

You can't keep good workers for long when you manage by fear. When jobs are scarce in your community or industry, workers might tolerate high-handed arbitrary bosses. But when the job market opens up, the best people will leave for companies with more pleasant working environments. Employee turnover can be expensive and often devastating.

Communication Breakdown

Praise *can* be overdone. If people are repeatedly praised for every trivial accomplishment, the value of praise is diminished to the point of superficiality.

Recently, I was retained by a company to help staff an entire office facility. As we reviewed the incoming resumes, we noticed loads of applications from one particular firm. My immediate assumption was that this other company was shaky and that its employees were seeking more stable employment. But the company was in excellent shape. Applicant after applicant told us that the company's arbitrary management style made their working environment unpleasant. Despite good pay and benefits, they wanted out.

The moral of this story is that you should use positive rather than negative techniques to motivate people (see Part 5).

"Give Them Some Praise and They'll Ask for a Raise"

People need to be praised. Everyone wants to know that his or her good work is appreciated. Yet many managers are reluctant to praise their employees.

Communication Breakdown

Don't promise employees raises or bonuses based on the accomplishment of a specific task. Financial reward should be based on overall performance over time. Promise a raise only if it's part of a compensation or management-by-objective plan that has been formally approved by your superiors, the human resources department, or others in your organization who have the authority to approve compensation changes.

Why? Some managers fear that if they praise a team member's work, that person will become complacent and stop trying to improve (certainly, some people do react this way). The key is to phrase your praise in a way that encourages the team member to continue the good work (see Chapter 16).

Other managers are concerned that if team members are praised for good work, they will expect pay raises or bonuses. And some folks might. But that's no reason to withhold praise when it's warranted. Employees should already know how salary adjustments, bonuses, and other financial rewards are determined. If compensation is renegotiated at annual performance evaluations, team members should be assured that the good work for which they are praised will be considered in the evaluation.

Some managers simply don't believe in praise. One department head told me, "The people I supervise know that they're doing okay if I don't talk to them. If I have to speak to them, they know they're in trouble." Offering no feedback other than reprimands isn't effective either. Remember, you want to use positive, not negative, reinforcement.

"The Best Way to Get People to Work Is a K.I.T.A. (Kick in the You-Know-What)"

Sure, some managers still kick their employees in the rear end—not literally, but verbally. Every year, James Miller, management consultant and author of *The Corporate Coach*, holds a contest for Best and Worst Boss of the Year. The employees do the nominating. Miller reports that nominations for worst boss always outnumber those for best boss. One of the chief reasons employees dislike their bosses, Miller found, is that the bosses use verbal K.I.T.A.s—continually finding fault with subordinates, expressing sarcasm, gloating over failures, and frequent hollering and screaming at employees.

No one really knows why people behave this way. Some people have always been screamed at—by parents, teachers, former bosses—so they think it's an effective communication tool.

We all raise our voices occasionally, especially when we're under stress. Sometimes it takes great self-discipline *not* to yell. Effective leaders, however, control this tendency. An occasional lapse is okay, but when yelling becomes your normal manner of communication, you're admitting your failure to be a real leader. You cannot get the *willing* cooperation of your associates by screaming at them.

The Golden Rule? Try the Platinum Rule

When you manage people, the Biblical rule "Do unto others as you would have others do unto you" is sound advice—to a point. Because people are *not* all alike, treating others as *you* want to be treated is not the same as treating them as *they* want to be treated.

For example, Linda prefers to be given broad objectives and likes to work out the details of her job on her own. But her assistant, Jason, is not comfortable receiving an assignment unless all the details are spelled out for him. If Linda delegates work to her assistant the way she likes to have work assigned to her, she won't get the best results.

Sol needs continuous reinforcement. He's happy on the job only when his boss oversees his work and assures Sol that he's doing a good job. Tanya, however, gets upset if her boss checks her work too

Meanings & Gleanings

When you work with your associates, rather than follow the golden rule, remember the *platinum rule*: Do unto others as they would have you do unto them.

often. "Doesn't she trust me?" she complains. You can't do unto Tanya as you do unto Sol and get good results from each of them.

Each of us has our own style, our own approach, and our own eccentricities. To "do unto others" as we would have them do unto us may be the poorest way of managing people.

To be an effective manager, you must know each member of your team and tailor your method of management to each individual. Rather than follow the golden rule, follow the *platinum* rule: "Do unto others as they would have you do unto them."

Compromises must be made, of course. In some situations, work must be done in a manner that may not be ideal for some people. By knowing ahead of time what needs to be accomplished, you can anticipate problems and prepare team members to accept their tasks.

Production, Performance, and Profit: The Manager's Job

Production, performance, and profit are important aspects of your job as a manager, but are these all you have to consider? Certainly, if a business is to survive, it must produce results. Equally important, however, is the development of its employees' potential. If you ignore people's potential, you limit your team's ability to achieve results. Instead, you reap short-term benefits at the expense of long-term success and even survival.

When Lee founded his computer components company, he was a pioneer in what was then a new and growing industry. Determined to be a leader in his field, he drove his employees to maintain high levels of productivity, always keeping his eye trained on the profit picture. But he paid no attention to the development of his staff. His technical and administrative staff members were given little opportunity to contribute ideas or initiate their own projects. Over the years, Lee's company saw reasonable profits but never grew to become an industry leader as Lee had hoped. Because he had stifled the potential and ambition of his employees, he lost much of his technical staff to other companies. And because he depended only on his own ideas, he missed out on all the innovative ideas his staff might have come up with.

Manager's Minute

Most employees have an exaggerated idea about the profits most companies make. Surveys indicate that people think companies make 20 to 30 percent profits. Truth be told, most companies make closer to a 5 percent profit.

P & L's Are Important, but So Are P & R's

Managers must keep track of their P & L's (profits and losses), but so must they balance their team's *P-factor* (potential of people) and *R-factor* (results desired). If you put too much emphasis on the R, you may attain short-range goals, but long-term goals will suffer. But if you tilt the scale too heavily in favor of the P (for example, if you overemphasize training and development and sacrifice results), your company may not be able to continue to stay in business. The P/R balance is shown in the figure below.

Your overall objective is to obtain superior performance from the entire team. This requires your keeping the P and R factors balanced. When people are given the opportunity to hone their skills, develop their own careers, and branch out in their fields, they are stimulated to work harder and achieve greater results. When they obtain their desired results, they are encouraged to try even harder—this cycle of positive reinforcement brings out people's greatest potential and higher levels of productivity.

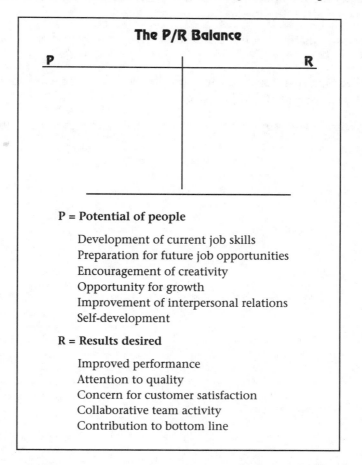

The P/R Balance

P   R

P = Potential of people

Development of current job skills
Preparation for future job opportunities
Encouragement of creativity
Opportunity for growth
Improvement of interpersonal relations
Self-development

R = Results desired

Improved performance
Attention to quality
Concern for customer satisfaction
Collaborative team activity
Contribution to bottom line

The comparison between people's potential and desired results. List potential factors on the left and results factors on the right to see whether they are in balance.

The Least You Need to Know

➤ Leadership abilities aren't necessarily inborn. They can be acquired.

➤ Managers are often influenced by misconceptions and myths about management. Don't assume you have to follow in your old bosses' footsteps.

➤ You should always use common sense when dealing with people. But no individual's experience is broad enough to cover all the bases. Seek out advice on leadership from experts.

➤ Don't rule by fear. Earn the respect of your associates, and they'll knock themselves out to please you.

➤ Praise people for work that's well done. Unrecognized work is like an unwatered plant. Productivity will wither away.

➤ Practice the platinum rule: "Do unto others as *they* would have you do unto them."

➤ Don't get so caught up in tracking profits and losses that you forget to balance your team's potential and performance.

Chapter 3

You Gotta Know Where You're Going and How to Get There

In This Chapter

➤ Setting realistic and attainable goals

➤ Planning for the long haul

➤ Scheduling day-to-day activities

➤ Assembling resources to get the job done

Now that you've cleared away the management myths that have been holding you back, you're ready to take the first steps toward becoming a modern manager. This process begins when you set goals. Like a good navigator, you determine how and when you want to reach those goals.

Some people like to set out on a journey without a map. They want to ride the currents and hope they'll find adventure and fortune—and sometimes they do—but managers can't afford to take those risks. Because managers have responsibilities to their teams, they must know where they want to go, what they want to accomplish, what kinds of problems they may encounter along the way, and how to overcome them.

This chapter helps you begin the process of setting short- and long-term goals and plan how to reach them.

Planting Your Goal Posts

Unless you know exactly what you want to achieve, there's no way to measure how close you are to achieving it. Specific goals give you a standard against which to measure your progress.

Meanings & Gleanings

Goal and *objective* are interchangeable terms that describe the purpose, or long-term results, toward which an organization or individual's endeavors are directed.

The goals you set for your team must be in line with the larger goals your company sets for you. If you don't coordinate the objectives of your job, department, or team with the objectives of your organization, you'll waste your time and energy.

Goals are the foundation of motivational programs. In striving to reach your goals, you become motivated. In knowing the goals of your team members and helping them reach those goals, you help motivate them.

In most organizations, big-picture goals are established by top management and filtered down to departments or teams, who use them as guides in establishing their own goals.

Goals Are More Than Hopes

The process of setting goals takes time, energy, and effort. Goals aren't something you scribble on a napkin during your coffee break. You must plan what you truly want to accomplish, establish timetables, determine who will be responsible for which aspect of the job, and then anticipate and plan a resolution for any obstacle that may threaten to thwart the achievement of your goals.

The suggestions in this section provide a systematic approach to setting goals.

Pipe Dreams or Goals?

Are you ready to set your goals? To prevent your goals from ending up mere pipe dreams, make sure they meet the following three conditions:

Clear and specific. It's not enough to state that your goal is "to improve market share of our product." Be specific: "Market share of our product will increase from its current 12 percent to 20 percent in five years."

Attainable. Pie-in-the-sky goals are self-defeating. If you can see your progress in reaching your goals, you'll have more incentive to continue working than if your goals seem completely unattainable.

Flexible. Sometimes you just can't reach a goal. Circumstances may change: What once seemed viable may no longer be. Don't be frustrated.

Here's a lesson in flexibility: An assistant manager set a goal to become a store manager in two years, but it didn't happen. Rather than quit his job in frustration, he reviewed his situation. He had based his goal on the premise that his company would continue to open 6 to 10 new stores every year. During the preceding year, business had been slow, and only two new outlets were opened. But business improved, and the company seemed likely to renew its expansion. He recognized that quitting would be the wrong solution and that he had to be flexible in the time limits he set for himself.

Secret Weapons

The way to achieve success is first to have a definite, clear, practical ideal—a goal, an objective. Second, have the necessary means to achieve your ends—wisdom, money, materials, methods. Third, adjust all your means to that end."—Aristotle

Changing Goals with Changing Circumstances

All of us set goals based on certain circumstances we anticipate during the life of our project. Circumstances do change, however, and original goals may have to be adjusted. To that end, many companies use a goal-setting program that involves three levels:

A main, or standard, goal: What you plan to accomplish if everything goes well.

Alternative 1: A slightly lower goal. If circumstances change and it becomes obvious that your main goal cannot be achieved, rather than start from scratch in redefining your goal, you can shift to this alternative.

Alternative 2: A higher-level goal. If you're making greater progress than you had originally thought you could, rather than be complacent about being ahead of target, shift to this alternative and accomplish even more.

Take, for example, CSC, a company in the metropolitan Philadelphia area that services and repairs computers. Its sales goal for one year was to open 10 new accounts. But when a national competitor opened a similar service in the same community, all of CSC's energies had to be redirected toward saving its current accounts. The goal for attracting new clients then had to be reduced.

Let's say CSC was having a good year. Its goals could have been accelerated. If CSC had gained eight new clients in the first half of the year, it could have automatically raised its goal to a higher level rather than using the next six months to open only two additional accounts.

Getting the Team to Buy into the Process

At a recent goal-setting seminar, one participant complained, "I have trouble getting people to buy into the big picture concept. They're so absorbed in their individual jobs that they can't see beyond their own problems."

Here's how you can overcome this type of situation:

➤ Bring everyone in your department or team into the early stages of the planning process.

➤ Discuss the major points of the overall plan.

➤ Ask each person to describe how he or she will fit into the big picture plan.

➤ Give each person a chance to comment on each stage of the project.

Breaking a long-term goal into bite-size pieces can help people see how their part in a project fits together with the others. It can also help them set overall team or project goals for the long run.

Communication Breakdown

Learn each of your team member's goals. If their goals aren't in line with those of your company, department, or project group, demonstrate to them that applying their skills to meeting the team's goals enhances the opportunity to fulfill their own expectations.

Sopping Up SOPs: The Company Bible

Your company may have a set of standard operating procedures (SOPs) or SPs (standard practices) that detail company plans and policies. Progressive companies usually restrict their SOPs to such matters as personnel policies, safety measures, and related matters. Many companies, however, incorporate specific job methods and procedures into their "bibles" or publish them in accompanying "instruction manuals." Providing policies and procedures for routine activities obviates the need to plan for them every time they occur. Because SOPs set standards that everyone must follow, they ensure consistent employee behavior in dealing with particular situations.

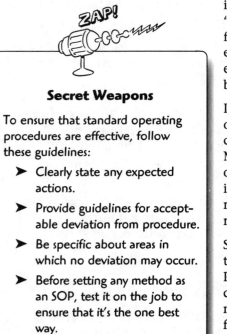

Secret Weapons

To ensure that standard operating procedures are effective, follow these guidelines:

➤ Clearly state any expected actions.

➤ Provide guidelines for acceptable deviation from procedure.

➤ Be specific about areas in which no deviation may occur.

➤ Before setting any method as an SOP, test it on the job to ensure that it's the one best way.

If you have to develop SOPs, keep them simple. Too often, managers draw up complicated SOPs in hopes of covering every possible contingency. *It can't be done.* Managers will frequently have to make decisions based on unforeseeable factors. SOPs should cover common issues in detail, but leave room for managers (or non-managerial people, where appropriate) to make spontaneous decisions when circumstances warrant them.

SOPs should also be flexible. Don't make SOPs so rigid that they can't be changed with changing circumstances. Plans may become obsolete because of new technologies, competition, government regulations, or the development of more efficient methods. Build into SOPs a policy for periodic review and adjustment.

Also keep in mind that not all plans are SOPs. Plans can be developed for special purposes, sometimes to be used only once or for projects that last several months or years.

Planning, Planning, Who'll Do the Planning?

Standard operating procedures are just one phase of planning. As mentioned, SOPs should cover only broad policy matters so that specific plans can be designed for each new project.

Your entire team should be involved in developing the team's plans. As team leader, you should coordinate and lead the process: Delegate particular aspects of the planning to the team members who know the most about them.

Professional Planners

Because many line managers are so bogged down in the day-to-day details of the job, they don't have the time and energy for planning. Because planning is so important, many organizations have planning specialists work with the managers in the development and coordination of this function.

The people who are closest to the work—who will be responsible for implementing the plans—should also be directly involved. Planning experts can help facilitate the process, but only the people who will carry out the project's duties can create a realistic and workable plan.

Hands-On: How to Plan

To illustrate how planning works, let's look at how Louise, the owner and manager of Featherdusters (a janitorial service company in Rock Hill, South Carolina), developed a plan to clean a five-story office building. The following list shows you the steps Louise deemed necessary to implement her plan:

Step 1: List what needs to be done. After consulting with her client, Louise made the following list:

Must be done daily	Must be done weekly
Empty wastebaskets into dumpsters	Sanitize telephones
Carry dumpsters to pick-up location	Polish brass railings
Dust furniture	Wax tile floors
Mop tile floors	**Must be done monthly**
Vacuum carpeted floors	Wash windows
Clean restrooms	Wash glass partitions
Clean lounges	

Step 2: Determine staffing. Louise hired two teams of three people. Each team was responsible for cleaning six floors. Each team was comprised of a trained floor waxer, a window washer, and a supervisor. The owner/manager oversaw the entire operation.

Step 3: Acquire supplies and equipment. Louise then acquired these supplies:

> vacuum cleaners
>
> dust cloths
>
> sponges
>
> a waxing machine
>
> floor wax
>
> disinfectant
>
> window washing solvent

Step 4: Estimate timing. Louise calculated that the cleaning job would take five hours (from 5 P.M. to 10 P.M.) five days a week to complete. The following list serves as a guide to Louise and the supervisors to ensure that scheduled tasks get done at the scheduled time:

> **Daily tasks:** All tasks are performed daily.
>
> **Weekly tasks:** The supervisor assigns one floor every day to one or more workers to complete each of the weekly tasks.
>
> **Monthly tasks:** The owner/manager and window washer schedule these tasks every month. The schedule must be flexible enough to account for weather conditions.

Step 5: Methods. All work will be performed according to the company's SOP for cleaning methods. Supervisors are responsible for quality of work, and the owner/manager will inspect work on an ad hoc basis.

Step 6: Budget. Specific figures should be included to cover cost of materials, equipment amortization, labor, transportation to and from the site, and miscellaneous costs.

Step 7: Contingencies. Things don't always work out according to plan. Unforeseen circumstances can develop that impede the completion of scheduled tasks. Louise anticipated the types of contingencies most likely to be encountered:

> **Truck or van breakdown:** Make arrangements for renting replacement vehicles.
>
> **Equipment breakdown:** Additional waxing machines are stored in a warehouse.
>
> **Personnel:** Owner/manager and supervisors have lists of substitutes available on short notice.

Step 8: Follow-up. Owner/manager makes periodic visits to site to inspect work and meets at least once per quarter with client to ensure satisfaction with work.

The following planning worksheet will enable you to plan and schedule your projects. Feel free to photocopy it or adapt it to meet your special needs.

Planning Worksheet

Objective: _____

Specific actions to be taken: _____

_____

_____

Staffing: _____

Equipment and supplies: _____

_____

Timing (include deadlines where required): _____

_____

Methods and techniques to be used: _____

_____

_____

Budget: _____

_____

_____

Contingencies: _____

_____

_____

Follow-up: _____

_____

_____

Converting Plans into Action

Plans similar to that of the Featherdusters are virtually self-starting. Implementing an already developed and tested plan with a new client is relatively easy. The introduction of a brand new product, however, requires a much more complex plan, which may involve several phases spread out over several months or even years.

For example, when Procter & Gamble (P&G) introduced Crest toothpaste to the market, it set up separate year-long plans for each of the main aspects of the project: manufacturing, marketing, and distribution. The product manager who coordinated the entire operation then developed, in collaboration with the manufacturing, marketing, and distribution managers, month-by-month plans. Each of the involved parties knew just what it had to accomplish in the specified period and were kept informed of the other parties' progress. By following this plan, P&G was able to introduce Crest toothpaste on time: Simultaneously, P&G supplied its retailers, placed ads on TV and in magazines, and mailed samples and discount coupons to consumers.

The Daily Grind: Planning for Daily Activities

You've set your goals, and now you must apply them to your day-to-day work schedule. You'll achieve your goals only if you break down, day-by-day, how you plan to reach them.

Unless your work is primarily routine and already standardized in the SOPs, the next step for you and your team members is to determine when and what task each member will undertake.

The $25,000 Suggestion

In the early 1900s, Ivy Lee, a pioneer in management consulting, paid a visit to Charles Schwab, the president of U.S. Steel. Lee told Schwab that he could help U.S. Steel become more effective. When Schwab expressed skepticism, Lee said, "I'll give you one suggestion today, and I want you to put it into effect for one month. At the end of that time, we will meet again, and you can pay me whatever you think that idea was worth to you. If it was of no value, you owe me nothing."

Meanings & Gleanings

When you *prioritize*, or put first things first, you determine the degree of importance a matter has in accomplishing your goals. Let your priorities dictate how you complete the tasks at hand.

Schwab accepted the challenge and implemented Lee's suggestion. When they met again, Schwab handed Lee a check for $25,000 and said, "That was the best advice I ever had. It worked so well for me that I passed it on to all my subordinate managers."

So, what was Lee's advice? Prioritize.

Every morning when you get to work (or every night before you go to bed), make a list of all the things you want to accomplish that day and put them in order of priority. Then work on the first item, and don't move on to the next one until you have done all you can. You'll be interrupted, of course—no job is free from interruption—so just handle the interruption, then return to what you were working on. Don't let any interruption make you forget what you were doing.

You probably won't have completed every item on your list at the end of the day. But the important tasks will have been accomplished. Take the remaining tasks, add them to the new ones that have developed, and compile another prioritized list for the next day. At the end of the month, you might notice that certain items remain on your list day after day. That's a sign that they weren't important enough to do. You should either delegate them to someone else or perhaps not do them at all.

What Do I Do First?

In his book, *The Seven Habits of Highly Effective People,* Steven Covey cautions that many managers confuse what is urgent with what is truly important. Urgent matters must be attended to immediately or else serious consequences might ensue, but if you spend all your time putting out fires, your truly important goals won't be met.

Scheduling Team Projects

After your team has planned the actions it will take to complete a project, you must develop a schedule. Lay out what will be done, who will do it, and when each task should be started and completed. Your schedule can be as simple as notes on a wall calendar, or as complex as specially designed planning charts and computer-based schedules (see Chapter 6).

The daily planning organizer below breaks down activities into categories.

You can print the planner on loose leaf paper and keep it in a binder, or you can blow it up to use as a wall chart. You can also format it for computer use.

When you use this type of planner, identify priorities in each category by number or color coding.

Secret Weapons

Set priorities and stick to them. When you get interrupted, deal with the interruption and then immediately get back to what you were doing.

Secret Weapons

Color code your calendar or planning chart so that you and your associates can tell at a glance the status of projects and assignments. This list suggests colors to use:

Red ink: High-priority items for that day.

Blue ink: Deadlines for projects (list in blue for two or three days before the actual deadline, then print in red on the day of the final deadline).

Green ink: Follow-up of other people's work.

Black ink: Routine work scheduled for that day.

Daily Planning Organizer

Date: _____

Priorities	Things to Do	Phone Calls

Correspondence	Appointments	Miscellaneous

A planning organizer helps your team schedule daily activities and achieve its goals.

Enough of This Preparation—Let's Get It Done!

The first step in setting plans to action is assembling the necessary resources—obtaining and allocating funds, accumulating equipment and materials, and acquiring pertinent information. The major tasks of choosing, training, and assigning personnel to the project are discussed later in this book.

Where's the Dough?

Inadequate funding will doom any project to failure. The most common reason that start-up companies fold is lack of capital. Even large, well-established organizations must determine how much money they should spend to get a project started and to keep it going until it pays off.

When figuring out the budget for a project, be careful not to underestimate costs just to make the numbers impressive. You don't want to be like Mike: Mike wanted to impress his boss, Sheila. He knew that she watched every dollar her department spent and was always boasting that she could get work done less expensively than other managers. When Mike was assigned a new project, he cut corners and came up with an impossibly tight budget. Sheila praised him for his business acumen and gave his project the go-ahead.

But Mike's lowball figures proved to be inadequate, and, shamefaced, he had to ask Sheila for additional funds. This mistake stalled not only the project but also Mike's career.

Communication Breakdown

If you're not sure how much money is necessary for a project, err on the high side. You'll look much better if you come in under budget than if you have to plead for more funds. Here's a safe rule: Underpromise and overdeliver!

Our Budget Is Too Low!

You may have no control over determining budgets for your department or team. If so, carefully study the budget you are given before starting a project. If the budget seems unrealistically small, discuss it with your manager. Whoever allotted the money for your work may not have been aware of certain factors. By presenting your case, you may persuade the company to provide a more realistic budget.

There are times you'll have to work with a less-than-ideal budget. That's when you have to sharpen your pencil and calculate how you can save money with minimal loss of productivity. Can some of the work you're farming out be done more cheaply in-house or vice versa? Can some of the work be re-engineered so that fewer costly hours are spent on it? Can deadlines be delayed to eliminate the need for overtime or additional temporary workers? Check all your costs. Saving small amounts of money in several areas can add up to your meeting the budget.

Everything in Its Place: Lining Up Your Tools

Do you need any special equipment for the job? Most departments have easy access to the company's machinery, computers, and other hardware, but sometimes access is limited.

In Angela's case, she was assigned to prepare a long-term market forecast for a new service proposed to her company. She created a software program especially for the project, but was stymied when the only computer sophisticated enough to

Secret Weapons

When you need special equipment or materials, make a list of them before you begin your assignment. Check availability. Arrange well in advance to obtain what you need when you need it.

deal with her program was tied up on a higher priority project. Angela was compelled to use an outside computer firm to run her program, which added cost and time to the project.

To avoid a glitch like Angela's, make sure all necessary equipment will be available to you as needed. Otherwise, consider your alternatives. Check to see whether another department has equipment you can use. Arrange to subcontract work you can't do in-house. Lease the equipment on a short-term basis. Budget for temporary personnel to augment your staff when necessary.

Information: The Golden Key to Accomplishment

The 19th century brought us the Industrial Revolution; the 20th century, the information revolution. Knowledge is now the key to accomplishment. Having an accurate, balanced, and unbiased picture of what is happening in your company, in your industry, and in the economy is essential to sound decision-making.

In the past, managers could wait for weekly or even monthly reports for the information necessary to run their companies or departments effectively. Today, *real time* is the magic formula for success.

Meanings & Gleanings

Real time refers to the actual time in which a process occurs (what's going on in the here and now).

Reports tell you what happened yesterday, last week, and last month. They're helpful, of course, because it's useful to review the past, but to be an effective manager today, you have to know what's going on *now*.

You need better and faster information. A report is a snapshot, a still picture of how things were at the time it was taken. Instead, you need a telecast—information that's reported as it happens. The tools are in place, but are you taking advantage of them? Take a look at what they can do for you:

If you're a sales manager, you can get up-to-the-minute sales information from field salespeople. Have them send the results of each sales call from their laptops directly to your home office.

In a branch facility, you can e-mail information about production, inventories, and special problems as often as necessary.

If you need materials, you can contact suppliers instantly by fax or e-mail to place orders, arrange shipments, or solve problems.

If you're a retail manager, you can continuously receive sales and stock information from the store's cash register computers.

If you're a general manager who needs specialized information, you can use the World Wide Web to obtain that information from anywhere anytime. You can subscribe to services that give you up-to-the-minute weather conditions worldwide, stock prices on foreign exchanges, transportation and shipping schedules, and virtually any other type of data you need.

Faster, Faster! Keeping Up with Current Techniques and Methods

Information goes beyond simple facts and figures. Managers must have in-depth knowledge of the most effective and cutting edge work methods. Team leaders and team members alike must keep up with the latest technologies.

You've been in your field for many years; you think you know your job and all the tricks of the trade. Do you really? The way you've been doing things works, of course, but are you sure it's the best way?

"If it ain't broke, don't fix it" doesn't apply anymore. A certain method may work, but that's no guarantee that it can't be done better. Equipment that didn't exist a few years ago may improve production or quality today. Techniques may have been refined or totally changed. This is a dynamic world, and you can never stop learning.

You Can Teach an Old Dog New Tricks

Here's another outdated saying: "You can't teach an old dog new tricks." Well, it may be true of dogs, but it certainly isn't true of humans. Don't let your team members tell you they're too old to learn new things.

When computers first became an essential management tool, many older managers and workers resisted learning how to use them, claiming, "Computers are for young people; I'll never be able to master them." But they *did* learn. Today you'll find a computer terminal on virtually every desk in an office, whether that desk is used by a computer whiz, a 50-year-old executive, a twentysomething clerk, or a middle-aged secretary. They have *all* learned.

The Least You Need to Know

➤ Make sure you set clear, specific, and attainable goals.

➤ Prioritize your tasks: Do first things first.

➤ Your calendar is a scheduling tool. Plan your day and work your plan.

➤ Set budgets that will provide adequate funds for your job to be completed in the specified timeframe.

➤ Arrange in advance to have the necessary equipment, computer time, and materials at your disposal.

➤ Get data in real time so that you're always on top of every situation.

Chapter 4

Talk the Talk—Communicating Like a Leader

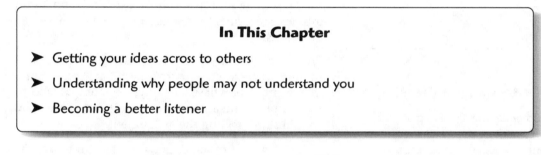

In This Chapter

➤ Getting your ideas across to others

➤ Understanding why people may not understand you

➤ Becoming a better listener

These days, *communication*—what you say and how you say it—can determine whether you succeed or fail. Take Ronald Reagan, for example. Many Americans believe he was reelected to office because he could communicate with voters so effectively (and telegenically).

This skill, shared by the most successful professionals, business executives, and government leaders, is a skill you, too, can acquire. All you need is will and determination. Once you've improved your ability to communicate, you can more effectively present your ideas to your boss, your associates, your customers, your team, even your friends and family.

In this chapter, you'll learn some strategies to better your oral and written communication—a major step toward becoming a more successful team leader.

What You Say

Suppose you call a team meeting to discuss a new project. Or you sit down with an associate for a serious discussion about performance. Or perhaps you're called upon to present a progress report to the executive committee. In all these situations, your choice of words and your delivery may determine your success or failure.

Whether you're addressing a group or having a one-to-one conversation, you should think out your message and how you plan to present it in advance. Sometimes you'll have to think on your feet with little or no time to prepare, but more often than not, when you're required to discuss something, you *can* prepare—even on short notice.

Know Your Subject

On the job, you'll usually communicate with others about subjects you're thoroughly familiar with: the work you're doing, matters in your own area of expertise, or company-related problems. Still, you should review the facts to be sure that you have a handle on all the available information and are prepared to answer any questions.

From time to time, you may be asked to report on matters with which you are unfamiliar. Your company may want to purchase a new type of computer software, for example, and ask you to check it out. Here's how you should start tackling the assignment:

➤ Learn as much as possible about the subject.

➤ Know 10 times more than you think you ought to know for the presentation.

➤ Prepare notes about the pluses and minuses of the proposed purchase, solution, and so on.

➤ Whether you will make this report to one person (your boss, for example) or to a group of managers or technical specialists, be prepared to answer questions about any subject that might come up.

Know Your Audience

Even the most skilled orator will fail to communicate effectively if his audience can't understand him. Half of good communication is understanding your audience. Choose words that your listeners will easily comprehend. If the people you address come from a technical background, you can use technical terminology to

Meanings & Gleanings

Communication takes place when persons or groups exchange information, ideas, and concepts.

Communication Breakdown

Unless your audience is familiar with it, don't use *jargon*—those special initials, acronyms, and words used in your field or company and nowhere else. A statement like, "We booked the perp on a 602A" won't mean anything to someone who's not a police officer.

communicate: Your listeners will clearly and readily understand these special terms. But if you talk about technical subject matter to an audience unfamiliar with it, drop the technical language. If your listeners can't understand your vocabulary, your message will be lost.

For example, suppose you're an engineer whose work primarily involves dealing with other engineers. You're accustomed to using technical terms all the time. Now let's say you're called on to make a presentation to your company's finance department to arrange the funding for a new engineering project. It's *your* responsibility, not your audience's, to ensure that your message gets across. If you can explain the technical matter in layperson's terms, do so. If you have to use technical language, take the time to explain a term the first time you use it and at least once again if you feel that it needs reinforcement.

How You Say It

No matter how well thought out your message is, no one will understand it if you don't express it clearly and distinctly.

Following are the five most common problems people have with speaking clearly:

➤ **Mumbling.** Do you swallow word endings? Do you speak with your mouth almost closed? Practice in front of a mirror. Open up those lips.

➤ **Speaking too fast.** Whoa! Give people a chance to absorb what you're saying.

➤ **Speaking too slowly.** Speak too slowly, and you'll lose your audience. While you're plodding through your message, their minds wander to other matters.

➤ **Mispronouncing words.** Not sure how a word is pronounced? Look it up.

➤ **Speaking in a monotone.** Vary the inflection of the tone and pitch of your voice. Otherwise, you'll put your listeners to sleep.

Communication Breakdown

Do you use "word whiskers," those extra sounds, words, and phrases peppered throughout speech? You know what they are—"er," "uhhhh," and "y'know" are just a few. They distract you from your thoughts. Listen to yourself, and shave off those "whiskers."

Have You Ever Really Heard Your Own Voice?

You don't hear yourself as others hear you. Get a tape recorder and record your voice when you talk to others in person or on the phone. Listen to yourself on tape. The recording will tell you whether you mumble, or speak too fast, too slowly, or in a monotone.

All you need to do to correct most of these problems is to be aware. If you're aware that you mumble, you'll make an effort not to mumble. If you're aware that you speak too fast, you'll make an effort to slow down. If you're aware that you speak in a monotone, you'll work consciously to speak in a more interesting tone.

Secret Weapons

All voice-mail programs give you the opportunity to listen to your outgoing message before making it final. Some programs also let you review a message you're leaving for someone before you hang up. Take advantage of these options. The more you listen to yourself, the better you'll hear how you sound to others. It will help you determine how to speak more clearly.

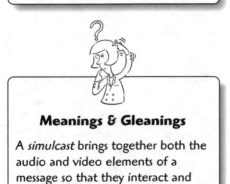

Meanings & Gleanings

A *simulcast* brings together both the audio and video elements of a message so that they interact and intensify the message.

Adding Video to the Audio

An old Chinese proverb says that a picture is worth a thousand words. People remember more of what they see than what they hear, and they remember even more of what they see and hear simultaneously. If people *see* something when you present your message (that is, if you use visual aids), it makes your message that much clearer, more exciting, and, most important, more memorable.

That's why TV is such an effective tool: It brings together, in a *simulcast*, both the video and the audio elements of a message. A perfect example of how this works is *Sesame Street* on public television. The program effectively teaches children to read, count, expand their vocabularies, and more through lessons that use words and pictures simultaneously.

You don't need a TV camera to be able to simulcast. Simply apply the philosophy behind simulcasting to your own presentation. These relatively inexpensive and easy-to-use techniques can help you broadcast your message more effectively:

➤ Use graphs or charts to clarify figures.

➤ Use photos, drawings, or diagrams to illustrate points.

➤ Use flow charts to describe processes.

Your company should also have many of the following visual aids available to you for larger group presentations:

➤ **Flip charts and chalkboards:** The least expensive and easiest items to use.

➤ **Overhead projectors:** Can be used to display prepared transparencies, which you can draw on and augment as you talk.

➤ **Slide presentations:** Colorful and dramatic slides can emphasize important points.

➤ **Videos or films:** A much more expensive aid, but worth it, particularly if your presentation will be repeated several times.

Even if you never make group presentations, you still can simulcast your message to an audience of one:

➤ Flip charts and chalkboards are just as easy to use and as effective whether your audience is one person or one hundred.

➤ Use your yellow pad (or any color pad you like). Anything that can be drawn on the flip chart can be drawn on a pad of paper.

➤ Charts, diagrams, and photos can be prepared before any meeting. Emulate salespeople who have successfully used these tools to make sales. Placed in acetate folders, usually in a loose leaf binder, these items make an attractive visual aid.

Are You Really Listening?

Suppose one of your colleagues brings a problem to you and asks for help. You begin listening attentively, but before you know it, your mind is wandering. Instead of listening to the problem, you're thinking about the pile of work on your desk, the meeting you have scheduled with the company vice president, the scuffle your son got into at school. You hear your colleague's words, but you're not really listening.

Does this happen to you? Of course, it does. It happens to all of us. Why? Our minds can process ideas 10 times faster than we can talk. While someone is talking, your mind may race ahead. You complete the speaker's sentence in your mind—often incorrectly—long before he or she does. You "hear" what your mind dictates, not what's actually said.

This is human nature. But that's no excuse for being a bad listener. Read on to learn how to listen more effectively.

Sorry, I Wasn't Listening

Now suppose your mind was wandering and you didn't hear what the other person said. It's embarrassing to admit you weren't listening, so you fake it. You pick up on the last few words you heard and comment on them. If you make sense, you're lucky. But you may have missed the real gist of the discussion.

When you haven't been listening, you don't have to admit, "I'm sorry, I was daydreaming." One way to get back on track is to ask a question or make a comment about the last item you did hear: "Can we go back a minute to such-and-such?"

Another method is to comment this way: "To make sure I can better understand your view on this, please elaborate."

Secret Weapons

As soon as you realize you haven't been paying full attention to someone—when you start hearing a droning sound instead of words, when you hear only words but not ideas, or when you're anticipating what you *think* will be said—stop! Then start listening!

Five Tricks to Make You a Better Listener

You *can* become a better listener. All you have to do is make a few changes in your work environment and in your approach to listening—a small effort with a big return.

➤ **Eliminate distractions.** The greatest distraction is probably the telephone. You want to give the speaker your full attention—*and the phone rings*. Answering the call not only interrupts your discussion but also disrupts the flow of your thoughts. Even after you've hung up, you may still be pondering the call.

If you know you'll be having a lengthy discussion at your desk, arrange for someone else to handle your calls or set your voice mail to pick up right away. If this isn't possible, get away from the telephone. Try an empty conference room.

➤ **Get rid of excess paper to reduce distractions.** If your desk is strewn with paper, you'll probably end up skimming them and realize too late that you're reading a memo instead of listening. Put those papers away in a drawer. Or go to a conference room and take only the papers that are related to your discussion.

➤ **Don't get too comfortable.** Some years ago I was discussing a situation with another manager. As was my custom, I sat in my comfortable executive chair with my hands behind my head. Maybe I rocked a little. Fortunately, I caught myself before I dozed off.

Ever since then, I've made a point of sitting on the edge of my chair and leaning forward rather than backward when I engage in discussions. This position brings me physically closer to the other person, enables me to be more attentive, and helps me maintain eye contact. It also shows the other person that I'm truly interested in getting the full story he or she is relating and that I take seriously what is being said. And because I'm not quite so comfortable, I have less of a tendency to daydream.

Meanings & Gleanings

An *active listener* not only pays close attention to what the other party says, but asks questions, makes comments, and reacts verbally and non-verbally to what is said.

➤ **Be an active listener.** An *active listener* doesn't just sit back with open ears. An active listener asks questions about what's being said. You can paraphrase ("So the way I understand it is that...") or ask specific questions about specific points. This technique not only enables you to clarify points that may be unclear but also keeps you alert and paying attention.

➤ **Be an empathetic listener.** Listen with your heart as well as with your head. Empathetic listeners not only listen to what other people say but also try to feel what other people are feeling when they speak. In other words, put yourself in the speaker's shoes.

➤ **Take notes.** It's impossible to remember everything said in a lengthy discussion. Take notes, but remember not to take stenographic transcriptions. If you're concentrating on what you're writing, you can't pay full attention to the conversation.

Jot down key words or phrases, write down figures or important facts—just enough to remind you of the principal points that were made.

Immediately after a meeting, while the information is still fresh in your mind, write a detailed summary. Dictate it into a recorder, enter it into your computer, or write it in your notebook—whichever is best for you.

Body Language: The Silent Signals

People communicate not only through words but also through gestures, facial expressions, and movements. Wouldn't it be great if you could buy a dictionary of body language?

Unfortunately, no such dictionary could exist because body language isn't standardized like verbal language. Some gestures—a nod or a smile—may seem universal, of course, but not everyone uses body language as you do.

Secret Weapons

Study the body language of people with whom you work. You may notice that when John smiles in a certain way, it has a specific meaning; if he smiles differently, there's a different meaning. Or maybe when Jane wrinkles her forehead, it means she doesn't agree. Make a conscious effort to study and remember people's individual body language.

Manager's Minute

Body language is a lot more important than people think. Take a hint from top salespeople. They make a practice of carefully studying the body language of a prospect during the first few minutes of the interview. They note how the prospect's expressions often emphasize what is really important to him. They especially note the prospect's body language in reaction to their sales presentation, adapting their pitches accordingly. All of us can benefit from following this practice. It will enable us to become better communicators, whether we are the speaker or the listener.

When people nod as you speak, for example, you might assume they're agreeing with you. But some people nod just to acknowledge that they're listening. When someone folds his arms as you speak, you might think his action is a subconscious show of disagreement. But it could simply be that your listener is just cold!

What You Send Might Not Be What's Received

Communication works like a two-way radio: Two parties sending messages and responding to each other. Sometimes, however, the message that's received may not be exactly the same as the message that was sent. Somewhere between the sender's radio and the receiver's radio, static may have intervened and distorted the message. This static may be generated from either end of the connection.

What causes that "static" in direct conversations? It might be rooted in your own mind. Everything you say and hear is filtered through your brain, and influenced by the attitudes you've acquired over the years. The following list details some of those attitudes.

➤ **Assumptions.** You've seen this situation repeatedly. For example, you have a pretty good idea about what causes a particular problem and how to solve it. In discussing it with others, you assume they know as much about it as you do, and you give instructions based on the assumption that they have know-how while they may not. The result is that you don't give them adequate information. Static!

➤ **Preconceptions.** People tend to hear what they expect to hear. The message you receive is distorted by any information you already have about the subject. So if the new information is different from what you expect, you might reject it as being incorrect.

What does this mean to you? Keep your mind open. When someone tells you something, make an extra effort to listen and evaluate the new information objectively instead of blocking it out because it differs from your preconceptions.

In communicating with others, try to learn their preconceptions. When you present your views to them, take into consideration what they already believe. If their beliefs differ from yours, be prepared to jump a few hurdles.

➤ **Prejudices.** Your biases for or against a person influence the way you receive his or her message. If you greatly admire the speaker, more than likely you'll be inclined to accept whatever he or she says. If you fervently dislike the speaker, you'll discount anything that's said.

Biases also affect the way subject matter is received. People turn a deaf ear to opposing viewpoints on matters they have strong feelings about.

Channels—The Message Distorter

Remember the game of "telephone" we all played as children? One person whispers a message to the next person, who in turn whispers it to the next, and so on. By the time it gets back to the originator, the message is usually entirely different.

This happens in real life whenever messages must be filtered through several people. Your company may require that you go through channels to deliver information: If you want to exchange information with a person in another department, for example, you first go to your boss, who goes to the supervisor of the other department, who in turn goes to the person with your information, gets a response, and conveys it back through the same channels. By the time you receive the message, it may have been distorted by a variety of interpretations.

For effective communication, try to eliminate, or at least minimize, the use of channels. Especially with routine matters that don't involve policy changes, people should be able to communicate directly with each other; this way, messages don't get distorted or held up in a cumbersome network of channels. One advantage of the flatter organizational structure is that it has fewer channels.

Conducting Effective Meetings

An effective way to exchange information is through meetings. But meetings can be a big waste of time—if they're not organized properly.

Have you ever left a meeting thinking: "What a waste of time. I could have accomplished so much more if I had spent this past hour at my desk!" In a recent survey, over 70 percent of the people interviewed felt they had wasted time in the meetings they had attended.

There is hope. Meetings can be made productive. In the following sections, I'll discuss a few ways to conduct your meetings more efficiently.

Players Only

Invite only appropriate participants. Some managers hold staff meetings on a regular basis—sometimes weekly or even daily. Quite often, many of the people who attend are not involved in the matters that are discussed. By inviting only those who can contribute to the meeting or will be affected by what is discussed, you can avoid wasting others' time and keep the meetings briefer.

Communication Breakdown

When people who are usually invited to meetings are not invited, they may worry: "Why wasn't I asked? Is the boss giving me a hidden message? Am I on the way out?" Avoid this concern by explaining beforehand your new policy and why you instituted it.

What's on the Agenda?

Prepare an agenda. An agenda is key to the success or failure of a meeting. Plan your agenda carefully, covering all matters that you want to discuss. By determining in advance not only what subjects will be addressed, but the order in which they will be covered, you'll make the meeting run more smoothly.

At least three days before the meeting, send the agenda to all people who will attend. This will allow them to study the topics of discussion and prepare their contribution.

Stick rigidly to the agenda. Don't allow people to bring up topics not on the agenda. If anyone tries, point out that unless it's an emergency, it cannot be discussed at this meeting. Suggest it be placed on the agenda for the next meeting.

Secret Weapons

In establishing the sequence of topics at a meeting, put the most complex ones at the beginning of the program. People come to meetings with clear minds and are able to approach deeper matters more effectively early on. If you schedule the important issues for later, participants are less likely to be attentive, and may be distracted by what has been discussed earlier.

Let's Hear It

Attendees should be encouraged to study the agenda and be prepared to discuss each item. If you need specific data to make a point, organize it into easy-to-follow visuals (for example, charts or hand-outs) and bring it to the meeting. Encourage discussion and create an atmosphere in which people can disagree without fear of ridicule or retaliation.

Manager's Minute

Provide "takeaway" photocopies of diagrams, flow charts, or whatever data you bring to the meeting. Distribute the copies to everyone at the meeting to ensure that they have a clear representation of the subjects you discuss. These copies also serve as permanent reminders of your message; participants can refer to them later if necessary.

If you have heftier handouts or other dense reading materials, distribute them far enough in advance of the meeting to enable team members to study them. The focus of a meeting should be on expanding, demonstrating, and clarifying information—not to introduce brand new concepts, particularly technical or complex material.

If you are the leader, ask questions that stimulate discussion. Be open to questions and dissension. It's better to have people butt heads during the meeting than let them stew over their problems over a long period of time.

Yap! Yap! Yap!

Don't you hate it when one person tries to dominate a meeting? It's usually the same one or two people who always have something to say—usually not important, often a personal pet peeve, and always distracting. Here are some tips on how you, as a meeting leader, can attempt to keep them quiet:

➤ Take the blabbermouth aside before the meeting and tell him or her, "I know you like to contribute to our meetings and I appreciate it, but we have a limited amount of time and some of the other people want a chance to present their ideas. So let's give them a chance to talk, and you and I can discuss your issues after the meeting."

➤ If the blabbermouth still insists on dominating the meeting, wait until he or she pauses for breath—which they inevitably must do—and quickly say, "Thank you. Now let's hear what Sue has to say."

➤ Announce that each speaker has only three minutes to make his or her point. Be flexible with others, but be strict with the blabbermouths.

Ending the Meeting

At the end of the meeting, after all the items on the agenda have been covered, the leader should summarize what has been accomplished. If any team members received assignments during the course of the meeting, have them indicate what they understand they will be expected to do and when they will do it.

Take Minutes

Take notes so that there is no misunderstanding of what has been decided at a meeting. These need not be detailed transcripts of the entire discussion, but a summary of the decisions made on each issue. After the meeting, distribute copies of the minutes not only to the attendees, but also to all people who may be affected by what was determined. The minutes will serve as a reminder to the participants of what was decided and as a communication to those who didn't attend.

Conferences, Conventions, and Retreats

In addition to team or department level meetings, managers often participate in company-wide conferences or conventions. These are more elaborate than local meetings, and if you are asked to make a presentation at one of them, you should prepare it carefully. Tips on making presentations of this sort will be discussed in

Chapter 10. A relatively recent innovation in company communications is the *retreat*. A group of managers is invited to a facility away from the company offices—usually a resort hotel—to relax and informally discuss company problems. You'll play golf or tennis, take nature walks, go canoeing, build campfires, or splurge on buffets. The hope is that staff members will loosen up and be more creative in presenting ideas and more receptive to receiving them.

If you are invited, of course, you should accept—it's less an invitation than a command. Sure, have fun. Participate in the discussions. But prepare what you will say and be businesslike in your demeanor. Dress informally, but not loudly. Drink moderately. Watch what you say.

Secret Weapons

You can use a retreat to get to know your boss better or make contacts with people in other departments. This can be very valuable to your work and the advancement of your career.

Communication Breakdown

When attending a convention or retreat, don't relax completely. Don't think for a minute that your offhand remarks will be considered "off the record." Everything you do and say will be noticed by the powers that be. This is not the time or place to gripe about the company or complain about people behind their backs. The other participants are not necessarily your buddies. They may be your bosses, your rivals for advancement, or your competitors for company funds or recognition of power.

Getting the Most out of Conventions or Conferences

Most managers who attend conferences often complain that they get little benefit from them. Here are 10 steps that will help make meetings more meaningful to you:

1. **Plan and Prepare.** Most conferences and conventions are announced months in advance. Usually an agenda accompanies the announcement. Study it carefully. Does any subject listed require special preparation? You may want to read a book or an article on unfamiliar subjects to help you comprehend and contribute to the discussion. You may want to re-examine your company's experience in that area so you can relate what is being discussed to your own organization's problems.

2. **Don't sit with your colleagues.** You can speak to them anytime. Here is your chance to meet new people. At many meetings, participants are seated at tables either for the entire program or for parts of it. Make a point of sitting with different people at various stages of the meetings. Especially at luncheon or dinner discussions, you can pick up more ideas from your tablemates than from the speakers. In addition, you can make new contacts who may be valuable resources for information after the conference.

3. **Open your mind.** You go to conferences and conventions to learn. To get the most out of what a speaker says, keep your mind open to new suggestions. They may be different from what you honestly believe is best, but until you hear it all and think it through objectively, you won't really know. Progress comes through change. This does not mean that all new ideas are good ones, but they should be listened to, evaluated, and carefully and objectively considered.

4. **Be tolerant.** Have you ever listened to a speaker who turned you off immediately? You didn't like his or her appearance, clothes, voice, or accent, so you either stopped listening or rejected what he or she said. Prejudice against a speaker keeps many an attendee from really listening to what is discussed or from accepting the ideas presented.

   During a conference break, I overheard one participant tell another: "This meeting is a waste of time. How can a woman tell us men how to market machine tools? She ought to stick to housewares or cosmetics." Sexism prevented him from acquiring valuable information, which could have been important to his company.

5. **Take notes.** Note taking has two important functions. It helps organize what you hear while you are at the conference, which leads to more systematic listening. It also becomes a source for future reference.

6. **Ask questions.** Don't hesitate to query a speaker when the opportunity arises. But don't waste other people's time with trivial questions.

7. **Contribute ideas.** Some people will always contribute more than others; some just sit and listen. When asked why they didn't participate, they say: "Why should I give my ideas to these people? Some of them are my competitors and I won't give away my trade secrets."

   Nobody expects you to say anything that would damage your firm or its competitive position, but most discussions are not of this nature. They're designed instead to promote the exchange of general ideas. The experience of one organization helps others. By contributing ideas, you provide richer experiences for everyone else, which in turn results in a more fulfilling experience for you.

8. **Summarize.** After the meeting, review your notes while the meeting is still fresh in mind. Write or dictate a report on the conference for your permanent files.

9. **Report.** Report on what you have learned to your boss or others in your organization who

Secret Weapons

Keep a record of the names and addresses of the speakers you hear at a conference or convention. You may want to contact some of them for additional information. Also list the names and addresses of people you meet at these events. They may be a source of information or guidance in the future.

might find the information valuable. By sharing what you have learned, you add to the value your firm receives from sending you to the convention.

10. **Apply what you have learned.** If you don't do anything with what you learned at the conference, it's been a waste of time and money.

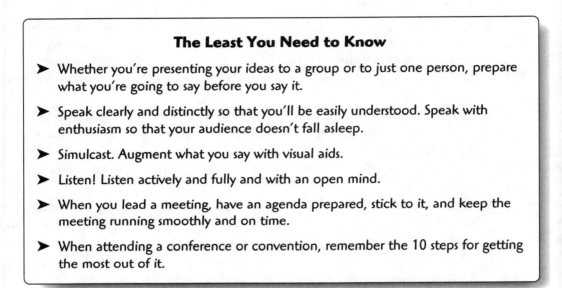

The Least You Need to Know

➤ Whether you're presenting your ideas to a group or to just one person, prepare what you're going to say before you say it.

➤ Speak clearly and distinctly so that you'll be easily understood. Speak with enthusiasm so that your audience doesn't fall asleep.

➤ Simulcast. Augment what you say with visual aids.

➤ Listen! Listen actively and fully and with an open mind.

➤ When you lead a meeting, have an agenda prepared, stick to it, and keep the meeting running smoothly and on time.

➤ When attending a conference or convention, remember the 10 steps for getting the most out of it.

Chapter 5

Put It in Writing!

> **In This Chapter**
>
> ➤ Making your letters and memos more effective
>
> ➤ Dealing with correspondence you receive
>
> ➤ Making your e-mail more exciting
>
> ➤ Writing reports that really report

Most of our day-to-day communication with team members, bosses, other team leaders, and even customers and vendors is done by telephone or personal contact. But written communication—letters, memos, faxes, e-mail, and reports—are still major ways to get and receive information, ideas, compliments, complaints, and instructions.

Write It Right

Because written communication tends to be more formal than speaking, you'll find it harder to accomplish. How often have you sat down to write something knowing exactly what you want to say, but the right words just won't come? People always say, "Just write the way you talk." Good idea, but when you put pencil to paper, your mind goes blank.

Secret Weapons

Clear thinking precedes clear writing.

Before you begin writing the first word, *TAB* your thoughts (see the "TAB Your Thoughts" list that follows). This will help you learn how to think clearly about what you want to write before you start writing.

Whether you're writing a letter to a customer, a memo to your boss, or a fax to a branch office, think out the content before you begin writing.

Ask yourself each of the questions on the "TAB Your Thoughts" list. Jot down the answers on a scratch pad or use a special form, such as the "Writing Guide" shown here. TAB-ing your thoughts will help you organize all the information concerning the situation you're writing about, indicate what you want done to deal with it, and describe how these actions will benefit your readers.

TAB Your Thoughts

Think about the situation _____

    What? _____

    Where? _____

    Who? _____

    When? _____

    How? _____

Action _____

    What do I want to be done? _____

Benefit _____

    How will this help: _____

        The company? _____

        Readers of this memo? _____

        Other people? _____

        Me? _____

Writing Guide

Think about the situation: Why am I writing this?

_____

_____

_____

Action: What do I want to accomplish?

_____

_____

_____

To do this, what do I want to say?

_____

_____

_____

Benefit: How will this be of value?

_____

_____

_____

The Three Cs

Now that you know what you want to write, you're ready to put it in writing. Whatever you write should be:

➤ Clear
➤ Complete
➤ Concise

Suppose you're writing a memo concerning the status of an order. Be sure to respond to any specific questions. Include the order number, date of the order, identification of materials, and other pertinent information. Avoid going into extraneous detail. Remain brief and to the point.

Keep It Short and Punchy

Steer clear of complex, multi-phrase constructions. Don't write, "Based on the research in this field, the program we offer will, in our opinion, promote the betterment of the writing skills of all employees who participate in the training." Just say, "This program will teach people to write better."

Short and punchy—yes! Short and dull—no! Rather than write the memo or fax in the usual narrative form, write it in the form of a bulletin:

➤ Headline your main point—use **bold print**.

➤ Break the story into separate sections for each subsidiary point.

➤ Use an asterisk (*) or bullet (•) to highlight key points.

➤ Where appropriate, use graphs, charts, or other visual aids to augment the impact of your words.

Manager's Minute

Vigorous writing is concise. A sentence should contain no superfluous words, a paragraph no unnecessary sentences—for the same reason drawings should have no gratuitous lines and a machine no extraneous parts.

Grammar and Spelling Can Make or Break You

You can't always depend on an assistant to correct your grammatical and spelling errors. Today, many managers don't have assistants and have to write their own letters and memos. Even if you're one of the lucky few who has an assistant, you should still double-check everything that goes out with your signature on it.

Your word processing program's "spell check" feature is a great asset, as it catches most typos and misspellings—but not all of them. Reread everything you write, whether it's you or your assistant who types it. The content and style of your written correspondence affect the image you and your company project.

Communication Breakdown

The spell checker can fool you—it checks for spelling, not meaning. You may have meant to write "break" and instead typed "brake." But brake is a word, so the spell checker won't catch the error. Don't depend completely on the spell checker. Proofread your documents before releasing them.

Know Your Reader

Your operations manager probably likes details. He or she wants to know facts and figures, statistics and technicalities. When you write a report, include all of these elements in it. Your marketing manager, however, may prefer terse, precise reports. He or she usually wants to see graphs rather than tables, and get an overall view rather than specific details. Tailor your style to what's most amenable to your readers.

Write the Way You Speak

I'll bet you've never received a letter that read like this:

Pursuant to our telephonic conversation of even date, transmitted herewith are the invoices for the work completed through the ultimate month.

But that was how a typical business letter might have read in the early part of this century.

Many people still use such stilted language because they believe one must be more formal when putting ideas on paper than when communicating them orally. Formal language comes across as artificial and often insincere. Your message will be clearer and more easily accepted by the reader if you write just the way you speak.

That letter would have been much clearer if it had been written this way:

As promised when we spoke on the telephone today, here are the invoices for the work completed through this month.

Secret Weapons

Be precise. Be concise. Think of your memo or fax as a cable for which you must pay a dollar a word.

Talk to Your Reader

Pretend you're talking face-to-face or on the phone with the person who will read the letter. Be informal. Relax. Talk in your regular voice, in your usual manner, with your own vocabulary, accents, idioms, and expressions. You wouldn't normally say *"Please be advised* that because of the fire in our plant, there will be a 10-day delay in shipping your order." Instead you'd get right into the message: "Because of the fire in our plant, your shipping order will be delayed 10 days." So why not write just that?

Don't Be Afraid to Use Contractions

Contractions are a normal part of our speech. We rarely use full phrases such as "I do not want this" or "I will not be able to attend." We say "I don't" or "I won't." Why not use these everyday contractions in our writing? They'll make your letters come across in a sincere and personal manner. Naturally, you should avoid slangy—and grammatically incorrect—contractions such as "ain't." Needless to say, you shouldn't use such language when speaking either.

Use Direct Questions

A conversation isn't one-sided. One person speaks, then the other interrupts, often with a question, such as "Yes, but how will this affect the quality?" By interjecting questions in your letter, you gain the attention of the reader to specific points. After making a point, you might ask: "What additional applications can you find by installing this software?" This gives the reader a chance to apply your message to his or her specific needs.

Communication Breakdown

Too many letters sound like form letters. Avoid this. Personalize your letter. Use the addressee's name. If you're friends, use the first name; if just business acquaintances, the last name. And instead of addressing the company in your comments, address the person you're writing to; use "you": "So, Beth [or Ms. Smith], you see how this will benefit you."

Use Personal Pronouns

In speech, we use *I*, *we*, and *you* all the time. They're part of the normal give and take of conversation. Everybody, it seems, who writes for a company or organization eschews the use of personal pronouns and clings desperately to the passive voice. They rarely say *we*, never say *I*, and even avoid the straightforward *you*. Instead they write phrases such as "It is assumed…," or "It is recommended…," and sentences such as: "An investigation will be made, and upon its completion, a report will be furnished to your organization." Why not just say, "We're investigating the matter and will let you know when we obtain the information."

There isn't much opportunity to say "I" when writing for an organization. You should use "I," however, when you express your own feelings or thoughts. "I'm sorry" or "I'm pleased" is better than "we're sorry" or "we're pleased."

Go Ahead, End a Sentence with a Preposition

Old grammarians caution against ending sentences with prepositions. This rule sometimes makes sentences sound awkward. We rarely think about such rules when we speak, but when we write, we try so hard to be grammatically correct that we make the sentences and entire letters sound artificial. Put prepositions at the end whenever it sounds right. Instead of writing, "The claimant is not entitled to the benefits for which he applied," it's okay to write, "The claimant isn't entitled to the benefits he applied for."

Another grammatical superstition tells us to avoid split infinitives. For example, "To better reduce costs, we should take the following steps" is stronger than "To reduce costs better, we should take the following steps."

Use Short, Snappy Sentences

Keep your sentences short. Readers can take in only so many words before their eyes come to a brief rest at a period. If a sentence is too wordy, readers tend to get lost and miss the point. Studies show that sentences no longer than 20 words are easiest to read and comprehend. Short sentences also have more impact.

Also, limit each sentence to one idea. Remember, your objective is to get your idea across to the reader—not to create undying prose. Another way to relate your message with more punch is to use short words. Readers might trip over long, cumbersome ones. Of course, feel free to use technical language when you write about technical matters to technically trained people. But if your reader isn't familiar with it, avoid jargon.

Manager's Minute

Lincoln's Gettysburg Address contained only 272 words. Each word a gem.

Avoid Business Clichés

Instead of churning out letters thick with overused and often meaningless business terminology, use simple terms. Here are some clunky business clichés, and their simpler counterparts:

Instead of writing	Write
In accordance with your request	As requested
At a later date	Later (or indicate the exact time)
The undersigned	I
We are herewith enclosing	Enclosed is
At your earliest convenience	As soon as possible
We are not in a position to	We cannot
At the present time	Now
Costs the sum of	Costs
For the period of one year	For a year
In the near future	Soon (or indicate when)

Dealing With Your In Box

You come in every morning to find your in box overflowing and you think you'll never see the bottom of it again. Just when you think you're making headway, somebody drops another huge pile of work into your basket. I'm sure you've wondered, as that mountain of paper continues to grow, how you can at least make a dent in it.

Secret Weapons

Give your letters a human touch. Express yourself. If it's good news, say you're glad; if it's bad news, say you're sorry. Be as courteous, polite, and interested as you'd be face-to-face with your reader. Remember, your reader is a human being, too. A friendly tone of voice will please him, and a cold one might annoy.

Set Priorities

To manage your in box effectively, establish priorities. This may be easier said than done. What you consider a high priority might be less important in your boss' eyes. You need to have a clear understanding of what higher management wants before you can determine the relative importance of the projects you're involved with.

Some time management experts recommend classifying work into categories A, B, and C. A for most important, B for the next level, and C for routine work. All extraneous matters are classified in the D category, and can be put off, delegated, or totally ignored.

Screening the In Box

When you come in each morning, remove all the papers from your in box, scan them rapidly, and prioritize them. A letter from a customer concerning a change in an order gets an "A"; a phone message from a supplier about some new items that may be of interest gets a "B"; a monthly sales report is categorized "C"; brochures, bulletins, newsletters, and so forth, are given a "D." This takes no more than 10 minutes in the morning, but will save you loads of time throughout the day. Now you can concentrate on the A list, go on to the Bs when you're done, and so on.

Focus on the Message, Not the Medium

When scanning the contents of your in box, you may note a few items that were faxed. Your first reaction might be to give them high priority. After all, they were *faxes*. Don't base priority on how the message was sent; judge it by its contents. Marshall McCluhan, an expert in communications, warns us that we should not be overly influenced by the medium through which we receive information—we should focus on the message instead.

Just because you receive the correspondence by fax, e-mail, Federal Express, or some other rapid delivery system does not mean it is more important than correspondence delivered through slower channels. Today many people and companies use these rapid delivery systems for even the most routine matters. Read the contents and deal with the item according to its real importance.

Interruptions

Once you've established priorities, begin working on the A list. But watch out! At 10 AM, the mail clerk will likely drop another load of papers into your in box. It's tempting to stop everything and look over the new papers. Don't. Instead, train yourself to complete a project whenever possible before going on to another one. There are enough unavoidable interruptions—telephone calls, personal visits from the boss, or others. More paperwork can wait.

When you've completed the task you're working on, screen the new material and quickly prioritize it. If something of an urgent nature is in the box, of course, you'll have to give it a higher priority than some of the work you classified earlier in the morning.

Unfortunately, this is not uncommon. Most companies are so bogged down with paperwork that employees who deal with it can't get through it all. Much of this paperwork can be streamlined or even eliminated by creative review of what is being done. Here are some suggestions on moving things out of your in box more rapidly:

➤ **Don't answer a memo with another memo.** You receive a memo from another manager in your company asking you to provide the current inventory of a list of items, specifying the items by name and stock number. Typically, you would respond by writing a new memo re-listing the items by name and stock number with inventory figures added. It would be much more efficient to just write the amount of inventory on the original document and return it to the writer.

   If you can respond to a memo with a few sentences, just pencil the response on the original memo, instead of writing a new one.

➤ **Use e-mail.** If people in your company rely heavily on computers to get work done, don't bother sending letters or faxes in response to correspondence—use your modem. In most cases, e-mail is less time-consuming and more efficient. I'll discuss using e-mail effectively in the next section.

➤ **Delegate correspondence.** Often information requested in a letter or memo must be obtained from a subordinate. Typically, you'll ask the subordinate to get you the information, then respond to the original memo once you've received the necessary information. To save time and reduce in box clutter, why not delegate the entire task to your subordinate? Have him retrieve the information *and* write the response. In the beginning, you may want to read and sign the final letter, but once your subordinates master this area, give them free reign.

Make Your E-mail E-xciting, E-xpressive, E-ngaging

More and more inter- and intra-office communication is now done via e-mail—you must give as much attention to writing e-mail messages as you do to the composition of standard letters and memos.

Remember that e-mail is a form of written communication. People sometimes think of it as a substitute for the telephone rather than the letter, so they'll dash off e-mail messages with little consideration of their style or even content. E-mails are kept on the computer or printed out and filed, so they should be carefully planned and composed. Here are a few tips:

➤ Think carefully about what you write. If the message is more than just casual chit-chat, plan it as you would a formal letter. If you're giving instructions, make sure the reader knows exactly what action you're requesting. If you're answering an inquiry, make sure you've gathered all the information necessary to respond to the questions asked.

Communication Breakdown

E-mail glut can result in your message being ignored or inadvertently deleted. Ask the receiver to acknowledge receipt of your e-mail (or use the "return receipt" function if your e-mail program has one). If the matters involved are very important, follow up with a telephone call to assure that the message was received and understood.

➤ Use an effective subject line. Your correspondent may receive dozens of e-mail messages each day. To assure that your message will be read promptly, use a subject heading that will be meaningful to the addressee. For example, instead of "Re your e-mail of 6/25," use the subject line to refer to the information you provide in your e-mail (for instance, "Media for new advertising campaign").

➤ Follow the suggestions given on writing letters and memos. Use the three Cs, the TAB approach, and short, punchy sentences. Keep to the point and be brief.

➤ If you attach files to the e-mail, specify in the text which files are attached, so the reader can make sure they come through.

➤ Read and spell check the message before you click send. If you are not happy with the message, postpone the transmission. Review it, rewrite it, then send it.

E-Mail Clutter

How many e-mail messages do you receive every-day? Participants in a recent Pitney-Bowes survey indicated that, on average, they each received about 178 messages each day. Many of these e-mails were "spam"—the computer term for junk mail—but they still cluttered up the in box.

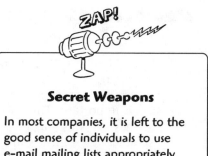

Secret Weapons

In most companies, it is left to the good sense of individuals to use e-mail mailing lists appropriately. But do what you can to restrict your employees' use of the "everyone" list.

In many companies, employees spend an inordinate amount of time on the computer e-mailing jokes, personal messages, offerings ("I have six cute kittens looking for a home"), and information that is usually unimportant to most recipients. Some companies alleviate such clutter by setting up special "classified ad" or bulletin board directories for these messages.

An example of clutter is sending an e-mail to an entire mailing list when only a few people on the list need the information. Some people who take a day off announce their plans to the "Everyone" list, thereby alerting 65 people, when only five or six people really need to know. Perhaps these people do so to puff up their own sense of self-importance. More likely, they're lazy. They find it easier to send a message to everyone than figure out who really needs to know and to type in all the names.

How Private Is Your E-mail?

It isn't. Sure, you may have a password and assume that it assures privacy, but hackers can easily break through even sophisticated systems. Assume anything you e-mail can be intercepted. If confidentiality is required, maybe e-mail is not the medium to use.

Remember that any e-mail sent via the company computer can be read by anybody in the company. Over the past few years there have been cases in which employees were fired because of e-mails they sent that violated company rules. The courts threw out the employees' claims of invasion of privacy.

More serious are the cases of people who made comments or jokes through e-mail, which were considered sexually or racially harassing. Printouts of such e-mail have been entered as evidence in suits against companies—even though the companies weren't aware of the e-mails. This has led to termination of the senders as well as legal action against both the senders and the companies.

Don't Lose the Personal Touch

Many people tend to resort to e-mail rather than make a phone call or a personal visit.

Using e-mail is often an easy way out. You don't have to leave your desk; it's less time-consuming than a telephone call—no need for small talk or lengthy discussion about a project. You just send the message. But often that small talk and pro-and-con discussion is important. The phone call allows for instant feedback. It not only helps clarify the message, but it assures that both you and the other person understand the matters involved in the same way.

In addition, phone conversations and, where feasible, personal meetings with people you deal with on a regular basis strengthen the personal relationship that is so important in developing rapport.

Charles Wang, the CEO of Computer Associates, found that e-mail's alleged efficiencies were ruining the interpersonal dynamics that had made his company so successful in the first place.

People stopped having face-to-face meetings and stopped speaking to each other altogether. His simple but shocking solution: Turn the whole system off for most of the day and force people to communicate in person. He follows this himself. When he wants you, he comes down the hall and finds you.

Ten E-mail Dos and Don'ts

1. **Do** carefully plan your e-mails.

2. **Do** read and re-read your messages before sending them.

3. **Don't** send off-color jokes or stories on company e-mail.

4. **Do** respond promptly to e-mail you receive, especially when immediate attention is required. Speed of communication is the chief advantage of this medium.

5. **Don't** use e-mail to replace telephone or personal contact. It is important to maintain voice-to-voice and face-to-face relationships with the people you deal with.

6. **Don't** play e-mail games or send or respond to chain letters or similar situations on company time and on company computers.

7. **Don't** download pornographic material or items that are derogatory to any racial or ethnic groups on company computers. Remember your e-mails can be read by anybody and may offend other people in the organization. It could lead to charges of sexual or racial harassment.

8. **Don't** spread gossip or rumors through e-mail. It's bad enough when gossip is repeated on the telephone or in person, but e-mail exponentially expands the number of people receiving such information.

9. **Do** check whether an e-mail has been received by asking the respondent to acknowledge it and/or by following up with a phone call.

10. **Don't** fully repeat the message you received when responding to an e-mail. This only adds to the length of the message and clutters the recipient's mailbox.

Writing Reports That Really Report

Just as the experienced carpenter will not put his saw to a piece of wood until he has thoroughly planned his work, you should not put a word on paper until careful preparation has been made. The words of your report may not be immortal prose, but once on paper or in the memory of the company's computer, it remains a more or less permanent record of what you have presented.

What should you do?

1. **Define the problem.** What is the objective of the report? A lot of people have wasted much time, effort, and money compiling a report without knowing what was really wanted. Unless the report writer is entirely clear on how the report will be used, she might spend more time on secondary aspects of the situation than on the really important areas.

2. **Get the facts.** Once the objectives are clear, get all the information needed. For example, if the assignment is to obtain information about some new software, your first step is research. First, speak to the people in your organization who will use the software and learn what they really want to accomplish by using it. Obtain literature about the software. Read what the technical journals say about it. Speak to people in other organizations who have switched to that product. Speak to the supplier's sales representatives. Speak to representatives from competing software vendors. Get all the information you can.

3. **Analyze the facts.** Once the information has been accumulated, assemble the facts and correlate and analyze them. One way is to list the advantages and limitations of the software under consideration and make similar lists for other software that might also be viable.

> **Secret Weapons**
>
> In assembling and analyzing facts, it's helpful to use some kind of system to keep information together and organized. One good technique is to make up separate folders for each major aspect of the study. As you accumulate information in each area (sales literature, reports of interviews, cost figures, and so on), put it in the proper folder. You can save hours of work by pre-sorting all your material.

What It Says

Once you've collected, assembled, and evaluated all your data, you are ready to put words on paper.

Remember that what you write must be easy to read. The language and form of your report should be familiar to its readers. An engineer writing a report for non-technical managers should try to couch the report in language as non-technical as the subject permits. If the use of technical language is essential to the report, the writer should define and clarify the meaning of such terms.

The report writer has an advantage when he knows what management expects in terms of language, details of content, graphic material, and the like. When writing a report for your boss or another manager with whom you have regular dealings, you should know whether he prefers terse, precise reports or a great deal of detail; whether that person prefers graphs or charts to statistical tables or likes to see both; whether rounded approximations are preferred to exact dollars and cents. The way you write your report should be tailored to the desires of the person who will read and act on it.

How It Looks

Although there's no ideal report style, here are a few suggestions for writing effective reports:

➤ **Briefly state the purpose of your report.** "As you requested, here's the information about the XYZ software programs."

➤ **Present a summary and some recommendations.** By providing a summary and stating your recommendations at the beginning of your report, readers get all the key information right away. Readers don't have to wade through reams of paper to discover your conclusions.

➤ **Provide a detailed backup.** A backup is the meat of your report, in which you present all the details that support your summary and recommendations. Use charts, graphs, and tables if they clarify or reinforce the information in the report.

How long should a report be? Long enough to tell the whole story—and not one word longer. Your objective is to provide the information—not write undying prose.

The Final Step

Before submitting the report, proofread it carefully. Even a good report loses credibility when it has spelling errors, poor grammatical structure, or sloppy typing. Figures

Communication Breakdown

Before submitting a report, proofread it thoroughly. Even a good report loses credibility when it has spelling errors, poor grammar, and sloppy typing. Figures should be checked and double-checked.

should be checked carefully. If possible, have another person who is knowledgeable about the subject read it. Make whatever changes are needed. Reread it. Then give it one more reading.

Attention to the finer points of obtaining and presenting information in writing will result in your being recognized as someone who can accomplish an assigned job. You will be seen as a person who can effectively communicate important ideas and necessary information.

The Least You Need to Know

➤ To write marvelous memos, fantastic faxes, lovely letters, and readable reports, use the TAB approach before writing and the three *Cs* when you're writing.

➤ Watch your grammar. Watch your spelling. Your writing style reflects your intelligence, personality, and authority.

➤ Talk to your reader. Pretend the person who will read the letter or report is sitting across from you or at the other end of the phone. Be informal. Relax. Write it as you would say it.

➤ Remember that what you write must be easy to read. Your written language and form should be familiar to your readers.

➤ In order to manage your incoming correspondence effectively, set priorities and stick to them.

➤ Give as much attention to writing e-mail as to standard letters and memos. Unfortunately, most e-mail writers dash off their messages with little or no thought to style or even content.

➤ Be careful in what you send via e-mail. Remember that any e-mail sent on company computers can be read by anybody in the company. There is no privacy in the cyberworld.

➤ Re-read and follow the 10 dos and don'ts of e-mail.

➤ Before writing a report, prepare carefully. Define the problem. Get the facts. Analyze the facts.

➤ An effective way to structure a report is to first state the purpose; then, present a summary and your recommendations; then present the details.

➤ To write right, prewrite, write, and rewrite.

I'M ALL EARS!

Open Your Ears, Open Your Mind

In This Chapter

➤ Getting people to contribute ideas

➤ Rejecting bad suggestions without causing resentment

➤ Developing suggestion programs that work

➤ Five ways to become more creative

Staff members have much more insight into what goes on in a company than many managers realize. You, as a manager, should continually ask your staff for ideas about cutting costs, improving techniques, and implementing innovations. No matter how smart you are, there's no way you can know everything.

My Mind Is Open, but Their Mouths Are Shut

Managers often complain that they're ready to listen to ideas but no one makes any suggestions. Whose fault is that? It's not likely that team members don't have any ideas—it's more likely that you just haven't established a climate of receptivity.

At a seminar I gave in Paterson, New Jersey, a participant named Stan came up to see me afterward. "I manage a tax service and have seven skilled accountants working for me. I run meetings at which I ask for their ideas, and I know that they must have some

Meanings & Gleanings

People in lower echelons of an organization participate in *upward communication* by making ideas, suggestions, and comments flow to those in decision-making positions.

good ideas, but I can't get them to come up with them. What am I doing wrong?"

I arranged to attend one of Stan's meetings, in which he presented a problem, suggested a solution, and then asked whether anyone had ideas that might also apply. He turned from one group member to another, and the typical response was, "No, I go along with what you said."

In a discussion with the accountants after the meeting, I learned that if they had, in the past, suggested any ideas that were different from what Stan had presented, he had greeted the idea with sarcasm or outright rejection. "Why disagree?" they asked. "It won't do any good."

Keeping an Open Door Open

Barbara supervised 12 clerks and boasted that her door was always open to staff members. They could come and see her anytime with any problems, complaints, or suggestions they had.

Right—they were *allowed* to come, but they didn't. The door was open, but when one of the clerks walked in, the look of annoyance on Barbara's face signaled that visitors were not welcome. It didn't take long for them to recognize that the door was open only in theory.

Some managers say that they want to be available to their associates but that there is so much work to do they can't let people barge in whenever they feel like it.

One solution is to have a *partially* open door. Set aside certain hours during which anyone is welcome to come in without an appointment to discuss problems, make suggestions, or just kick around ideas. In this way, you can plan your time so that your work gets done and your associates still have the opportunity to bring you their concerns.

To avoid giving the impression that you feel your work is more important than your concern for the work of other team members, point out that by setting aside special hours for discussing their problems, you are able to give them full, uninterrupted attention.

Managing by Walking Around (MBWA)

You can learn a great deal by walking around. If you're always in your office or hiding behind the papers on your desk, how can you expect to know what's going on? You have to get out there with your associates, talk to them, and develop their confidence.

It's not just walking around—it's what you *do* when you walk around. Lou made a practice of walking around the factory floor and stopping to speak to some of his employees—usually the same old-timers whom he had known for years. He asked how they were doing and about their families. It was good for morale, but he never learned anything of real value.

Carmen also walked around her department, but she took a different approach: Before her tour, she reviewed which projects were being performed, the assignments each person had, and the work problems she was particularly concerned about. The questions and comments she presented to her colleagues were specific. She asked whether the new computer program that had just been installed was giving them any problems. She asked whether they had any ideas for change and elicited comments about progress being made and what could be done to expedite the processing of back orders. Her MBWA-style paid off for her: Her associates knew that she wanted to hear their ideas.

Secret Weapons

When you solicit ideas from your team members, never present your view first. Because of your position, what you say may influence what team members had planned to say. *Listen with an open mind.* Their comments may give you new insights into the problem and result in a better solution.

Rejecting Ideas Without Causing Resentment

Suppose Keesha comes to you excited about a great idea she believes will help the department, but in your opinion, her idea isn't practical. You know she will not only be upset if the idea is rejected but may also wonder why she even bothered to suggest anything. She may not ever make another suggestion. But you know that just because this idea wasn't a good one doesn't mean her future ones won't be winners.

Rather than reject a poor suggestion, ask questions about it. With good questioning, you can get people to rethink their ideas and see the weak points they had initially overlooked. They will then reject their own bad ideas without your having to make a single negative comment.

To see how this technique might work, look at what happens when Don rushes into Lisa's office:

> **Don:** I have a great idea. We could save time processing these orders if we didn't have to have accounting check them against the invoices. They rarely find discrepancies, and, those few times they do, adjustments can be made later.

> **Lisa:** It *would* save time, Don. Would you happen to know how many orders are returned by accounting with errors in them?

> **Don:** Last week, there were 15. That's only about five percent of the orders we handled.

> **Lisa:** What would happen if those 15 orders had been processed with the errors in them?

Don: They would have been caught down the line.

Lisa: How much time would it take to correct them then?

Don: Actually, it would be very time-consuming. I guess in the long run it would take more time than we would have saved in the beginning.

Lisa knew that Don's idea was impractical. By asking questions that made Don reach the conclusion himself, the suggestion was rejected without arguments or resentment.

Encourage Idea Sharing

Some people are bubbling with ideas and can't wait to share them. But many people need some prodding to get them to bring their suggestions to you.

Various programs have been developed to make it easier for employees to bring their ideas to the company's attention. Some, such as suggestion boxes, have been around for a long time. This section discusses others that have been introduced more recently.

Feeding the Suggestion Box

Suggestion boxes have been around for decades. Do they generate good ideas, or are they just receptacles for gripes and grievances?

Secret Weapons

Make suggestion programs exciting by incorporating some of these rewards:

➤ Run periodic special award contests.

➤ Conduct a lottery. All persons who make suggestions participate in a drawing for a big screen TV.

➤ Have a monthly or quarterly luncheon for all winners.

➤ Send award winners' photos to local newspapers.

Suggestion systems can be as good as you want them to be. All it takes is a sincere commitment and a real effort to make them work. Companies have received from employees many suggestions that have enabled them to solve difficult problems, eliminate waste, improve quality, create new products, and save people millions of dollars annually.

The use of an employee suggestion form (see the following) encourages people to participate.

Follow my suggestions below to help ensure the success of your suggestion program:

➤ Make sure senior management is fully behind the program.

➤ Publicize the program with creativity and flair. Place colorful posters promoting the program around the building, and send letters to employees to encourage participation. Some companies have special promotions to increase the number of suggestions made for a specified period.

Suggestion Form

Contributor: _____ Date: _____

Department: _____ Team leader: _____

Situation: _____

_____

_____

_____

Your suggestion (use additional pages if necessary): _____

_____

_____

_____

Estimate of first year's savings: _____

Other benefits to be derived: _____

Please attach supporting documents to this form.

You will receive acknowledgment and comments from the Suggestion Committee within 10 working days. Thank you for your suggestion.

➤ Make awards commensurate with the value of the suggestion. Many companies determine the amount of the award as a certain percentage of the money the company earns or saves.

➤ Acknowledge all suggestions promptly. Unless contributions are acknowledged immediately and contributors kept informed of the status of their suggestions, they lose interest in the program and are loath to make suggestions in the future.

➤ Have all suggestions evaluated by a suggestion committee and, where applicable, technical specialists. The suggestion committee should be composed of representatives of various departments and should be chaired by a senior executive, such as the human resources manager or operations manager. The committee should be empowered to accept or reject suggestions expeditiously.

➤ Make decisions and notify the contributor as soon as possible.

➤ Give public recognition to persons receiving awards—in the company newspaper, on bulletin boards, and at staff meetings.

Eyeing Ideas for "I" Meetings

The letter *I* in "I" meetings stands for *idea*. Several days before a meeting, the people who will attend are given the agenda (usually only one or two items). They are asked to think about the matters to be discussed and be prepared to present at least one idea about each item.

At the meeting, the ideas are presented and discussed. Because the participants often approach problems from different angles, they're likely to offer a variety of ideas.

Meanings & Gleanings

A *quality circle* is a group of employees who voluntarily meet on a regular basis to discuss ideas for improving the quality of their products or services.

Unlike brainstorming (discussed later in this chapter), in which the sole purpose is idea generation with no critiques or discussions, suggestions made in "I" meetings are discussed in detail and decisions about their viability are made.

Marty, the owner of a chain of hair styling salons, adds some excitement to his "I" meetings by handing out crisp $10 bills to anyone who comes up with an especially good idea. Once in a while, if he thinks that an idea has merit but is not well thought out, he tears a bill in half and says to the person who made the suggestion, "I'll give you the other half when you work out the kinks in your concept."

Running Around in Quality Circles

The Japanese people mostly attribute the high quality of their products to quality circles. Workers, usually without management participation, are free to discuss any and all aspects of their work. They are given access to any information they feel is necessary to their discussions.

Manager's Minute

The concept of quality circles didn't originate in Japan. It originated right here in the United States in the 1950s but failed to catch on then. When workers were asked to participate in quality circles, the typical response was, "It's not my job. Someone else is responsible for quality." Today, most people recognize that quality is everyone's business.

Because the meetings are informal and managers don't oversee them, ideas flow freely and are then passed on to management. A high percentage of these suggestions are accepted and instituted. Although the concept of "quality circles" was conceived to discuss quality problems, these discussions have expanded over the years to productivity, performance, the working environment, and other aspects of business.

Focusing on Focus Groups

Market researchers developed *focus groups* to learn about typical consumers' reactions to a company's product or service. Many consumer product manufacturers have focus groups try out a product, then discuss their opinions about it. Likewise, service organizations use focus groups to evaluate the service they are providing.

Over the past few years, human resources consultants have used this approach to reveal the true attitudes of employees about their company, their department, their managers, and specific aspects of their jobs.

A group of employees is selected as a focus group to discuss a particular situation—for example, the proposed changes in the health insurance program. The participants represent several departments and vary in length of tenure at the company. Before the meeting, they are given copies of the current and proposed plans to study. The first step is to explain the plan and answer any questions from the group. Then ask for their comments and reactions. Assure them that the proposed plan hasn't as yet been adopted and no decisions will be made until after much further study, beginning with this focus group. Participants must be assured that their ideas and feelings will be considered.

Although focus groups are most effective when restricted to specific areas, they can also be used as a means of identifying basic problems that can be explored in other groups.

It is absolutely essential that no member of management observe the meeting in progress or view or hear tapes later. Anonymity of the participants is key to frank discussion. But it's okay to study written transcripts that don't identify who said what.

Meanings & Gleanings

Focus groups created to discuss how proposed company changes will affect workers represent a broad cross section of employees.

Confidential Employee Surveys

Employee attitude surveys have long been used to determine employee morale and locate problem areas. In recent years, these surveys have been refined and have become quite sophisticated diagnostic tools.

To obtain honest and meaningful information from employees, surveys, like focus groups, must be conducted by an impartial outsider. Surveys can range from a series of broad questions about company policies or employee satisfaction (or lack thereof) to specific questions about special matters.

Communication Breakdown

It's not a good idea to try to conduct your own survey. Unless the employees truly believe that the information they give will be kept confidential, you'll only get what they think you want to hear.

Inasmuch as such surveys should be designed to fit each company's special needs, they should be developed and conducted by organizations geared for that purpose. Getting the most from an employee survey goes beyond just obtaining information. A lot of planning has to go into the design of an employee survey, and it is best if it is geared toward a specific industry. For instance, a survey that is designed for use by a publisher would not be appropriate at all for use by a trucking company. Some of the best employee surveys are specially designed by a consulting firm that understands and specializes in the industry being examined. In addition, once you have answers to the questions asked, they must be interpreted intelligently, or else you haven't really learned anything. In essence, this is something that must be done by specialists.

Trials and Tribulations of the Town Meeting

Town meetings are open-ended meetings to which all employees are invited and encouraged to express their thoughts and ideas to management. Generally, this is not a good idea. Companies that run town meetings often find that they become little more than gripe sessions. People with personal agendas tend to dominate the meetings. At one such gathering I attended, a small group of employees attempted to use the meeting to voice their opinions about a grievance that had already been adjudicated—just not to their satisfaction. This distracted from the objectives of the meeting, wasted most of the participants' time, and soured everybody on the concept of town meetings.

Stimulating Creativity

"If it ain't broke, don't fix it." Wrong! Today's world is tough and competitive. You can't wait for things to break before fixing them. If you're not constantly coming up with better ideas—better ways to do things—your competitors will overwhelm you. Use constructive discontent to look at everything you're doing. Keep asking yourself, and encourage other people to ask themselves, "Is there a better way?"

It's easy to get into a rut: You become so comfortable with the status quo that you resist change. Change hurts. If you change the way you physically do something, new muscles are brought into play—and it hurts. If you change a mental process, you get real headaches. That's why so many people resist new ideas—and avoid suggesting them.

Five "Creative Thinking" Stimulators

Most people don't consider themselves to be creative. They assume that only a chosen few—inventors, artists, and writers, for example—have that talent. But all of us have the seeds of creativity within us. Those seeds just need to be developed.

As a manager, you can establish a climate that nurtures those seeds. Then, watch the creative ideas flow from the people in your department. By becoming aware and helping associates become aware of some of these creative approaches, you and your team members can dramatically increase the team's creativity levels.

One: Lateral Thinking—Looking At It Sideways

When you face a problem, you'll usually attack it logically—and that's good. But sometimes logical doesn't necessarily mean straightforward or direct. Often the best answer to a problem isn't right in front of you. You'll have to look at the problem from different angles to find the solution.

Alexander Fleming, a biologist, studied certain microbes. Periodically, when he would select a tray in which the microbes were kept for study, he'd find the germs were dead. This disturbed him because he would then have to redo his work. After finding several times that the germs had died mysteriously, Fleming wondered, "My goal is to find ways to kill germs, but these germs are already dead. Now I have to find out how they died. What killed them?"

Additional study proved that a mold that had developed in the tray had killed the germs. Thus came the discovery of penicillin. This story illustrates lateral thinking: To find the answer to his original question, Fleming redirected his focus in ways he hadn't ever considered.

Training yourself to think laterally isn't easy. The first step is to be aware that problems aren't always what they seem and that solutions aren't always straightforward. For more pointers, take a look at the book *Lateral Thinking: Creativity Step by Step*, by Edward deBono. In it, deBono provides a detailed program to help you learn how to think laterally.

Manager's Minute

The answers to your problems aren't always found by looking at them head-on. Learn to think laterally. Learn to look at, over, under, and around a problem.

Two: Being Flexible—Observation and Adaptation

Everyday you observe things happening around you. Sometimes, by adapting lessons you learn in one context to other areas of your life, you can solve myriad problems.

While Jeff was waiting for his car to be serviced at a quick lube shop, he thought about his own company, which had a fleet of delivery vans. Whenever one of the vans needed servicing, a driver had to take it to the dealer's service center and leave it there for the day. Another driver would follow along to take the first driver back to the shop. In the late afternoon, two drivers had to be dispatched again to retrieve the vehicle.

Jeff realized that, because it took half an hour to get from his shop to the service center, his company lost four person-hours just for transportation every time a van was serviced. This, in addition to the van being out of service for the entire day. Also, the company had to pay the drivers at their regular rates, even though they were doing less productive work, and had to pay for the cost of the van's servicing. Jeff knew that if those vans could be serviced at a quick lube shop, his company could save a considerable amount of money. He made the suggestion. The company implemented it, saved thousands of dollars, and gave Jeff a substantial suggestion award.

Three: Modify, Modify, Modify

By modifying something you already have, you may come up with something new, different, or better. Victor Kiam, the CEO of the Remington Electric Shaver Company, tells this story:

ZAP!

Secret Weapons

Every time you receive a form or a report, ask these questions: "Is it worth keeping? Can it be eliminated? Can it be combined with another form or made better?"

One of the members of his office staff returned to work after undergoing surgery. When Kiam went over to welcome her back, she told him, "Mr. Kiam, when I was in the hospital, I thought of you. Before the operation, the nurse shaved the body hair around the area of my abdomen where the operation was to be performed. She used a double-edge razor and nicked me three times. I said, 'You should use a Lady Remington.'"

Kiam brought that idea to his research people, who developed a modified Lady Remington, designed to be used as a surgical shaver. It's now doing well in the marketplace.

Four: Elimination—Getting Rid of Things

Most people think that in order to be creative, they have to invent something new. You can be just as creative by getting rid of things. Because most companies are bogged down with paperwork, a truly creative approach to paring down the paper hassle would save companies considerable time and money.

Evaluate by asking the following questions of every form, record, and report that is generated on a daily, weekly, or monthly basis:

➤ **Is this paperwork really necessary?** Every month when Susan received a copy of a certain report, she skimmed it briefly, then immediately filed it away because it wasn't of much value to her. When she mentioned the report to a colleague, he agreed that it was no help to him either. A survey of all the people on the distribution list showed that although the report had had some use several years earlier, it had outlived its value. By eliminating the report altogether, the company saved time and money.

➤ **Can it be combined or consolidated with other forms?** Many forms or reports contain similar or even identical data in a different format. In one company, a team of clerks spent hours each week compiling a sales report for the marketing manager and then, at the end of the month, more hours compiling the same data in a different form for the controller. At the suggestion of one of the clerks, the computer was programmed to convert the weekly reports to a monthly format, which freed up the clerks' time for more productive work.

➤ **Can it be improved?** By redesigning a form, you can often make it easier to compile and understand.

➤ **Can it be reviewed electronically?** Specialized software for creating forms and reports lets you redesign or create better forms quickly on the computer.

Communication Breakdown

Brainstorming isn't appropriate for all types of problems. It works best when you're dealing with specific situations rather than with long-term policies: naming a new product, improving a procedure, probing for new channels of distribution, making jobs more interesting, or developing new approaches to marketing a product or service.

Five: Brainstorming—Encouraging Group Creativity

A brainstorming meeting may be exciting, hectic, and totally chaotic, but it does generate ideas. The goal of brainstorming is to develop as many ideas as possible—not to critique, analyze, or discuss them or make decisions.

Suppose you are participating in a brainstorming session in which participants call out ideas that are hurriedly listed on a flip chart. Some of the ideas seem totally ridiculous, but no one scoffs, rebuts, or comments. No matter how stupid or inane an idea seems, it's listed on the chart.

Why is the group encouraged to bring out all these ideas, even the absurd ones? The psychological principle behind brainstorming is called *triggering*. Any idea, no matter how dumb it seems, can trigger more viable ideas in other participants' minds. By allowing participants to think freely and express their ideas without fear of criticism, brainstorming draws out a maximum amount of valuable ideas from people. After the session, a committee analyzes the better ideas in more detail.

The Least You Need to Know

➤ Create a climate that is open to upward communication.

➤ Use focus groups and attitude surveys to learn how employees really feel about projected changes in company policies.

➤ Rather than reject a bad idea, ask questions. Your questioning will help people think more clearly about their ideas and discover any inadequacies.

➤ Well-designed suggestion programs generate productive ideas.

➤ "I" meetings and quality circles can stimulate your team members to think constructively about their work.

➤ You can develop your own creativity and the creativity of your staff by training yourself and your team to employ lateral thinking, observation and adaptation, modification, elimination, and, when appropriate, brainstorming.

OK, JOHNSON I WANT YOU TO HANDLE THE MARKETING. LEE, YOU CRUNCH THE NUMBERS, AND PEREZ DO R&D...

You Can't Do It All Yourself

In This Chapter

➤ Overcoming your fears of delegating

➤ Understanding the five elements of effective assigning

➤ Scheduling the workload

➤ Managing multiple priorities

Your team has lots of work to do. What will you do yourself, and what will you assign to other team members? When you delegate, you assign to your team members not only tasks but also the power and the authority to accomplish them.

Effective *delegation* means that a team leader has enough confidence in his or her team members to know that they'll carry out an assignment satisfactorily and expeditiously.

This chapter looks at some techniques and approaches to help you become a better delegater.

Don't Hesitate—Delegate!

Sure, you're responsible for everything that goes on in your department or team, but if you try to do everything yourself, you'll put in 12 or more hours a day. That can lead to burnout and ulcers, or even heart attacks and nervous breakdowns.

There are certain things, of course, that only you can do, decisions that only you can make, critical areas that only you can handle. That's where you earn your keep. Many of the activities you undertake, however, can and should be done by others. This list discusses some of the reasons you may hesitate to delegate and explains why you should reconsider:

➤ **You can do it better than your associates.** That may be the case, but you should spend your time and energy on more important things. Each of your team members has talents and skills that contribute to your team's performance. By delegating assignments, you give team members the opportunity to use those skills.

How often have you thought, "By the time I tell a co-worker what to do, demonstrate how to do it, check the work, find it wrong, and have it done over, I could have it completed and go on to other things"? Showing someone how to perform a certain task will take time now, of course, but after your co-worker masters the task, it will make your job easier later.

➤ **You get a great deal of satisfaction from a certain aspect of the work and hesitate to give it up.** You're not alone. All of us enjoy certain things about our work and are reluctant to assign them to others. Look at the tasks objectively. Even if you have a pet project, you must delegate it if your time can be spent handling other activities that are now your responsibility as a manager.

➤ **You're concerned that, if you don't do it yourself, it won't get done right.** You have a right to be concerned. The following section explains how to minimize this risk. You won't have to be afraid of delegating work to others if you follow the principles I describe.

Meanings & Gleanings

Delegation enables you to position the right work at the right responsibility level, helping both you and your team members expand skills and contributions. You also ensure that all work gets done on time by the right person who has the right experience or interest.

Who's Gonna Do the Work?

You know the capabilities of each of your associates. When you plan their assignments, consider which person can do which job most effectively. If you're under no time pressure, you can use the assignment to build up another person's skills. The more team members who have the capabilities to take on a variety of assignments, the easier your job is for you. If no one on your staff can do the work, then of course you'll have to do it yourself. You should train one or more team members in several areas so you can delegate work in those areas when necessary.

Tell 'em What to Do—The Right Way

After you give detailed instructions to one of your team members, your usual question is probably "Do you understand?" And the usual answer is "Yes."

But does the employee really understand? Maybe. But maybe that person isn't quite sure, but in good faith says "I understand." Or maybe the person doesn't understand at all but is too embarrassed to say so.

Rather than ask "Do you understand?" ask "What are you going to do?" If the response indicates that one or more of your points isn't clear, you can correct it before the employee does something wrong.

When it's essential for an employee to rigidly conform to your instructions, you should make sure that he or she thoroughly understands them. Give a quiz. Ask specific questions so that both you and your team member completely agree about what he or she will do. When it's not essential for a delegated activity to be performed in a specific manner, you can just get some general feedback.

Tailor the way you make assignments to the preferences of the person to whom you're delegating. Some people like to have responsibilities spelled out explicitly, perhaps in the form of a written list of items. Others prefer simple, concise instructions. Some people prefer e-mail, and others would rather have you delegate in person.

Meanings & Gleanings

Some people use the word *assigning* when they're talking about short-term projects and the word *delegating* for long-term projects. The terms are usually interchangeable.

Make Sure They Understand—and Accept—Your Instructions

Your instructions must be both understood *and* accepted by your team member. Suppose that on Tuesday morning, Janet, the office manager, gives an assignment to Jeremy with a deadline of 3:30 that afternoon. Jeremy looks at the amount of work involved and says to himself, "There's no way." It's unlikely that he will meet that *deadline.*

To gain acceptance, let your team member know just how important the work is. Janet might say, "Jeremy, this report must be on the director's desk when she comes in tomorrow morning. She needs it for an early morning meeting with the executive committee. When do you think I can have it?" Jeremy may think, "This is important. If I skip my break and don't call my girlfriend, I can have it by 5:00."

Why did Janet originally indicate that she wanted the report by 3:30 when she didn't even need it until the following morning? Maybe she thought that if she said 3:30,

Jeremy would knock himself out and finish the report by the end of the day. But most people don't react that way. Faced with what they consider to be an unreasonable deadline, most people won't even try. By letting people set their own schedules within reasonable limits, you get their full commitment to meeting or beating a deadline.

But suppose that Janet really did need that report by 3:30—so that it could be proofread, photocopied, collated, and bound. To get the report completed on time, she could have assigned someone to help Jeremy or allowed him to work overtime.

Be realistic when you assign deadlines. Don't make a practice of asking for projects to be completed earlier than you need them—people will stop taking your deadlines seriously.

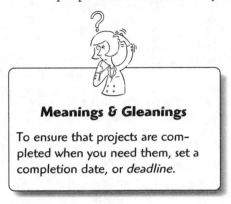

Meanings & Gleanings

To ensure that projects are completed when you need them, set a completion date, or *deadline*.

Control Points—Your Safeguard

A control point is the point at which you stop a project, examine the work that has been completed, and correct any errors. Control points can help you catch errors before they blow up into catastrophes.

A control point is *not* a surprise inspection. Team members should know exactly when each control point is established and what should be accomplished by then.

Suppose Gary, a team leader, gives a project to Kim on Monday morning. The deadline is the following Friday at 3 P.M. They agree that the first control point will be at 4 P.M. Tuesday, at which time Kim should have completed parts A and B. Notice that Kim knows exactly *what* and *when*. When Gary and Kim meet on Tuesday, they find several errors in part B. That's not good, but it's not terrible. The errors can be corrected before the work continues. If Gary and Kim had not scheduled a control point, the errors would have been perpetuated throughout the entire project.

Communication Breakdown

Some managers make decisions in every phase of an assignment and look over everyone's shoulders checking for dotted *i*'s and crossed *t*'s. When you *micro-manage*, you stifle creativity and prevent team members from working at their full potential.

Provide the Right Tools— Delegate Authority

You can't do a job without the proper tools. Providing equipment, computer time, and access to resources is an obvious step, but giving away *authority* is another story.

Many managers are reluctant to give up any of their authority. If a job is to be done without your micro-management, you must give the people doing the job the power to make decisions.

If they need supplies or materials, allot them a budget so that they can order what they need without having to ask your approval for every purchase. If a job might call for overtime, give them the authority to order it. If you have to be around to make every decision, the work will get bogged down.

When You Delegate, You Don't Abdicate

Team or workgroup members almost always have questions, seek advice, and need your help. Be there for them, but don't let them throw the entire project back at you. Let them know that you're available to help, advise, and support, but not to do their work.

Putting Delegation to Work

Now that you know the principles of delegation, you're ready to apply them on the job.

To help you systematize your approach to delegation, use the sample delegation worksheet below. You may photocopy it or adapt it to your needs.

Secret Weapons

When people bring you a problem, insist that they bring with it a suggested solution. At best, they will solve their own problems and not bother you. At the very least, they'll ask you, "Do you think this solution will work?" which is much easier to respond to than "What do I do now?"

Delegating to Teams

When an organization is structured into teams, work should be delegated and assigned as a team activity. When people have some control over the assignments they get, they approach their work with enthusiasm and commitment.

When your boss gives you a complex project, present it in its entirety to your team. You should discuss with your team how to break the assignment into phases. Delegating each of the phases to individual team members will follow easily. Most members will choose to handle the areas in which they have the most expertise. If two members want the same area, let them iron it out with each other. But if it gets sticky, you should step in and resolve the problem diplomatically: "Abdul, you did the research on our last project, so let's give Carol a chance to handle it this time."

Certain phases of the assignment are bound to be tough or unpleasant. No one's really going to volunteer to do them. Have your team set up an equitable system for assigning this type of work.

As team leader, be sure that every member of your team is aware of everyone else's responsibilities as well as his or her own. In this way, everyone knows what everyone else is doing and what kind of support he or she can give or receive from others.

To keep everyone informed, create a chart listing each phase of the assignment, the person handling it, deadlines, and other pertinent information. Post the chart in the office for easy referral.

Delegation Worksheet

Delegated to: _____

Date of assignment: _____   Deadline: _____

Brief description of assignment: _____

_____

Communication:

Assignee's comments: _____

_____

_____

Areas that must be clarified: _____

Control points:

First control point will be on _____ at _____

Phase to be completed: _____

_____

Performance standards: _____

_____

_____

Date this phase completed: _____

(Use separate pages for each subsequent control point)

Assignment completed: _____   Date: _____

Comments: _____

_____

_____

How we can make this person more effective in the next assignment:

_____

_____

Manager's Minute

If you have a difficult task, assign it to a capable, but lazy person. He or she will find an easy way to do it.

Delegating by Using Teams

Before companies began using the team concept, work was done interdepartmentally. That is, the department manager would schedule production for his or her department with the assistance of support departments (for instance, production control, inventory control, and purchasing). The order department would process customers' orders and send the orders on to production scheduling. The production department would then determine priorities and assign various aspects of the job to the appropriate departments. Each department head would then assign specific phases of the task to individual employees.

As you can imagine, this process would often result in bottlenecks. If one department fell behind, it would cause delays in all the others.

The multi-departmental team can successfully handle projects that require coordination among many diverse workgroups within a company. An effective team has these characteristics:

➤ It is composed of representatives from all relevant internal departments, such as Sales and Production. Team members are usually chosen by the team leader in coordination with managers of the involved departments.

➤ Outside representatives, such as customers, suppliers, and subcontractors, are invited to participate in team discussions. Although these people aren't members of the team, their input is important in helping the team accomplish its goal.

➤ Production schedules are determined based on customers' needs. Team members are given detailed information about these needs and

Meanings & Gleanings

In a *multi-departmental team*, also called a *cross-functional team*, representatives from different departments, who are temporarily assigned to work as a team, combine their expertise to work collaboratively on a project.

are encouraged to deal directly with customers to keep up to date on necessary adjustments.

➤ Delivery of materials is arranged on a just-in-time basis. To avoid unnecessary inventory costs, arrangements are made for delivery of materials and supplies as close as possible to the time they'll be used.

➤ Work assignments are planned collaboratively and control points are established. Some projects require teams to meet daily to coordinate and maintain attention to the assignment. Other projects require only occasional meetings to check on progress and deal with problems.

The key to the success of multi-departmental programs is communication. Team members are encouraged to communicate in person, on the telephone, or by writing, faxing, or e-mailing each other on a timely basis. Problems can then be addressed without delay.

Project Management

When companies are faced with special types of projects, usually one-time tasks (such as introducing a new product to the market, moving to a new location, or developing a new product or service), they often create a project management team, rather than assign it to one or more operating departments.

This new group handles all matters related to the project. Project managers have the authority to obtain from various departments in the company all necessary personnel, equipment, and anything else to complete the assignment. Project team members are often temporarily relieved of their regular duties for the duration of the project.

The person chosen to be *project manager* is usually a senior or middle manager who has expertise in the activities the project involves. Some of the project manager's first tasks are listed below:

➤ Assemble a multi-departmental team that includes representatives from various parts of the organization to plan and implement the project.

➤ Together with these representatives, plan the project and set timetables for each phase.

➤ Work with team members to coordinate the work of everyone involved, from the inception of the design phase, to the final distribution, to customers. The people involved may include engineers, production supervisors, marketing and sales staff, and shipping and distribution personnel.

Meanings & Gleanings

A *project manager* is a team leader assigned to head up a specific project, such as the design and manufacture of an electronic system or the development and marketing of a new product.

The result is that you get cooperation in place of turf wars. Rather than time-wasting red tape, you get fast decisions. By crossing over traditional departmental barriers, project managers can get quick action, shift gears when necessary, and react immediately to urgent problems.

Using the Computer as a Scheduling Tool

As work scheduling becomes more and more complex, computers will be integral to helping you keep the details organized.

Scheduling programs, such as Microsoft Project, enable you to define the various project tasks and their relationships to one another. Microsoft Project lets you concentrate on major phases of a project or on specific detailed tasks. It also enables you to allocate and track resources and to set working hours and days for groups and individuals. The program will alert you to deviations from the schedule so that you can take immediate action.

When you use this type of software, it's easy to see whether your project is progressing as planned. You know which tasks must be given special attention to avoid delaying the completion of a project.

Microsoft Project also has a variety of report formats you can use to communicate your progress to your own staff, customers, and anyone else involved.

Managing Multiple Priorities

If you're a typical '90s manager, you're probably loaded down with more work than it seems possible to do—and so are your team members.

Darlene, for example, is not only working on a project for you but is also on the quality assurance team and is involved in the research for a new product. Hans, a member of your functional team, has been asked to work on a special project for another manager. All these assignments are important, but you're responsible for getting the work on your project accomplished.

What can you do when members of your team have other assignments that are equally important or when your team is facing several high-priority tasks that must be completed in the same timeframe?

Communication Breakdown

Putting in more hours, bringing more work home, and going to the office on weekends may help, but it often results in stress, fatigue, and low morale, which can reduce performance and productivity. Don't forget that most people have families, other interests, and the need to rest and refuel.

Communicate, Communicate, Communicate

You can't pull rank. It used to be that you could force your priorities on others because you were higher on the totem pole. Occasionally, this is still acceptable, but in most progressive organizations such power plays are discouraged.

Work it out. Talk to team members and to other team leaders to schedule work that will enable all of you to make the best contribution you can to your organization. This process takes diplomacy and a willingness to compromise.

Working Smarter Beats Working Harder

A limited number of hours is available for work, and no matter how you look at it, there are only 24 hours in a day. For most people, the 8-hour workday is a mere pipe dream. Many people spend 10 or 12 hours at the office, and then take work home with them at night. There's a limit, however, to the amount of time a person can spend working.

Secret Weapons

When you say "no" to an assignment, explain how taking on the assignment would inhibit completion of other higher-priority projects. Suggest alternative solutions.

Overwork *does* exist. In the past few years, as more and more companies downsize, overworking has become a serious problem. Employees who remain in an organization after a downsizing have to take on their ex-colleagues' assignments in addition to their own workload.

As you learned in Chapter 6, you should seek new and creative approaches to your work—that is, work smarter, not harder. Ask yourself: What kind of work can be eliminated? Which work processes can be re-engineered? Which can be delegated? The time you spend learning about new approaches will pay off through expedient performance.

Don't Be Afraid to Say No

You can't do everything. At times, your team gets so bogged down with work that taking on another assignment would simply be impossible. How can you turn it down diplomatically?

Sometimes you can't. The project may have a high priority and must be completed. In that case, re-examine all your other projects. Determine which of them can be put on the back burner until you complete the new assignment. Some projects may be ahead of schedule and can be temporarily postponed; others may not be as important as the new job. Discuss these issues with your boss, and work together to reschedule other priorities.

Often, you can just reschedule. The new assignment may not be a high-priority project and can be put on hold for a while. Or maybe the project can be done more effectively by another team. It's no shame to admit that your group may not have the necessary background for a project. Know your limitations.

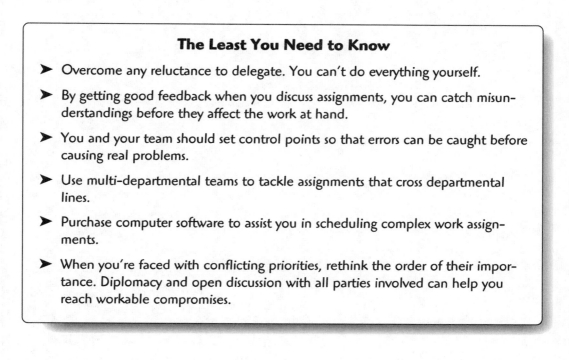

The Least You Need to Know

➤ Overcome any reluctance to delegate. You can't do everything yourself.

➤ By getting good feedback when you discuss assignments, you can catch misunderstandings before they affect the work at hand.

➤ You and your team should set control points so that errors can be caught before causing real problems.

➤ Use multi-departmental teams to tackle assignments that cross departmental lines.

➤ Purchase computer software to assist you in scheduling complex work assignments.

➤ When you're faced with conflicting priorities, rethink the order of their importance. Diplomacy and open discussion with all parties involved can help you reach workable compromises.

Part 2
The Supervisor as Coach

Your team is in place. Now comes the real work: molding those men and women into a dynamic, interactive, high-performance unit. That's what a coach does for athletic teams, and that's your job now.

How do you do it? By helping the members of your team develop their talents to optimum capacity. You have to keep your team aware of your organization's goals and on top of the latest methods and techniques that will enable them to reach those goals. You have to help them learn what they don't know and perfect what they do know.

In this part of the book, you'll pick up some suggestions for the training and development of the people on your team.

Chapter 8

PUSH YOURSELVES!!
C'MON, FEEL THE BURN!!

Developing Your Team for Optimum Performance

In This Chapter

➤ Identifying what your team needs to learn

➤ Understanding the four-step approach to imparting know-how

➤ Using your entire team as a training vehicle

➤ Using techniques that make training fun and effective

➤ Training people to work under changing conditions

One thing's for sure: Things change. Nothing in this dynamic world stays the same for long. The way we approach our jobs, the way a job is performed, and even the type of work we do changes with the times. As a team leader, you must keep up with these changes and help team members learn how to do their jobs and keep up with changing methods and techniques.

Planting the Training Seeds

Like everything, training starts at the beginning. It's your job to make sure your team members have the know-how to do their jobs. New associates may bring with them skills they acquired through education and not experience. It's a plus, of course, if a new team member has done similar work in another company, but even work experience isn't enough to eliminate the need for training. Every organization has its own way of doing things. To ensure consistency in the way your group works, all new associates should be given basic job training or retraining.

When's the Harvest?

New people may need basic training, but training and development aren't limited to newcomers. All members of your team need ongoing training. They should continually acquire new techniques and renew established skills. Always encourage self-development.

As a leader and a coach, you are the guide and stimulus of your team's growth. By working closely with each of your team members, you can suggest areas in which additional training will be helpful and skills they should acquire. You can also provide the resources for this process.

How much time, effort, and money should you invest in training? There's no question that well-trained, high performance teams are major ingredients in a company's success, but (as mentioned in Chapter 2), there must be a balance between the P (*potential* of people) and R (*results* desired).

Few companies have unlimited training budgets—companies aren't universities. People in professional and high-tech jobs must acquire necessary skills before joining an organization. A company's responsibility is to help these people adapt their knowledge to meet its particular needs.

Communication Breakdown

If your new associate has done similar work in another job, don't assume that training is unnecessary. Observe the way a new employee approaches his job, and discuss any differences between it and his previous work. To ensure consistency, retrain the person. But keep an open mind: Your new associate may be able to teach you a better way to do a job.

Some jobs, however, are unique to a company. In such cases, the company is the only source employees have for training. The amount of time and money a company spends on training, then, depends on the complexity of the tasks that need to be performed.

America is moving rapidly from a production-based to a service-based economy. More and more people are eschewing blue collar jobs for jobs in offices, stores, restaurants, and other service oriented industries. The required skills differ, and the need to train the people who perform them presents new challenges to management. Whether a job calls for skills in computer operations, telemarketing, claims processing, cooking, or customer service, mastery of specific tasks must be taught. The trainers—team leaders and managers—are the coaches who will develop the skills necessary for their team's optimum performance.

Train for What?

Training may be important, but it is only cost effective if the selected training areas pay off in higher productivity and a better bottom line.

Assessing Training Needs

Many companies only guess as to what type of training is needed. Sure, training in the specific skills required to do the work is obvious, but skills alone do not ensure productivity. Too often, companies implement unnecessary training programs, ignoring the more valuable areas where people would actually benefit from some training.

Before choosing any training programs, the company should conduct a needs analysis. Professional training experts apply systematic approaches to needs assessments, but you can also make some basic assessments on your own.

Secret Weapons

As jobs change, people must also change. Anticipate the types of jobs you think your company will eventually need. If your company doesn't provide training in those areas, find your own ways to acquire the necessary skills. Take computer training, enroll in interpersonal-relations courses, or learn a foreign language. Take the initiative—your career is in your own hands.

Ten Questions About Your Training Needs

Study the jobs involved and ask yourself questions like these:

1. What is the gap between desired and actual performance?
2. Is the problem caused by lack of technical skills?
3. Is the problem caused by employees' attitudes?
4. Can you close the gap through supervisory attention, or do you think special training is needed?
5. If you do require training, which employees need the training?
6. Do you have the internal capability to provide the training? If so, who will do it and when?
7. If not, and you choose to go outside, what sources are available?
8. What performance results should you expect from the training?
9. What is the cost of the training?
10. What financial benefits will result?

Once you have the answers to these questions, you can determine the type of program to institute. If you choose to do the training internally, prepare to be the best instructor you can be. Techniques and tools of effective instruction will be covered in Chapter 9.

Manager's Minute

"Training people is often a one-way process. The teacher presents information and hopes the student absorbs it. When training is replaced by learning, the emphasis is on developing the capability of trainees to identify and solve problems, to seek knowledge, and to take the initiative in continuing self-development."

—Erwin S. Stanton

Keeping Up with the State-of-the-Art

Basic skills training still has its place in the business world. The fundamentals of a job must be acquired as a start, but we can't stop there. Continued training must be an ongoing concern. Continued training to teach new technologies is already in place in most companies, but even that's not enough. The following list shows five ways to bring your training and development up-to-date:

➤ Instead of teaching employees how to deal with specific problems, give them a general understanding of how to identify and solve all problems.

➤ Place the ultimate responsibility for learning on the individual (or, in team learning, on the team). The person who conducts the training is a facilitator: Rather than spoon-feeding information to trainees, he or she guides them through the process and summarizes and reinforces the resulting insights.

Communication Breakdown

Steer clear of training programs that promise miracles. If they sound too good to be true, they are too good to be true. Your best bet is to use well-established, proven training programs.

➤ Make sure that people who will learn together share a common vocabulary, are trained to use the same analytical tools, and have communication channels available so they can work together and with other people or teams within an organization. A company, through its training or HR department, should provide these tools.

➤ To learn to solve problems, trainees should be encouraged to tap resources in other departments or outside the company, such as customers, suppliers, and trade or professional associations.

➤ Avoid having professional trainers do the training. Let people from all job categories (managers, team leaders, human resource specialists) be the facilitators. This technique not only expands a company's training resources but helps develop future leaders.

In-House Universities—Training Medium of the Future

Have you heard of Hamburger University? It's no joke. McDonald's created it to train its management people, and it was the forerunner of many other "company universities." So why was a university created to teach people how to flip a Big Mac? If that was all there was to managing a McDonald's outlet, it would be considered overkill. McDonald's recognized early on that developing managers who know how to lead teams, market products, and increase sales pays off in making its units profitable.

In an article titled "Five Top Corporate Training Programs" in *Successful Meetings* magazine, Robert Carey says that a number of other companies have converted their training departments into autonomous schools with the latest teaching equipment, faculties drawn both from within the company and from outside sources, and curricula planned as carefully as (or more carefully than) those of many colleges. Most of these organizations call their schools "universities." According to the American Council on Education (ACE), more than 40 of these company universities have been established in the United States.

This section looks at some of the most successful of these "universities."

At Walt Disney, Training Is Show Biz

Disney University isn't a campus, but a process for training all employees of Walt Disney World Resorts. The first week of training includes a workshop called "Traditions," in which multimedia techniques are used to give trainees an overview of Disney history and culture and the vision of the organization. Facilitators for the sessions are Disney employees themselves. They share with trainees their own personal experiences working for Disney. Professional facilitators are also used, but only for technical and executive sessions.

What makes this program unique is that trainees are allowed to mingle among the visiting crowds at the parks and observe Disney employees in action. The result is that Disney's front-line attrition rate is only 15 percent compared with 60 percent for the rest of the hospitality industry.

Saturn Company: GM's Training for the Next Century

The key to Saturn's structure is its use of teams. The goal of the Saturn University training program is to teach employees to operate as continuously learning, fully independent work teams. The teams are responsible for their own development. The teams manage their own budgets, order their own materials, and gauge their own educational progress.

Each employee is responsible for creating his or her own training and development plan. It may involve brushing up on current skills or acquiring new ones, attending seminars, completing computer-based training programs, or even teaching a training session or cross training a team member. Half of all Saturn training is in interpersonal relations and communications.

The best example of Saturn's commitment to education is that all executives, including its CEO, teach at Saturn University.

Meanings & Gleanings

In-house "universities" are not traditional degree-offering colleges. They are structured curricula designed to train employees, enhance their job skills, prepare them for career growth, and keep them on the cutting edge of industry technology.

Motorola University

Motorola, an award-winning international electronics manufacturer, is committed to customer service. Motorola University was created to make sure all employees kept their technical skills sharp, but that was only the beginning. Motorola programs also help trainees develop creativity and leadership, work in teams, and improve customer relations.

The program's success has resulted in Motorola's amazing growth in a highly competitive industry—not just in the United States, but also in the global marketplace. The training program has become a model for many other organizations.

Manager's Minute

Motorola University invites other companies to learn about its training. Write to Motorola University at 2 Century Center, 1700 East Golf Road, Schaumburg, IL 60173. Or call (708) 538-4404.

Finding Training Expertise Outside the Company

When should you go outside the company for help in training? When others can do it better. Review your needs assessment. Determine what type of required training you cannot do yourself. Then look for the organization that can do it for you.

If the training need is computer skill development, your best source may be the hardware manufacturer or software provider. These firms usually have training facilities. Either they will send trainers to your office or offer classes at their own offices. Costs vary. Many suppliers offer free training with a purchase; others charge per hour or day.

Manufacturers of technical equipment also usually provide free or low cost training upon equipment installation and reasonably priced training for new employees later.

Training in the soft skills is more complicated. You can implement in-house programs in selling, leadership, self-confidence, communications, public speaking, and more or send team members to public seminars and classes. These programs are offered by individual consultants, college professors, training organizations, and others. They vary from one-day seminars to week-long retreats to weekly classes over several months. Costs vary. Some places charge per attendee; others ask for a flat fee.

Manager's Minute

The National Organization of Executive Secretaries offers periodic seminars on developing management skills for secretaries and executive assistants. They include programs for leadership, communication, human resources development, and related topics. The seminars are open to both members and nonmembers. For information, write to 900 South Washington Street, Suite G13, Falls Church, VA 22046, or call (703) 237-8616.

Eight Tips for Picking the Right Trainer

1. Select a firm with professional credentials. The firm should be a member of the American Society for Training & Development (see Appendix C), or affiliated with a university or appropriate professional associations.

2. Ask managers of other companies for referrals. If they have used training organizations for similar problems, their recommendations will be valuable.

3. Check out the firms you are considering with other companies in your industry or area. Even if these other companies haven't used the training firms you're considering, they may know of others that have.

4. Ask for references. Get the names of several past and present clients. Make sure you speak with clients who used the service several years ago. Ask them about the long-term value they feel the training has offered. Ask if they would use the firm again.

5. Sit in on a current training class. If the firm gives public programs, either attend a session yourself or send one of your managers. If the type of program you want isn't offered publicly, but at another company, ask the company's permission to attend.

6. Ask to see a random selection of past program evaluations. Look for patterns of positive and negative factors. For example, I recently read a batch of evaluations that indicated the instructor was a dynamic, exciting speaker, but also noted that he did not encourage group participation. As participation was key to my client's objectives, we didn't select that trainer.

ZAP!

Secret Weapons

Many companies that have regular needs for people with certain skills team up with local community colleges to train people—often providing financial aid, equipment, materials, and instructors.

7. Make sure the instructor is an expert in the field you need help with. One of my clients needed training in Total Quality Management and retained a prestigious consulting firm. But the trainer they assigned had only a superficial knowledge of that area. Interview the principal of the firm *and* the assigned instructor.

8. Be wary of programs that advertise training "gimmicks" and claim to give your employees motivation or improved interpersonal skills. Many of these programs are truly fun and exciting, but rarely provide long-term benefits. Over the years, programs such as EST and Sensitivity Training have come and gone.

Using Local Schools and Colleges

Some training can be provided inexpensively through local schools. These facilities are especially helpful with training in basic skills, such as English as a Second Language, computers, typing, and business practices. Some companies, such as Eastman Kodak, arrange for the schools to send teachers to company facilities to conduct classes after working hours.

Many community colleges develop special programs to meet the needs of companies in their communities. For example, in South Carolina, several community colleges offer courses geared toward the textile industry. In New York City, there is a community college located near LaGuardia Airport that offers training in various skills used by the aviation industry.

Many universities offer undergraduate and graduate degree programs that can be valuable to local employees. They also have non-degree courses in their continuing education divisions designed for people who either don't have a degree or already have a degree in one area and want to acquire knowledge in other areas.

Companies can encourage employees to participate in such programs by paying directly for them or reimbursing tuition.

Bells Ring, Lights Flash, but Does the Training Work?

Often the training program generates excitement among the participants. They enjoy the class, are amused by the instructor's stories and stimulated by the case studies, games, and interactive programs. Great! But have they learned what they were sent to learn?

Over the years, many senior executives have expressed skepticism about the value of training because they could not quantify the results. Attempts to measure the effectiveness of training programs were generally done superficially, usually by asking the trainees to fill out a questionnaire reflecting their reaction to the program.

In 1959, Donald L. Kirkpatrick, now professor emeritus at the University of Wisconsin, first proposed a model for measuring training programs. This model was recently revised and updated in his book, *Evaluating Training Programs: The Four Levels*.

> *Level 1: Using the traditional trainee evaluation forms.* Getting immediate feedback from trainees allows you to gauge their reaction to the program. You'll learn the trainee's feelings about course content, instructor effectiveness, and whether the course met the trainee's expectations. You can get this feedback through questionnaires and evaluation reports immediately or shortly after the completion of a training program.

> *Level 2: Determining what the trainee learned.* Just as schools have always tested students on what they learned in class, you can test what your employees learned during training. Administer a written or oral exam, or ask for a demonstration of skills acquired. Follow up a few months later to see how much of the material the trainee has retained.

> *Level 3: Evaluating the application of learned skills to the job.* This can be a significant tool in determining the value of training. Have the trainees applied to their jobs what they learned during training? With hard skills, you should be able to assess application by checking for such things as reduction in number of rejects and increase in productivity. Of course, it is much more difficult to measure application of soft skills. Behavioral scientists have developed instruments to measure this, but such studies must be conducted by specially trained professionals.

Secret Weapons

A company's training investment is most likely to pay off when the training department is held accountable for results, used only when it is the appropriate tool, and linked to the company strategy.

Level 4: Tying training to the bottom line. Did the training result in a measurable improvement in business results?

Manager's Minute

A recent variation of Kirkpatrick's four levels of training evaluation is Jack J. Phillips's *"Level 5"*—Measurement of ROI, or Return on Investment. Here, you evaluate whether the monetary value of the results exceeds the cost of the program.

The Least You Need to Know

➤ The first step in the training process is to assess your training needs.

➤ Learning never ceases. You and your team must keep up with the state-of-the-art not only in your areas of specialty, but in the business and industry as a whole.

➤ Creating in-house universities, as Motorola, McDonald's, and Disney did, adds credence to the value your organization places on training.

➤ Equipment and software suppliers are excellent sources for training in the products they provide.

➤ Check backgrounds and references of consultants and training organizations carefully before signing on.

➤ Be wary of companies that offer gimmicky approaches to motivational or interpersonal relations training. Stick to well-established programs.

➤ Local schools, community colleges, and universities are excellent sources of training.

➤ Measure the effectiveness of your training using Kirkpatrick's "Four Levels of Training Evaluation."

Chapter 9

Training Tools and Techniques

In This Chapter

➤ The four Ps of job training

➤ Training as a team activity

➤ Problems in learning

➤ Training and development techniques

In most organizations, training is done on the job by team leaders and supervisors—not professional trainers. Training is not an innate talent. It can be learned. In this chapter, I will discuss several successful techniques that can be used in most types of skill training.

The Four Ps

Training cannot be a haphazard process. It must be planned and systemized. Many organizations have used an effective and simple four-step training program for several years: job-instruction training, or *JIT*. Job-instruction training, a systematic approach to training people to perform tasks, involves four steps: preparation, presentation, performance, and post-work.

Preparation

Preparation is both physical and psychological. All *physical* equipment and facilities that are necessary for training should be in place before you begin. If you're training someone in a computer process, you should have on hand a computer, the software, a training manual, the data, and any other materials necessary to show someone how to use a computer. After you begin, you don't want to be interrupted by having to look for items you need.

In the *psychological* part of the process, you should tell a trainee, before the training begins, what will be taught, why it's performed, and how it fits into the overall picture. When people can see the entire picture, not just their small part in it, they learn faster and understand more clearly, and they're more likely to remember what they've been taught.

Presentation

You can no longer say to a trainee, "Just watch me, and do what I do." If it were only that simple. Work today is much too complex to learn just by observation. The following four steps can guide you in showing someone how to perform a task:

1. Describe what you're going to do.

2. Demonstrate step by step. As you demonstrate, explain each step and explain why it's done (for example, "Notice that I entered the order number on the top right side of the form to make it easy to locate").

3. Have the trainee perform the task and explain to you the method and reason for each step.

4. If the trainee doesn't perform to your satisfaction, have him repeat the task. If he performs well, reinforce the behavior with praise or positive comments.

Performance

After you're satisfied that a trainee can do a job, leave her alone and let her do it. The trainee needs an opportunity to try out what she has learned. She will probably make some mistakes, but that's to be expected. From time to time, check out how things are going and make necessary corrections.

Post-Work

The post-work step is important because people tend to change what they have been taught. Careless people may skip some steps in a procedure, causing errors or complications. Smart people may make changes that they believe are better than what they were taught. Although you should encourage your associates to try to find more effective approaches to their job, caution them not to make any changes until they have discussed them with you. They often may not be aware of the ramifications of their suggested changes.

Schedule post-work discussions of new assignments three to four weeks after the presentation step. At that time, review what the associate has been doing, and, if changes have been made intentionally or inadvertently, bring the person back on track.

Training Is a Team Activity

Just because you're the team leader doesn't mean you have to train all your team members. The training function should be shared by everyone on the team. Some organizations encourage an entire team to share in the task of training new members; others assign one person to act as a mentor.

Determining who will train new members or be assigned to retrain others depends on what people are being trained to do. *Caution:* A person who knows the job best isn't always the most qualified person to train others. It takes more than job knowledge to be an effective trainer.

Job know-how *is* essential for the person who will do the training, but it's only part of the picture. Look for these additional factors:

➤ **Personal characteristics:** Patience, empathy, and flexibility are good qualities to look for.

➤ **Knowledge of training techniques:** If a team member has the personal characteristics, he can learn the training techniques. Some companies provide "Train the Trainer" programs to build up the communications skills of people who will do the training.

➤ **A strong, positive attitude toward the job and the company:** If you assign a disgruntled person to do your training, that person will inject the trainee with the virus of discontent.

Communication Breakdown

Practice does *not* make perfect. If people practice doing things wrong, they become perfect in doing things wrong. Practice makes *permanent.* When you train associates, periodically check out what they're doing. If it's wrong, correct it immediately, before it becomes permanently ingrained as a bad habit.

Scheduling Training

When training must be accomplished in a short time, you should set up a training schedule. Before you can do so, you must determine whether the training will be done on or off the job.

On-the-job training is done at the work site during regular working hours, usually by the supervisor or another team member. Off-the-job training is conducted in a classroom or a special facility rather than at the regular place of work, and it has many advantages over on-the-job training:

➤ **People learn faster.** Because trainees devote all their time and effort to training, no other work interferes with the learning process.

➤ **It's usually conducted by a professional trainer.** This person has not only the know-how and the personal characteristics to train, but also has no other duties to distract from the training.

Secret Weapons

Carefully plan the sequence in which you will present the subject. Begin with the simple stuff, and work up to complex subjects. Build a foundation before you attempt to construct the framework.

➤ **It doesn't interfere with production.** Because trainees are in a classroom and not on a job site, they don't slow down work in progress or interfere with co-workers' performance.

Despite these major advantages, off-the-job training has a limitation: It isn't cost-effective unless you're training several people at the same time. Because most managers usually train only one or two people at a time, off-site training may not be feasible. Another limitation is that you can't really learn the full scope of a job outside the job environment. Therefore, off-site training generally enables you to train only for a particular task or skill, not for the entire job. Many companies use a combination of on- and off-site training.

Setting the Training Schedule

When you prepare a training schedule (see the following on-the-job training schedule), indicate the subjects that must be covered, determine how long it should take an average person to learn the subject matter, and allot the necessary time for the training. Also, give the trainer enough flexibility to handle any snags that could arise. Give the trainer all the required training aids and spell out the training methods that should be employed.

Communication Breakdown

Never purchase a training tape before you preview it. Most companies that sell tapes charge a fee for the preview, but it's worth it. Catalog descriptions give only limited information; previewing enables you to determine whether the tape will serve your purpose.

Whether you or an associate is assigned to do the training, review the training schedule before you begin. Be sure that everything to be learned is scheduled. The sequence of the subject matter is often a problem, so be sure to check it, too. You should introduce new subjects only when the trainee is ready to learn them.

On-the-Job Training Schedule

Job: _____

Trainer: _____ Trainee: _____

Equipment necessary for training: _____

_____

_____

Time scheduled Day/hour	Subject	Training methods	Training aids	Completed

"They Just Don't Get It"

Everyone responds differently to being taught new things. Some people are slow to learn, some are reluctant to change their ways and resist training, some believe they're not good at learning and give up easily.

Slow Learners

Margaret, the team leader, was about to give up on Mark, who was trying hard to learn new material, but just couldn't quite get it. Margaret asked a colleague for help with the problem: "When Mark worked in your department, did he have difficulty learning new things? "Yes," the other team leader responded, "He's a slow learner, but after he did learn the material, he became one of my best workers." Margaret followed up:

107

"What did you do to help him?" He responded: "I watched his learning patterns and recognized that he needed to have the tasks broken down into smaller segments so that he could absorb each step individually. Then we worked to bring them together. I also noted that he responded best when I gave him immediate feedback about his performance and praised him each time he was successful with a given task."

The Learning Curve

Have you ever made great progress in learning something new only to realize that your mind suddenly seems to stop? You can't move beyond a certain point, but why?

Secret Weapons

Being a slow learner doesn't mean that a person is stupid. Be patient, and try different approaches! Slow learners often can develop into productive team members.

The human mind can absorb only a limited amount of new information at any time. At some point in the learning process, you have to stop and integrate the new material with what you already know. While this process is in place, you're at a plateau: Nothing new can enter your system. After the new material is absorbed, however, your mind opens again and—boom!—off you go. This process is known as the *learning curve*.

Whether you're the learner or the teacher, keep the learning curve in mind. When you or your trainee seem to be unable to go beyond a certain point, *stop*. Wait an hour or a day or longer. Depending on the complexity of the material and the learner's background, the duration of the plateau varies.

The Know-It-All

You've run into know-it-alls. You can't tell them anything. They believe that they know best and oppose *any* type of change.

But change they must. Because know-it-alls resist learning new things, you have to learn how to overcome their attitude:

➤ Listen to their objections. Point out the advantages of the new changes and how they will make the system more efficient, less expensive, or easier to maintain.

➤ Get other team members to back you up.

➤ Use patience, reinforcement, and diplomacy to make your point.

The Fear of Learning

How often have you heard someone say, "It's too hard for me—I'm too old to learn new things"? Eric, a bookkeeping machine operator for 20 years, was the fastest and most accurate operator in his department. When his company replaced its old

Burroughs machines with PCs, he was devastated. "What will I do?" he asked. "I'm 50 years old. I'm too old to learn about computers."

When the computer company's trainer began the training program, Eric froze. He didn't seem to absorb even the basic elements of his work. The trainer spent extra time with him and paid special attention to his efforts. His manager talked to him to build up his confidence, but nothing helped. Eric's request for a transfer to another department was denied because computers were used everywhere.

When Eric was at his lowest, Lillian, one of the other bookkeeping machine operators, took him aside. "Eric, you *can* learn. I'm older than you, and I had no trouble learning to use the PC. Try it. I'll help you. *All* of us will help you." The help and support of his peers gave Eric the incentive to learn. Now he's a productive PC operator and proudly boasts about his new skills.

Training and Development Techniques

Today's leaders have available to them a variety of aids and techniques to facilitate their training efforts. Some have been around for years; others were developed more recently.

Training Manuals—Gobbledygook or the Real Stuff?

Training manuals, or "do it by the numbers" handbooks, are helpful for teaching routine tasks. They make the training process easy for both the trainer and the trainees; you can always refer to them when you're in doubt about what to do.

Unfortunately, training manuals can be poorly written and confusing; some are laced with technical terminology intelligible only to the engineers who wrote them.

Because jobs today are becoming less and less routine, training manuals are often inadequate—to the point that they even stifle creativity. Don't rely on a book because it's easy; rather, think out new and possibly better approaches to training.

Communication Breakdown

Make sure any training manual you write or approve is written to the level of the trainees and is clear, concise, and complete.

Interactive Computer Training

Many companies have developed a variety of interactive computer programs to train employees. Such programs were initially designed for use in schools to enable students to learn at their own pace. Slower learners could take their time and repeat sections until they understood them. Fast learners or students who had more background could move ahead quickly, and students could test themselves as they progressed.

Because most companies have their own ways of doing things, generic programs, such as the ones used by schools, haven't been of much value. But some generic programs, such as those that teach basic accounting skills and various computer operations, can be an asset to any organization. Check software catalogs to determine which programs might be valuable to you.

Some larger organizations have customized programs to suit their own needs. These programs are usually proprietary, and aren't made available outside the companies that developed them. Perhaps you can customize programs to meet your own requirements.

The Internet—the School of the Future

The personal computer has moved training from the classroom to the desk, the kitchen table, and even the lap of each individual.

Universities and private organizations offer courses and individual study programs on hundreds of subjects. You can study a foreign language, learn basic or advanced math, acquire technical know-how, and even obtain a college degree. The Internet makes it possible for students to engage in classroom interaction, even when they're participating from home.

Teleconferencing

Sometimes the most effective way to train or retrain staff members is to hold classes that bring together employees from several locations. This is a common practice among national and global organizations. It's also one of the most expensive ways to train. Not only do the participants take time off from their regular work, but they also spend additional time getting to and from the training site. Travel, hotel, meals, and often the cost of renting the training facility (for example, a conference center) add to the expense.

One way to reduce the cost and time involved is teleconferencing. Using specially designed computer and TV equipment, participants can see, hear, and interact with the instructor and each other without going far from their base. Larger organizations may have teleconferencing technology available on-site. Smaller companies can use the services of teleconferencing firms that can set up such conferences wherever needed.

At the University of Notre Dame, for example, executive M.B.A. courses are held simultaneously via satellite at three corporate facilities, Ameritech, Carrier Corporation, and Owens-Illinois.

Meanings & Gleanings

Training people is a one-way process. The teacher presents information; the student absorbs it (you hope). When training is replaced by *learning*, the emphasis shifts to developing the trainee's ability to identify and solve problems, seek knowledge, and take the initiative to continue self-development.

CD-ROMs

Interactive programs are also available in CD-ROM format. Walk into any computer store and you will find a variety of standard courses on CD-ROM. These can be used at the workplace or given to employees to use at home.

On CD-ROM, you'll find courses in all types of computer functions, typing, general office skills, accounting, marketing, business planning, and general management.

Case Studies

A *case study* is a description of a real or simulated business situation presented to trainees for analysis, discussion, and solution.

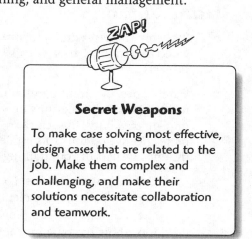

Secret Weapons

To make case solving most effective, design cases that are related to the job. Make them complex and challenging, and make their solutions necessitate collaboration and teamwork.

Case studies are used in graduate schools, seminars, and corporate training programs to enable trainees to work on the types of problems they're most likely to encounter on the job. The studies are often drawn from the experiences of real companies. The experience of working out these types of problems in a classroom instead of learning by trial and error on the job pays off in fewer trials and less costly errors.

A significant advantage of using case studies in management development is that trainees work on the case collaboratively. They learn how to organize and use teams to solve cases.

Role-Playing

In today's companies, most jobs require interaction with other people. Perhaps the best way to train people for this type of interaction is through role-playing.

As in case studies, role-playing should be based on realistic situations a trainee may face on the job: dealing with a customer, resolving a dispute among team members, or conducting a performance review. Role-playing should be fun, but if it's only fun and not a learning experience, you're wasting your time.

Effective role-playing must be carefully structured. Participants should be briefed on the goals of the exercise, and each participant should be given a specific part to play. Don't give people scripts—improvisation makes the exercise more spontaneous and allows for flexibility. Just make sure you establish limits, so participants don't stray from the goal of the exercise.

To get everyone—not just the players—involved, give each role to a group of people. The group studies and discusses how the role should be played. Then one member of the group is appointed to play the role. The other group members may step in to supplement the primary player. For example, if the person playing the role of a personnel interviewer fails to ask a key question, one of the members of that group can intervene and ask the question.

After the role-playing is completed, all the groups critique what has transpired and discuss what they've learned from the experience.

Using Video

Probably the most dramatic innovation in training and development is the use of video as a training tool. Check video catalogs; you'll find tapes that cover a variety of subjects.

Video tapes, like training manuals, are most appropriate for training people to do routine jobs. For situations in which flexibility and initiative are necessary, tapes can impede creativity. In such cases, customizing videotapes to meet your own needs is a more effective option. This list describes some ways to use customized video to enhance the effectiveness of your training programs:

➤ **Tape demonstrations:** For work of a physical nature (most factory or maintenance jobs and some clerical jobs), a good demonstration is an important part of the training. You can tape yourself or one of your team members performing the job. Show the tape in real time to demonstrate the pace at which a job should be carried out. Use slow motion to better explain each step of the task. Once you have a good demonstration on tape, you can show it to any of your trainees at any time.

➤ **Tape job performance:** One of the best ways to help people recognize exactly what they're doing on the job is to videotape them at work. Rather than trying to verbalize your associate's strengths and weaknesses, let the associate review the tape and see for himself.

➤ **Tape team meetings:** One employee's team leader videotaped several team meetings. By studying the tapes, the employee noticed that she tended to dominate group discussions. She pushed her ideas across, shut off opposing arguments, and was sometimes rude to other team members. She told her team leader that although she was an assertive person, until she saw the tape she didn't realize the way she came across to others and agreed to attend a human relations training course.

➤ **Tape role-playing:** Role-playing is an excellent way to develop interpersonal relations. By videotaping role-playing and reviewing the tapes, role-playing becomes an even more effective training tool.

➤ **Tape presentations:** If you're required to make presentations at internal meetings or outside functions, there's no better way to improve your oratory skills than to study videos of your practice deliveries.

Using Audio

One of the best ways to train people whose jobs require lots of telephone use—telemarketers, customer service representatives, order clerks, credit checkers—is to record telephone conversations.

You can purchase a component that connects the telephone to a voice-activated tape recorder. Some voice mail and answering machines have this capability built in.

Tape several conversations, and then review them with each team member. Listen to what is said and how it's said. Pay close attention to the way your associate reacts to what the other party says—and how that person reacts to your associate.

Communication Breakdown

In some states, taping telephone conversations is illegal without the consent of the party being recorded. Check your state laws.

Cross Training

When teams are the operating units in an organization, it's helpful for everyone on a team to be able to perform the work of any other member. The whining comment "It's not my job" is no longer valid.

In cross-functional or multi-departmental teams, this capability isn't always feasible. If your team consists of people from various disciplines, you cannot always expect them to be able to do work in other areas: A team consisting of people from marketing, engineering, and finance doesn't easily lend itself to cross training.

Most teams, however, are made up of people who do similar work. One sales support team consists of order clerks, customer service representatives, and computer operators. All are trained in every aspect of the team's work and can move from job to job as necessary.

Although that team's order clerks spend most of their time processing orders and the customer service reps are almost always on the phone, if the pressure is on processing orders, customer service reps can work on order processing between calls. If a customer service rep is out of the office, any team member can fill in at a moment's notice.

Preparing for Advancement

Training isn't limited to teaching job skills. Training team members to become team leaders is an important aspect of organizational development.

The Cadet Corps

For many years, training for management positions was limited to people who were on a special management track. They usually were hired as management trainees after graduating from college and went through a series of management training programs within an organization, often supplemented by seminars, courses, and residencies at universities or special training schools.

One of the most commonly used cadet programs was job rotation. After basic orientation, trainees were assigned to work for a short period in each of several departments. The objective was to give them an overview of the company so that when they moved into regular positions, they would have a good concept of the entire operation.

Makes sense? Sometimes. In many companies, the time spent in each training assignment was not long enough to give the trainees any more than a superficial knowledge. They never really got their feet wet. They wasted the time of the department heads, who had to divert their energies from working with their own teams. The regular team members, knowing that the trainees would be gone shortly, often resented their intrusion. Resentment was compounded by people's feelings that these cadets were of a privileged class and would someday be their bosses without having worked their way up.

Meanings & Gleanings

A *mentor* is a team member assigned to act as counselor, trainer, and "big brother" or "big sister" to a new member.

Everybody Is a Potential Manager

In recent years the special management track has been supplanted by team development, in which training for management is open to any team member. And why not? Even the military has learned that graduation from military academies isn't essential to be a top leader. (Two of the recent Chairmen of the Joint Chiefs of Staff—Colin Powell and John Shalikashvili—weren't West Pointers.) Companies have recognized that latent leadership talent exists in most people and can be developed in them. (Chapter 10 discusses some of the programs that companies have used to encourage people to move up in their careers.)

Mentor, Mentor—Where Is My Mentor?

It's a well known fact that when a high-ranking manager takes a younger employee under his or her wing—becomes that person's mentor—the protégé not only has a head start for advancement, but will acquire more know-how about the work, the workings of the company, and the "tricks of the trade" than others.

Why shouldn't everybody have a mentor? Why leave it to chance that some senior managers choose a protégé while others do not? Why not make mentoring a job requirement—not only for senior executives, but for all experienced team members? By structuring a mentoring program and assigning the best people on your team the responsibility of mentoring a new member, you take a giant step forward in encouraging productivity and growth in the newcomer.

A structured mentoring program requires that chosen mentors be willing to take on the job. Compelling someone to be a mentor is self-defeating. Not everybody is interested in or qualified for this assignment. New mentors should be trained by experienced people in the art of mentoring.

Manager's Minute

Both the mentor and the mentored benefit from the process of mentoring. Those who are mentored learn the new skills while mentors sharpen their skills in order to pass them on. It heightens the mentor's sense of responsibility as he guides his protégé through the maze of company policies and politics. It also makes the mentor more effective in his interpersonal relationships.

Ten Tips for New Mentors

If you're a first-time mentor, you're probably unsure of how to deal with this new responsibility. If you have had your own successful experience with a mentor, use that as a guide. If not, seek out a member of your organization who has a reputation as a great mentor and ask for advice, counsel, and guidance. Ask him to be your mentor in mentoring.

In any case, here are 10 tips to start you on the right track:

1. Know your work. Review the basics. Think back on the problems you've faced and how you dealt with them. Be prepared to answer questions about every aspect of the job.

2. Know your company. One of the main functions of a mentor is to help the trainee overcome the hurdles of unfamiliar company policies and practices. More important, as a person who's been around the organization for some time, you know the inner workings of the organization—the true power structure—the company politics.

3. Get to know your protégé, To be an effective mentor, take the time to learn as much as you can about the person you are mentoring. Learn about his or her education, previous work experience, current job, and more. Learn his or her goals, ambitions, and outside interests. Observe personality traits. Get accustomed to his or her ways of communicating in writing, verbally, and, most important, non-verbally.

4. Learn to teach. If you have minimal experience in teaching, pick up pointers on teaching methods from the best trainers you know. Read articles and books on training techniques.

5. Learn to learn. It is essential that you keep learning—not only the latest techniques in your own field, but developments in your industry, in the business community, and in the overall field of management.

6. Be patient. Your protégé may not pick up what you teach as rapidly as you would like. Patience is key for successful mentoring.

7. Be tactful. You are not a drill sergeant training a rookie in how to survive in combat. Be kind. Be courteous. Be gentle—but be firm and let the trainee know you expect the best.

8. Don't be afraid to take risks. Give your protégé assignments that will challenge his or her capabilities. Let her know that she won't succeed in all the assignments, but that the best way to grow is to take on tough jobs. We learn through failure, after all.

9. Celebrate successes. Let the trainee know you are proud of the accomplishments and progress he makes. When he achieves something especially significant, make a big fuss.

10. Encourage your protégé to be a mentor. The best reward you can get from being a mentor is that once the need for mentoring is done, your protégé carries the process on by becoming a mentor.

Laying the Foundation for Self-Training

It wasn't long ago that when you were trained for a job, you were considered fully trained after you mastered the skills and functions of the job. This training was augmented by occasional technology updates. But now, just a few years later, many formerly routine and highly structured jobs are dynamic and flexible.

Look at the position of "secretary." It used to connote a woman taking dictation, making appointments for her boss, answering the phone, filing papers, and acting as a gofer. Today that secretary is more of an executive assistant. He may prepare the agenda for a meeting, supervise clerks, compile information and write reports, and make important business decisions. It's a considerably different job. Traditional secretarial training isn't adequate preparation for this type of work.

Training must be replaced by learning. The difference between training and learning is that training is a one-way transfer of information from trainer to trainee. Learning involves not only absorbing information but also knowing how to identify potential problems, seeking the knowledge and information that are necessary to solve problems, and creating new concepts. This process is the focus of modern training and development.

The Least You Need To Know

➤ The four Ps in training are preparation, presentation, performance, and post-work.

➤ All members of a team should be trained to train. Then you must let them do it.

➤ Set up training schedules to ensure that what must be taught *is* taught.

➤ Everyone learns in different ways. Seek different approaches to which they can relate. Everyone has management potential. Encourage self-development as a step toward career growth.

➤ Incorporate into your training program techniques such as case studies, role-playing, interactive computer programs, and audio or video taping to make the training experience more exciting, more meaningful, and more productive.

➤ Encourage experienced team members to become mentors for new employees, and experienced managers to mentor potential team leaders.

➤ Redesign your training programs to meet today's challenges. Emphasize problem solving and creative thinking and help participants become self-learners.

Chapter 10

When Do You Graduate? You Don't!

In This Chapter

➤ Understanding that continued learning leads to continued growth

➤ Developing your team's skills, talents, and potential

➤ Ensuring career development

➤ Conducting effective training meetings

"So many books—so little time." I recently saw this phrase on a T-shirt and thought how true that is, not only of books but of all the things we want to learn. Even if we limit what we learn to material that's relevant to our jobs, there's no way we can ever learn it all.

But we must continue to learn. Successful people make a practice of allocating time, no matter how busy they are, to keeping up with developments in their fields.

This chapter discusses some of the things you can do to help yourself and your team members develop skills that will facilitate success both in your current jobs and in the future.

The need for training never ends. The following list of reasons can help you understand why:

➤ As technology changes, you have to keep up with the state-of-the-art in your field.

➤ Changing circumstances in your company or industry require your team to acquire knowledge in unfamiliar areas.

➤ You and your team members want to strengthen your weaknesses and add to your strengths, not only to do a better job now but also to prepare for career advancement.

Manager's Minute

"The recipe for perpetual ignorance is to be satisfied with your opinions and content with your knowledge."

—Elbert Hubbard

Upgrading Current Job Skills

It's essential for job survival that you keep up with the latest developments in your field. You must not only be on the cutting edge of technology and other developments but also ensure, as team leader, that your team members are trained in those areas.

Secret Weapons

When continued learning is an integral part of a company's culture, employees seek out opportunities to hone their skills—not just to do today's job but also to meet tomorrow's challenges.

Sharpening the Saw

Just as good carpenters must keep their saws sharpened, good managers must keep their tools and those of their teams in tip-top condition. To do this, set up a program for yourself and for your team members to continually develop current skills and acquire additional ones. In your program, make sure to do the following:

➤ Identify the skills of each team member.

➤ Investigate new equipment and methods.

➤ Determine which additional skills are necessary.

➤ Arrange for training in these areas.

Manager's Minute

Managers are often asked what they look for when they choose people for promotion. They acknowledge that knowledge of the technical or specialized aspects of a job is important. But they also realize the importance of personal skills on the job. Such skills include the ability to communicate both orally and in writing, and the ability to relate with other people both within and outside an organization.

Becoming a Better Presenter

You or another member of your team may be called on to make a presentation to another team, a vendor, customer, or even to a higher level management committee.

People who communicate well one-on-one often freeze when they have to speak to a group. Others may do well when they're talking to their own team, but are on tenterhooks when they have to address others.

Overcoming a fear of public speaking is best accomplished by getting up and doing it. One man learned this the hard way: After researching the potential market for a new product, his assignment was to present his team's findings to the executive committee. He was so nervous that he rushed through the report, fumbled for words, and—even though he knew the answers—was unable to respond to their questions.

A manager who attended the meeting called the man aside and said, "When I had to make my first presentation, I was just as nervous as you. But I did something about it. I joined Toastmasters."

Toastmasters International is a worldwide organization created to give people the opportunity to speak in front of audiences. It isn't a formal training

Secret Weapons

Learn how to make dynamic and exciting talks by reading *The Complete Idiot's Guide to Speaking in Public with Confidence,* by Laurie Rozakis, Ph.D.

Communication Breakdown

When giving a presentation that includes slides, never look away from your audience to read from the slides. Keep in front of you what is on the slides so you can refer to the information without turning away from the group.

program—it's just a group of men and women who meet weekly. Each one gives a short talk about any subject he or she chooses. The experience of speaking in public, augmented by support and helpful hints from others, has helped countless people overcome their fear of public speaking. Toastmasters offers many benefits, including the opportunity to network and learn discipline, leadership skills, and how to think on your feet. Look in the phone book or call Toastmaster's International at (800) 993-7732 to find the chapter nearest you.

More formal training is also available. Most universities and community colleges have public speaking courses, and public schools offer adult education programs. These classroom presentations are often videotaped and followed by critiques. Some companies retain private training organizations, such as Communispond, to run in-house programs on public speaking. Others hire experts to personally coach managers or associates in presentation preparation.

Learning a Foreign Language

If your company is expanding into the global market, knowing a foreign language can be a significant asset. Although business people in most countries speak English, you'd be at a great advantage if you could conduct your business in your overseas associates' native tongues.

Universities and special training centers throughout the country conduct intensive language programs. Pioneered by the U.S. State Department, these programs teach foreign languages by immersing participants in English-free environments.

In preparation for a tour of duty in Jordan, a man enrolled in an intensive language program to learn Arabic. After the first few days, in which he was given a thorough grounding in the Arabic language, the remainder of the program was conducted solely in Arabic. All English language signs in the area were replaced with Arabic signs, and the instructor spoke only Arabic. Participants were at first requested and later instructed to speak only Arabic among themselves. Arabic texts, newspapers, and magazines were distributed. At the end of the three-week program, the man had become fully conversant in Arabic.

In addition to learning the language, members of the class learned about Near East customs, foods, religion, and history—helpful knowledge for doing business with the residents of that area.

If you have the discipline to work on your own, audio tapes and CD-ROM language programs can teach you a language. But access to a teacher and interaction with classmates are much more effective in helping you learn a new language.

Using Other Programs

A variety of training and development programs can be valuable to you and your organization. The following list shows some of the types of available programs:

➤ **Computer literacy.** As a team leader, you may realize that you and your team members would benefit from learning how to use new computer software. Arrange for it to happen.

➤ **Writing skills.** One of your team members may express an interest in improving her writing skills. If your company provides an in-house writing program or if a local school has a similar course, send her to it. Your company's tuition reimbursement plan may pay for this type of program.

➤ **English language skills.** If one of your team members is a new immigrant and better English skills could increase his or her value to your team, help the person locate a suitable program.

➤ **Dale Carnegie course.** If the aggressive behavior of one of your team members is affecting your team's work, discuss the matter with the person and suggest this or a related program to improve his or her interpersonal relations.

Improving Your Long-Term Career Opportunities

As a result of the flattening of organizational structures, career paths that were formerly common roads to company advancement have changed radically. A young person used to be hired at an entry level position, and—with diligence, hard work, and a little luck—could move gradually up the company hierarchy. Career-oriented people joining a relatively large company in the 1970s could expect to move up three to four steps in their first 10 years with a company. But their younger counterparts entering the workforce in the 1990s don't have such an easy path into management.

With fewer layers of management in the reengineered company, opportunities for vertical advancement have been severely curtailed. The opportunities for career growth are still available, but the road to management is much different now.

You Can Earn More Money

Although it's not the only reason, many people seek advancement for the financial reward that comes along with it. With fewer management level positions required in a flattened structure, many companies—to keep good people from quitting and to encourage good work from all team members—have adjusted their compensation systems.

The traditional method of paying employees was to establish base pay for a job. Employee performance was evaluated annually, and most workers received some type of raise, either a cost-of-living adjustment or a higher amount for good performance.

Meanings & Gleanings

Most companies give employees an *annual raise* if they meet minimum performance standards, and many employees consider it an entitlement. The amount of the increase is usually based on the cost of living. A more meaningful system is based on a *merit raise*, which is determined by each person's performance.

123

Employees usually continued to receive this salary until their next review. One of the inequities of this type of system was that long-term employees were paid significantly more than newer—and perhaps more productive—people. These people were rewarded for longevity rather than for performance.

This system is being replaced in many organizations by a system of pay based on performance. All team members, regardless of tenure, are paid a base salary. Additional income comes in the form of bonuses or profit sharing. This amount is measured in some companies by a team's productivity: The entire team shares in bonuses commensurate with increased production, and bonuses are based on monthly calculations. Although the base pay doesn't change, total income may vary significantly from month to month.

A more common system is some variation of profit sharing. If a company makes a profit, all employees share in it. If they don't, no one receives a bonus. Bonuses based on profit are distributed either quarterly or annually to serve as an incentive for employees to be concerned about production, quality, waste, and customer satisfaction.

Communication Breakdown

Profit sharing plans are sometimes based on formulas so complex that employees cannot understand them and often feel frustrated.

A growing form of the profit sharing plan is an *ESOP,* or *employee stock-ownership plan,* in which employees are given the opportunity to buy shares in the company and become its true owners. Among the better known are TWA, United Airlines, and Avis. These companies play up this ownership in their advertising, by letting the public know that, inasmuch as their employees are, in a sense, their own bosses, they'll knock themselves out to satisfy customers. (And they do!)

Keep in mind that money is a primary reason people seek advancement. They're satisfied as long as they have the opportunity to make as much or more money through the compensation system as they might have made by upgrading their position.

What's Keeping You Back?

Karen's goal was to move into a leadership position. An outgoing, ambitious, and capable marketing specialist, she was a valuable contributor to her team's success. Her bonuses were more than satisfactory, but that wasn't enough: She was ready for team leadership. Looking around, she noticed that her team leader and others in marketing were doing fine work and weren't about to move up, either in or out of the organization. It seemed that she was stalled in her career—and she was only 32 years old.

Unusual? Not at all. One of the major challenges to management is what to do with high potential, ambitious people such as Karen, who are frustrated because of a lack of upward mobility.

If you can't depend on moving step-by-step up the ranks in your current department or job category, you have to seek other channels that may help you reach your goal. Two successful approaches are horizontal growth and outsourcing.

Stepping Sideways on the Way Up

Karen asked her team leader and her human resources manager what she could do to move into a more responsible role. The company fortunately had a career development program for people with Karen's goals. Karen met with a career counselor who told her that people able to function in several areas have more career opportunities than people who specialize in only one. Karen then took additional training courses in aspects of the business outside marketing. She was given in-house training in operations and enrolled in outside classes in computer technology and finance. She was then assigned to a cross-functional team in which she was able to interrelate with specialists in other departments.

By expanding outside her specialty, Karen participated in *horizontal growth,* opening several doors that may lead her to higher management spots.

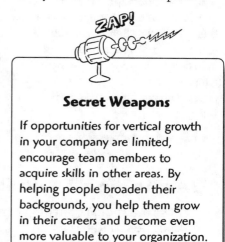

Secret Weapons

If opportunities for vertical growth in your company are limited, encourage team members to acquire skills in other areas. By helping people broaden their backgrounds, you help them grow in their careers and become even more valuable to your organization.

The Outsource Option

Part of the restructuring process has involved *outsourcing.* In this process, a company subcontracts work that formerly had been performed in-house to outsiders. This allows the company to get the work done less expensively and also frees company management to concentrate on areas in which it is most competent.

Robert had been in the traffic department of his valve company for 17 years. He had moved up to the number two position in the department and reported to the vice president for distribution. One day he heard a rumor that the company was planning to eliminate the traffic department and subcontract it to an outside source.

Panicked, Robert confronted his boss, who verified that the company was seriously considering that option. "But what will happen to me?" Robert asked. His boss responded that the move was at least a year away and asked him to consider being the subcontractor. Because Robert knew as much about traffic as anyone in the company, the boss suggested that the company would probably become Robert's first customer and that he was then likely to get additional customers. The boss also suggested that Robert continue in his present job during the transition period but begin the process of developing his new company on his own time. In this way, he could keep things moving smoothly during the transition and be ready to begin functioning as a subcontractor immediately when the new system went into effect.

Communication Breakdown

Many "development" programs develop little else than income for their promoters. Before you subscribe to a program, send team members to a course, or purchase audio or video tapes, ask for references from current users. *Check it out.*

Companies planning to outsource are often happy to assist one of their own employees in becoming a subcontractor. They can then work with someone they know and trust and who knows their special problems. This process offers ambitious people a career opportunity the company cannot provide internally.

Being an independent entrepreneur isn't for everyone. Risks are involved: You have to raise capital, lease work space, purchase equipment, and hire staff members. And there's always a risk that it won't work out. Being your own boss may sound appealing, but it often involves longer hours and harder work than being employed by a company. In addition, you have to provide your own benefits. Contractors aren't covered by a company health plan, pension fund, or group insurance. People who feel more comfortable under a corporate umbrella may find it difficult to adapt to being in business for themselves.

Developing Team Leaders

Organizational flattening has led to the elimination of many middle management positions and has reduced the number of layers within companies. But companies will always have a CEO, senior officers, and some middle managers. And the chief source for filling these openings will be team leaders.

Secret Weapons

If your goal is upper management, prepare for it now. Tomorrow's leaders won't be specialists—they'll have experience in several management functions and probably in more than one industry. They'll be comfortable working with computers, statistics, financial and marketing figures, and international business relations. They'll also have superior communication and public relations skills.

Any member of a team is a potential team leader, and any team leader is a potential higher level manager. The selection and development of team leaders can therefore be the single most important personnel activity a company undertakes.

Identifying Potential Team Leaders

As a team leader, *you* are the most important source for identifying potential team leaders in your company. This list shows some things you should remember as you evaluate your fellow team members:

➤ Be a keen observer of their behavior, skills, and personalities.

➤ Know the goals of each person, and help each one clarify his or her career goals.

➤ Give each person an opportunity to lead a project, make a report, or chair a meeting.

➤ Encourage them to take in-house training and enroll in seminars or educational courses.

➤ Keep your managers aware of your team members' abilities and goals.

Preparing People for Advancement

As mentioned in Chapter 7, the restricted "management track" approach to promotion has been supplanted in most organizations by a more open attitude.

To accomplish this openness, most companies have instituted management development programs or arranged for management candidates to take outside training. Some programs begin by having employees consult with human resource specialists trained in career counseling. Using in-depth interviews, aptitude testing, assessment centers, and discussions with managers and peers, career counselors can evaluate your team members' strengths and limitations. They develop a plan of action to provide internal training, and offer recommendations for outside schooling.

This list mentions some of the available management development programs:

➤ **Special skills.** Training in areas such as statistics, computers, and specific technical fields.

➤ **Leadership.** Seminars and courses in psychology, applied leadership, and management techniques through either in-house or outside sources.

➤ **Problem solving and decision making.** Effective seminars and special programs such as the ones offered by Kepner-Tregoe (Princeton, New Jersey).

➤ **Graduate degrees** in management or a technical specialty. Tuition reimbursement.

Another way to facilitate training for yourself or team members is to purchase materials that people can study on their own time, such as audio or video tapes or CD-ROM programs (and, although it may seem old-fashioned, books).

You have no assurance that any of these programs by itself will guarantee success, but companies that have invested large sums of money in this type of training continue to do so—one indication that they work, at least for those companies.

Introducing the T & D Meeting

A team meeting for T & D (training and development) can be an easy and effective vehicle for ongoing learning—or it can be a complete waste of time. A well-thought-out training meeting can reinforce old knowledge and introduce new ideas. It can serve as a means of getting feedback about how earlier training has been applied and as a guide to what changes should be made. It also gives team members an opportunity to participate in the training process.

Prepare for training meetings by following these suggestions:

➤ **Set clear objectives.** State clearly the purpose of the meeting: to teach participants a new method, perfect a technique, or develop skills.

➤ **Choose the method to be used.** You can choose, for example, a demonstration followed by practice, a participatory workshop, or a problem-solving discussion.

➤ **Assemble training aids.** Use flip charts, an overhead or slide projector and slides, handouts, videos, computers, and other items to make your meetings more "user friendly."

➤ **Use your team members as trainers.** Take advantage of the expertise of your own team members. Assign one or more team members to lead the discussion about different aspects of the material. This technique not only provides information and expertise you may not possess yourself but also leads to a more participatory atmosphere.

➤ **If it's helpful, arrange for backup instructors.** If your background in what's being taught isn't adequate, bring in an expert to conduct the meeting or at least to assist. When you train people in the use of a new piece of equipment or computer program, have a representative from the supplier lead the meeting.

Secret Weapons

A team leader's role in T & D includes the following tasks:

➤ **Communication:** Ensure that team members are made aware of information that affects their jobs.

➤ **Observation:** Keep tabs on team members to identify training needs.

➤ **Assessment:** Measure accomplishments against goals.

➤ **Counseling:** Work with team members to shore up strengths and strengthen weaknesses.

➤ **Helping:** Train team members to develop their full potential.

Tips for Conducting Better Training Meetings

Conducting a training meeting is a challenge to a team leader. Meetings must be informative: Participants should leave with more knowledge about the matters that were discussed than they had before the meeting. Meetings should also be exciting: Everyone should participate, by asking questions, expressing their agreements and disagreements, and sharing their ideas. And, finally, meetings should be motivating: Attendees should leave a meeting eager to put into practice what they have learned.

Here are some suggestions for making your meetings more effective:

➤ **Treat team members as knowledgeable people, not as schoolchildren.** Team members are adults who are willing to learn.

➤ **Avoid lecturing.** A lecture is deadly. Make the meeting a participatory experience for all who attend.

128

➤ **Don't just repeat what's in the training manual or handouts.** Team members can read it for themselves. You're there to expand, illustrate, and elucidate.

➤ **Prepare for each session.** You should know 10 times more about the subject than you present at the meeting.

➤ **Keep the sessions short.** Keep them short, but not so short that the material can't be adequately covered.

➤ **Use drama and humor.** Use your imagination to keep attendees awake, alert, and excited about what they're learning.

➤ **Use visual aids.** Use appropriate materials to augment what is spoken.

➤ **Set aside the last five minutes of each session for a summary.** Be sure to clear up any misunderstandings made obvious by participants' questions and comments. If a class lasts more than a day, spend 10 or 15 minutes summarizing the preceding day's discussion.

The Least You Need to Know

➤ Training never ceases. It's an ongoing part of every job.

➤ Job skills and personal skills are essential for success. Skills you should develop include the ability to make public presentations, knowledge of a foreign language, and improved interpersonal relations.

➤ Organizational flattening and restructuring have lessened the opportunity for advancement. Rather than take the direct vertical route, ambitious people must find new approaches, such as the acquisition of skills outside their current specialty or becoming independent contractors.

➤ Well-designed career counseling programs can help team members assess their future opportunities and prepare for them.

➤ Seek out college courses, seminars, and special training to supplement in-house programs to develop your own leadership skills in addition to those of your team members.

➤ Periodic training and development meetings, if they're well-planned and conducted effectively, are an excellent way to establish a climate for continuing education.

Part 3

Understanding and Complying with Equal Employment Laws

You're not a bigot. You believe in fair treatment of everybody regardless of their color, gender, ethnic background, or age. But you are concerned that somewhere along the line you might inadvertently make a comment, ask a question, or do something in good faith, but still be accused of violating the law.

Like all laws, the laws governing equal employment opportunity are subject to interpretation. What appears clear and simple, therefore, easily becomes vague and complex.

This part of the book looks at these laws and provides you with some suggestions and guidelines to help you cope with some common problems, such as questions you can and cannot ask an applicant, how to prevent sexual harassment, and making accommodations for people who have special challenges.

Chapter 11

How Equal Employment Opportunity Laws Affect Your Job

In This Chapter

➤ Hiring under the civil rights laws

➤ Avoiding age discrimination in hiring, firing, and retiring

➤ Adhering to the ADA: Abilities, not disabilities

➤ Understanding the penalties for violating the laws

Your efforts to comply with any law aren't as simple as just reading and understanding the statute. Administrative rulings and various interpretations of the law based on court decisions determine how a law should be applied.

As a manager, the laws governing equal employment opportunity affect most of the decisions you make about the way you hire, supervise, compensate, evaluate, and discipline personnel.

This chapter looks at these laws and discusses some of the problems you may have in applying them in your job. It explores some of the problems that have plagued other employers and what you can do to avoid similar troubles.

What the Laws Say—An Overview

The laws governing equal employment affect every aspect of your job as a manager. It begins even before your first contact with an applicant and governs all your relations with employees: how you screen candidates, what you pay employees, how you treat employees on the job—all the way to employees' separation from the company, and sometimes even after that.

The main federal laws that apply to equal employment are shown in this list:

➤ The Civil Rights Act of 1964, as amended, prohibits discrimination in employment on the basis of race, color, sex, religion, or national origin. The section of the law that covers employment (Title VII) is the Equal Employment Opportunity (EEO) law and is administered by the Equal Employment Opportunity Commission (EEOC). The EEOC also administers the Age Discrimination in Employment Act (ADEA) and the Americans with Disabilities Act (ADA).

➤ The Age Discrimination in Employment Act of 1967, as amended, prohibits discrimination against individuals 40 years of age or older. Some state laws cover all persons over the age of 18.

➤ The Americans with Disabilities Act of 1990 prohibits discrimination against people who are physically or mentally challenged.

➤ The Equal Pay Act of 1963 requires that an employee's gender not be considered in determining salary (equal pay for equal work).

Most states have similar laws. Because some state laws are stricter than the federal laws, make sure that you know what your state requires.

In addition, several Presidential executive orders require that certain government contractors and other organizations receiving funds from the federal government institute affirmative-action programs to bring more minorities and women into the workplace (see Chapter 10).

It's important to remember that an employer isn't obligated to hire an applicant just because he or she is in a protected category (such as a person covered by the ADA). An employer can still hire another, better qualified candidate. But the employer cannot use discriminatory information to *exclude* a candidate who is otherwise most qualified for a job or promotion. Managers must, therefore, avoid doing, asking, or saying anything that could possibly be construed as discriminatory.

What to Watch For When Hiring

Suppose you have an opening in your department and you ask personnel to line up some potential interviewees. To find the ideal candidate for your team, you tell personnel:

"We're an aggressive, hard-hitting bunch of young guys. Get me a sharp, up-and-coming recent college grad. Most of my boys are Ivy Leaguers, so that will be an asset. And, oh yes, no hippies—get me a clean-living churchgoer."

How many violations of the equal employment laws are in that statement? Let's review it:

➤ "Young guys." Violates the prohibition of both age and sex discrimination. Avoid terms that even hint at gender, such as "guys" or "boys."

➤ "Recent college grad." "Recent" usually means "young." Of course, some people graduate from college in their 40s or older, but they're still the exceptions to the norm. Specifying *or even implying* that a candidate be "young" violates the age discrimination laws.

➤ "Ivy Leaguer." Discriminates against people who, because of their race or religion, have chosen to attend primarily minority colleges or religion-sponsored schools. Also, because minorities are likely to be less affluent and attend less expensive schools, hiring only "Ivy Leaguers" has the effect of discriminating against minorities.

➤ "Churchgoer." This phrase violates the prohibition against religious discrimination. It can be interpreted as discriminating against people who choose not to belong to any organized religion or as "Christian only" because members of other religions may not attend "church."

Communication Breakdown

The interpretation of EEO laws comes from both administrative rulings and court decisions. As in many legal matters, what seems simple is often complex. I strongly urge you to consult an attorney to clarify any actions you take under these laws.

"I Didn't Know That Question Was Illegal"

Who does the interviewing? In today's companies the human resources department does preliminary screening, but team leaders and often other team members interview applicants (see Part 4). Every team member must be thoroughly familiar with EEO laws because an improper question from any interviewer can lead to a formal complaint.

To test yourself, take the following quiz.

The following quiz answers are based on federal law, but states interpret laws differently. In addition, because new laws, administrative rulings, and judicial interpretations are promulgated from time to time, the reasoning on which these answers are based may change. Keep in mind the job-relatedness of the questions and what kind of effect they have when asked of ethnic minorities. These are key factors in determining the legitimacy of the questions.

What Do You Know About EEO?

To function as a manager today, you must be thoroughly familiar with various state and federal laws concerning equal employment opportunity. To help you measure your knowledge of these laws, we have prepared the following quiz. It covers only a few of the key factors in the laws but should give you some insight into understanding this important area.

Answer Yes or No:

On an application form or in an interview, you may ask:

1. "What are the names of your nearest of kin?" ____

2. "Do you have a permanent immigration visa?" ____

3. "Have you ever been arrested?" ____

Indicate whether each of these help-wanted ads is legal:

4. "Management trainees: College degree; top 10 percent of class only" ____

5. "Accountant: Part-time opportunity for retiree" ____

6. "Sales: Recent college graduate preferred" ____

Other areas:

7. Companies may give tests to applicants to measure intelligence or personality as long as the publisher of the test guarantees that it is nondiscriminatory. ____

8. A company may refuse to employ applicants because they are over 70. ____

9. A company may refuse to employ an applicant if she is pregnant. ____

10. A company may ask whether a woman has small children at home. ____

A company may indicate an age preference if:

11. It is for a training program. ____

12. Older people cannot qualify for the company pension program. ____

13. The job calls for considerable travel. ____

Miscellaneous questions:

14. A company may specify that it requires a man for a job if the job calls for travel. ____

15. The company may specify that it requires an attractive woman to greet customers and visitors. ____

1. **No.** You cannot ask about next of kin because the response may show national origin if the name differs from the applicant's. You may not even ask whom to notify in case of emergency until after you hire an applicant.

2. **Yes.** Immigration laws require that legal aliens working in the United States have a permanent immigration visa (green card).

3. **No.** Courts have ruled that because ethnic minorities are more likely than non-minorities to be arrested for minor offenses, asking about an arrest record is

discriminatory. You *can* ask about convictions for felonies (see the section "Criminal Records," later in this chapter).

4. **No.** Unless you can substantiate that students from the top 10 percent of their class have performed significantly better than students with lower grades, this ad isn't job-related.

5. **No.** Because most retirees are over the age of 60, specifying a "retiree" implies that persons between the ages of 40 and 60 are not welcome. The Age Discrimination in Employment Act protects persons older than 40 against discrimination because of their age.

6. **No.** The phrase "recent college graduate" implies youth. As noted, even the implication of "youth" violates the terms of the ADEA.

7. **No.** The Supreme Court, in *Griggs vs. Duke Power Co.*, upheld the EEOC's requirement that intelligence and personality tests must have a direct relationship to effectiveness on the job for the specific job for which the test is used. Because only the company using the test can verify this relationship, it must be validated against each company's experience.

8. **No.** The Age Discrimination in Employment Act prohibits discrimination against people who are 40 years or older. There is no top age limit.

9. **No.** Pregnant women may not be refused employment unless the work might endanger their health (such as heavy physical work or exposure to dangerous substances). Employers cannot ask an applicant whether she is pregnant or comment that the company doesn't hire pregnant women. If a pregnant woman were rejected, she would have to prove that the reason for the rejection was her pregnancy.

10. **No.** Because men aren't usually asked whether they have small children at home, it has been interpreted as a means of discriminating against women.

11. **No.** Training programs may not be limited to young people.

12. **No.** Participation in a pension program is not an acceptable reason for age discrimination.

13. **No.** Ability to travel is not related to age.

14. **No.** Ability to travel is not related to gender.

15. **No.** A company's desire to have an attractive woman as a receptionist doesn't make it a bona fide occupational qualification (see the following section).

Every manager who hires people should, ideally, score 100 percent on this quiz. Failure to comply with any one of these rules may result in complaints, investigations, hearings, and penalties.

Bona Fide Occupational Qualifications (BFOQs)

There are some positions for which a company is permitted to specify only a man or only a woman for the job. Clear-cut reasons must exist, however, for why a person of only that gender can perform the job. In the law, these reasons are referred to as *bona fide occupational qualifications*, or *BFOQs*.

If a job calls for heavy lifting, for example, is it a BFOQ for men only? Not necessarily. Certain strong women may be able to do the job, and certain weak men may not. It's legitimate to require that all applicants—both men and women—pass a weightlifting test.

Meanings & Gleanings

The only undisputed *bona fide occupational qualifications* are a wet nurse (for a woman) and a sperm donor (for a man).

And that's not all. Suppose that a job calls for driving a forklift truck and that the operator is occasionally required to do heavy lifting. A woman applicant may be able to drive the truck but not be able to do the lifting. If the lifting is only a small part of the job, you cannot reject her. She is capable of performing the major aspect of the work, and other people can be assigned to handle the lifting.

Suppose that you have always had an attractive woman as your receptionist and that the job is now open. Is this a BFOQ for a woman? Of course not. There's no reason that a man—with the personality for the position—cannot be just as effective.

Things I'd Like to Know, but Can't Ask

To make sure that the person you hire will, in your judgment, be effective, you believe that there are certain questions you *must* ask. Although civil rights laws vary somewhat from state to state, federal law governs all organizations doing business in the United States. The "lawful and unlawful" questions in Table 11.1 are presented as general guidelines that apply under federal laws and the laws of the strictest states. To ensure that you're in compliance with legal requirements and interpretations in any specific state, however, check with local authorities and an attorney specializing in this field.

(Note that questions that would otherwise be deemed lawful may in certain circumstances be deemed as evidence of unlawful discrimination when the question seeks to elicit information about a selection criterion that isn't job-related and that has a disproportionate effect on the members of a minority group and cannot be justified by business necessity.)

Table 11.1   Legal and Illegal Pre-employment Questions

Subject	Lawful	Unlawful
Age	"Are you 18 years or older? If not, state age."	"How old are you?" "What is your date of birth?" "What year did you graduate?"
Arrest record	"Have you ever been convicted of a crime? (Give details.)"	"Have you ever been arrested?"
Birth control	None.	Inquiry into capacity to reproduce or advocacy of any form of birth control or family planning.
Birthdate	None. (After person is employed, proof of age for insurance or other purposes may be requested.)	Requirements that applicant submit birth certificate, naturalization, or naturalization, or baptismal record Requirement that applicant produce proof of age in the form of a birth certificate or baptismal record.
Birthplace	None.	Birthplace of applicant. Birthplace of applicant's parents, spouse, or other close relatives.
Citizenship	"Are you a citizen of the United States? If not a citizen of the United States, do you intend to become a citizen of the United States? If not a citizen of the United States, have you the legal right to remain permanently in the United States?" (See Chapter 10.) "Do you intend to remain permanently in the United States?"	"Of what country are you a citizen?" Whether applicant is naturalized or native-born citizen. "On what date did you acquire citizenship?" Requirement that applicant produce naturalization papers or first papers. "Are your parents or spouse naturalized or native-born citizens of the United States?" "On what date did your parents or spouse acquire citizenship?"
Disability	"Do you have any impairments (physical, mental, or medical) that would interfere with your ability to perform the job for which you have applied?"	"Do you have a disability?" "Have you ever been treated for any of the following diseases?" (followed by list of diseases)
Driver's	"Do you possess a valid driver's license?"	Requirement that applicant produce a driver's license prior to employment.

Table 11.1 Continued

Subject	Lawful	Unlawful
Education	Inquiry into applicant's academic, vocational, or professional education and schools attended.	None.
Experience	Inquiry into work experience.	None.
Gender	None.	Any inquiry about gender on application form or interview. "Do you wish to be addressed as Mr., Miss, Mrs., or Ms.?"
Language	Inquiry into languages applicant speaks and writes fluently.	"What is your native language?" or any inquiry into how applicant acquired ability to read, write, or speak a foreign language.
Marital status	None.	"Are you married, single, divorced, or separated?" Name or other information about spouse. Where spouse works. "How many children do you have?" "How old are your children?" "What arrangements have you made for child care when you're at work?"
Military experience	Inquiry into applicant's military experience in the Armed Forces of the United States or in a state militia. Inquiry into applicant's service in specific branch of United States Armed Forces.	Inquiry into applicant's general military experience (for example, a military unit of another country).
Name	"Have you ever worked for this company under a different name?" "Is any additional information (a change of name or use of assumed name or nickname) necessary to enable a check of your work record? If yes, explain."	Original name of applicant whose name has been changed by court order or otherwise. Maiden name of married woman. "Have you ever worked under a different name? State name and dates."

Subject	Lawful	Unlawful
National origin	None.	Inquiry into applicant's lineage, ancestry, national origin, descent, parentage, or nationality. Spouse's nationality. "What is your native tongue?"
Notify in case of emergency	None.	Name and address of person to be notified in case of an emergency. (This information may be asked only after an applicant is employed.)
Organizations	Inquiry into applicant's memberships in organizations that the applicant considers relevant to ability to perform job.	"List all clubs, societies, and lodges to which you belong."
Photograph	None.	Requirement or option that applicant affix a photograph to employment form at any time before being hired.
Race or color	None.	Complexion, color of skin, coloring.
Relatives	Names of applicant's relatives other than spouse already employed by company.	Names, addresses, number, or other information concerning applicant's spouse, children, or other relatives not employed by company.
Religion or creed	None.	Inquiry into applicant's religious denomination, religious affiliations, church, parish, pastor, or religious holidays observed. Applicants may not be told "This is a Catholic (or Protestant or Jewish) organization."

Marriage and Children

In your desire to obtain as much information as you can about an applicant so that you'll make the right hiring decision, you may ask questions that seem to be important but that violate equal employment opportunity laws. The most frequently asked illegal questions relate to marriage and child care. "But this stuff is important," you might say. "I *need* to know."

Suppose your team puts in a great deal of overtime—often on short notice. One applicant is a married woman (you noticed the ring on her finger), and you think that you have to know whether she has children at home. You reason that everyone knows that women with children have to pick them up at day care and can't work overtime. Another applicant isn't wearing a ring. Maybe she's divorced. Maybe she has children. You have to find out in order to know her availability, right?

Wrong, in both cases. Of course it's important to know whether applicants can work overtime on short notice, but you cannot assume their availability to work based on their responsibility for child care. In many families the father picks up a couple's children from a day care facility. The inability to work overtime isn't limited to child care matters. Anyone—single or married, man or woman—may not be able to work overtime for many reasons.

How do you deal with this issue? You tell both men and women applicants about the overtime and then ask whether that will be a problem.

Here's a good rule of thumb: Don't ask questions of one gender that you wouldn't ask of the other. "Okay," you think, "I'll ask both men and women about their children, and then I'll be safe." Nope, even this method can be interpreted as discrimination.

Secret Weapons

In choosing interview questions, ask yourself whether knowing the answers to those questions are necessary to determine an applicant's suitability to the position. Steer clear of questions that even hint at relating to a person's race, religion, national origin, gender, age, or disabilities.

If you ask a male applicant how many children he has and he says that he has four, your reaction may be, "Good, here's a stable family man. He'll work hard to support his family."

If you ask a woman applicant the same question and she gives the same answer, do you have the same reaction? Usually not. Managers often think that a woman will stay home from work every time one of her children gets sick, but such assumptions are unfair. In many families, both spouses share child care responsibilities or make arrangements for it.

Here's another good rule of thumb: Don't ask applicants any questions about marriage or family. Period. These types of questions elicit information that may be used to discriminate against women.

Criminal Records

You cannot ask applicants whether they have ever been arrested. Surprised? You shouldn't be. In our judicial system, after all, a person is innocent until proven guilty. Because police are often tougher and more likely to make arrests in minority neighborhoods, asking about arrests has an adverse effect on some minority groups.

You can ask about *convictions* for a felony; however, you cannot refuse to hire a person solely on the basis of a conviction—unless it's job-related. You might, for example, disqualify an applicant from a cashier's position if he was convicted for theft, but not if he was convicted for disorderly conduct.

Lie Detector Tests

Employees handle cash or confidential information in many companies, so employers want to do their best to weed out dishonest people. For years, companies used polygraphs to screen applicants for sensitive jobs, but no more! A federal law now restricts the use of these lie detector tests.

Exempt from this law are government agencies, defense contractors, companies providing armed security guards, and a few others.

Although lie detector tests are not legal in the hiring process, they can still be used as part of an investigation for theft, embezzlement, industrial espionage, and similar offenses. Before using polygraphs for any purpose, check with your attorney to ensure compliance with all applicable federal, state, and local laws.

Age Discrimination

The one equal employment law that will eventually cover you and everyone else is the Age Discrimination in Employment Act. Despite federal and state laws, the accent on youth in many companies has kept productive men and women from getting and keeping jobs or from functioning at their highest levels in a job. Studies have shown that mature people are at least as productive and creative, are more reliable, and make better judgments and decisions than their younger counterparts.

Manager's Minute

The majority of complaints filed with the Equal Employment Opportunity Commission deal with age discrimination.

Avoiding Age Discrimination in Hiring

Even though most company application forms don't ask a person's age or date of birth and most people omit that information from their résumés, it's still easy to guess an applicant's age range within a few years. A team leader who prefers that young people join his or her team may overlook, just because of age, potential members who could be of great value to the team.

When you interview older applicants, avoid the stereotypes that may keep you from hiring highly qualified people for the wrong reason:

➤ **"The applicant is overqualified."** The term "overqualified" is often a euphemism for "too old." Some people may have more know-how or experience than a job requires, but that doesn't necessarily mean that they won't be productive. Discuss the details of the work with the applicant. It may be an opportunity for the person to learn new things. Or he or she may be able to contribute to the job some expertise that makes it more challenging. Judge the person as an individual, not as a member of an age group.

Secret Weapons

Your team will benefit from a mix of men and women of all ages and various cultural backgrounds—all contributing their talents, expertise, and experience to your team's activities.

➤ **"The applicant made more money in the last job."** People with many years of experience often have earned more money than those with less experience. If the amount of salary your company can offer is a factor in your hiring decision, discuss it with the applicant—he or she should be the one to determine whether the salary is satisfactory. You may worry that if a better-paying job comes along, the new member will jump to it. That may happen, of course, but a younger person would probably do the same.

➤ **"This person won't fit in with my team."** Being of different age levels isn't necessarily a barrier to cooperation and collaboration. Make that determination on the basis of the candidate's personality, not on his or her age.

Encouraging Retirement

One method companies use to cut costs when they downsize is to compel higher-paid workers (who are most often older men and women) to retire early. Under current law, employees cannot (with a few minor exceptions) be forced to retire, no matter how old they are, unless they're not capable of performing their work.

Although forcing out older workers is illegal, companies often persuade people to retire by offering them bonuses, benefits, or other rewards. You can use this strategy as long as you do it in good faith and according to the law. Because it's a legal matter, an attorney should prepare the appropriate documents.

The Americans with Disabilities Act (ADA)

The newest and probably least understood civil rights law is the Americans with Disabilities Act (ADA). This section discusses some of the highlights of the law and how it applies to you as a manager. Your company must adhere to this law if it has 15 or more employees.

What You Can Do—What You Don't Have to Do

The ADA makes it illegal to discriminate in hiring, in job assignments, and in the treatment of employees because of a disability. Employers must make *reasonable accommodation* so that these people can perform the essential duties of their jobs.

This accommodation can vary from building access ramps for wheelchair users to providing special equipment for people who are seeing- or hearing-challenged, unless this type of accommodation is an *undue hardship* for the company. Undue hardship is usually defined in monetary terms. If an applicant who uses a wheelchair applies for a job with a small company, the cost of building an elevator or a ramp to give access to the floor on which the job is located may be a financial hardship. Because of this undue hardship, the company could reject the applicant or provide a less expensive accommodation if possible. If the same applicant applied for a job in a more affluent company, however, it may not be considered undue hardship to do the necessary construction.

Accommodation doesn't always require expensive construction. The hypothetical examples in this list examine some other ways to meet this requirement:

➤ The small company you work for wants to hire someone who uses a wheelchair as an accountant, but the accounting department is on the second floor of your building. The building has no elevator or ramp, and providing one would cost more than the company can afford. Must you do it? No. That would be an *undue hardship* for your company. There may be other ways to accommodate this person, however. Use your imagination. Why not let him work on the ground floor? His work could be brought to him. It may be an inconvenience, but it would qualify as reasonable accommodation—and it would enable you to hire this particular competent accountant.

➤ A highly skilled word processor operator is legally blind and walks with the aid of a white cane. She can transcribe from dictated material faster and more accurately than many sighted people can. You want to hire her, but you're concerned that in case of a fire or other emergency she would be a danger to herself and others. The accommodation you can make is to assign someone to escort her in case of an emergency.

➤ An assembler in a factory was badly injured in an automobile accident, and his job requires him to stand at a workbench all day. When he was ready to return to work, he was unable to stand for long periods. His supervisor sent him home and told him that until he was able to perform the work as he did before, he could not return. The supervisor

Communication Breakdown

If you suspect that an employee cannot perform a job because of alcohol or drug abuse, have the person tested. Employees should be made aware that this policy will be followed, and it should be clearly stated in the company's policy manual.

was wrong. Accommodations should have been made. Perhaps a high stool could have been provided so that the employee could reach the workbench without having to stand. If that option wasn't feasible, his hours might have been adjusted so that he could work part time on that job and do other work that didn't require standing for long portions of the day.

Must I Hire Substance Abusers?

Alcohol and drug users are considered disabled under the ADA. If a person can perform a job satisfactorily, a previous record of alcoholism or drug addiction is not reason enough to refuse hiring, or to discipline or terminate a current employee. If an applicant is still addicted, however, and the addiction manifests itself in a recent history of poor attendance or poor performance, you can reject or discipline the person—not because of the addiction, but because of poor work habits.

It's legal to discipline employees who use drugs or alcohol in the workplace or who report to work under the influence of an illegal substance.

Secret Weapons

When you interview a candidate for a new job or consider someone for a promotion, don't focus on disabilities. Concentrate on that person's *abilities*.

The Plus Side: Utilizing the Talents of Physically and Mentally Challenged People

Even in this day of computers and technological sophistication, many types of work are still routine and repetitious, resulting in high turnover among workers who are assigned to that work.

Many companies have found that people who are mentally challenged can do this work and are not bored by it. These people are often capable of learning much more than you might expect. It takes more patience, and some tasks may have to be simplified, but trainees who master these tasks retain the skills and often improve on them. Coaches who are specially trained to work with mentally challenged people are available in many communities. Your local mental health association can tell you whether this type of help is available in your area.

AIDS in the Workplace

You may be concerned about hiring people who have AIDS (acquired immunodeficiency syndrome) or retaining employees who have become infected with this disease. The courts have ruled that people with AIDS are covered by the ADA.

If your team members see this policy as a problem, point out that all medical reports show that HIV is not spread by casual contact. To overcome this unjustified fear, follow the example of many companies that have instituted HIV/AIDS-awareness programs: Using videos, pamphlets, company newspaper articles, and talks by doctors, they teach their employees the facts about how HIV is spread.

Ouch! What Happens When You Violate the EEO Laws?

If, after hearings before state or federal agencies responsible for enforcing civil rights laws, a company is found to be in violation of these laws, any or a combination of the following penalties may be invoked:

➤ If the complainant is an applicant, you may be required to hire that person with back pay to the date of the interview. If no job is available, a financial settlement will be negotiated.

➤ If the complainant is a discharged employee, you may have to reinstate that person with back pay from the date of termination.

➤ If the complainant has been denied a promotion, raise, or other benefit, you will be required to make that person "whole" (promote or give him or her the raise or benefit retroactively).

Manager's Minute

When the Civil Rights Act of 1964 was introduced in Congress, it covered only race, color, religion, and national origin. An opponent of the act added sex discrimination to it because he believed that such a radical provision would make the law unpassable. As they say, the rest is history.

➤ If it's a class action, in which a pattern of discrimination is found, all parties to the class action may be awarded a financial settlement (frequently hundreds of thousands of dollars).

➤ In addition to financial penalties, companies have been required to institute an affirmative action plan to correct imbalances of minorities or women in the organization.

➤ Government contractors who violate the law or executive orders may lose their contracts or be banned from receiving future contracts.

➤ Companies that don't comply with orders from administrative agencies can be prosecuted in the courts and fined. Executives who defy the orders can be jailed.

➤ Companies can be sued by persons whose rights have been violated under these laws. Damages may be awarded for lost pay. In addition, companies can incur punitive damages, which can amount to tens or even hundreds of thousand dollars.

The Least You Need to Know

➤ Equal employment opportunity laws prohibit discrimination in employment based on color, race, religion, national origin, gender, age, and disability.

➤ Job specifications should be determined by what's necessary for success on the job, not by preconceived stereotypes.

➤ Don't ask any applicants—male or female—questions relating to their marital status or family.

➤ You cannot refuse to hire or force to retire anyone over the age of 40 just because of age.

➤ In screening people for hiring, transfer, training programs, or promotion, focus on their abilities, not on their disabilities.

YOU LOOK TENSE.

Chapter 12

EEO Problems on the Job

In This Chapter

➤ Preventing and dealing with sexual harassment

➤ Making accommodations for religious requirements

➤ Working with people from diverse cultures

➤ Complying with affirmative action laws

➤ Understanding the family leave law

The various laws that relate to equal employment opportunity were discussed in Chapter 11. This chapter explores some of the major issues you face in applying these laws to the day-to-day management of your team.

During the first 20 years these laws were in effect, most complaints were made in the areas of hiring and firing. Although complaints in these areas are still prevalent, more and more complaints over the past 10 years have involved on-the-job problems, such as sexual harassment and the treatment of minorities and women in the workplace.

Sexual Harassment

You've read about it in the papers; you've heard of it on television: The president of a famous cosmetics company is accused of sexually harassing 15 female employees, and the company pays the women $1.2 million in an out-of-court settlement. Then a U.S. senator is forced to resign because he is accused of sexually harassing at least 26 women who worked for him.

It's not only company presidents and senators who are accused of sexual harassment. Organizations of all sizes and types have faced charges brought against them by both female and male employees claiming sexual harassment.

Manager's Minute

Sexual harassment on the job has been illegal since 1965, but relatively few cases were filed until Anita Hill brought the sexual harassment charges against Clarence Thomas during his Supreme Court confirmation hearings. In the three years preceding these hearings, 18,300 sexual harassment complaints were filed with the EEOC. In the three years following the hearings, 40,800 cases were filed.

In 1998, the Mitsubishi Company settled a sexual harassment suit by agreeing to pay $34 million to 360 women who had been harassed in their plant in Normal, Illinois.

The women reported that they had been fondled by male workers, propositioned by supervisors, called crude, sexually explicit names, subjected to viewing pornographic graffiti on the walls, and generally mistreated. Complaints to management were ignored.

In Long Island, New York, several women employees of Smith Barney, one of the top stock brokerage firms, accused their managers of creating a hostile and offensive working environment. They reported that the employee lounge was nicknamed the "boom-boom room"—male employees made passes at women there and considered it "good fun" to make sexually oriented remarks. Women in other Smith Barney offices joined the class action. A federal court ordered the firm to submit the claims to an arbitration board to determine how much each individual claimant should be paid. The total cost to the company: in the millions. In addition, the company was ordered to institute a diversity training program to recruit, train, and promote women to jobs within the company where they were under-represented. The total cost: $15 million.

The Supreme Court Says...

In 1998, the Supreme Court handed down two other decisions related to sexual harassment. In one case, they ruled that a company can be forced to pay damages to workers who are sexually harassed by a low-level supervisor, even if the company knew nothing of the harassment.

The Court said the general rule is that companies and public employers are automatically liable for a supervisor's sexual harassment. But if sued, companies can sometimes defend themselves by proving that they have a strong policy against sexual harassment and respond quickly to complaints. They must also show that the victim failed to complain. But the burden of proof remains on the employer. The court said, in effect, that companies must prove their innocence when a worker claims sexual harassment on the job. When in doubt, the company is liable.

In another case, a Chicago woman claimed that her boss made repeated comments about sex, urged her to wear shorter skirts, and told her that she was not "loose enough" to suit him. He commented he could make her life very hard or very easy.

After a year the woman quit and sued the company, Burlington Industries. A federal judge threw out her claim because she had not suffered a "tangible job consequence," such as a demotion, for refusing her supervisor's advances.

The U.S. Court of Appeals in Chicago overturned the lower court's decision, holding Burlington liable for the supervisor's harassment even though no specific job consequence had been involved.

The Supreme Court agreed. Although the woman had not suffered a tangible job employment action at the hands of her employer, Burlington was still subject to vicarious liability for her manager's action. To defend itself, the company would have had to prove that it "exercised reasonable care" to prevent harassment in the workplace.

What Is Sexual Harassment?

The commonly accepted definition of sexual harassment isn't always the same as the legal definition. The legal definition of sexual harassment covers much more than just demanding sexual favors for favorable treatment on the job (naturally, these types of demands are included).

Here's the way the courts and the EEOC define sexual harassment: Any unwelcome sexual advances or requests for sexual favors or any conduct of a sexual nature when:

➤ Submission is made explicitly or implicitly a term or condition of initial or continued employment.

➤ Submission or rejection is used as a basis of working conditions including promotion, salary adjustment, assignment of work, or termination.

➤ Such conduct has the purpose or effect of substantially interfering with an individual's work environment or creates an intimidating, hostile, or offensive work environment.

Secret Weapons

Unless you know someone well, other than the traditional handshake, don't hug, don't pat, and certainly don't kiss. Remember the platinum rule (refer to Chapter 2): "Do unto others as they would have you do unto them."

But what does this mean in plain English? This section looks at how this concept works on the job.

"Explicit" Is Clear, but What's "Implicit"?

You would think that corporate presidents and senators would have common sense enough to refrain from making *explicit* sexual demands. Most do. Most people in general have such common sense. That's why people in positions of authority who sexually harass their subordinates use much more subtle tactics. They don't make any actual demands; instead, they imply them. They make references to other employees who have benefited by being "more friendly" or they comment about people's physical attributes.

"Wait a minute," you say. "If I tell a woman she's attractive, *that's* harassment?" It depends on what you say and how you say it.

The comment "That's an attractive dress" is different from the comment "That dress is sexy." The statement "I like your new hairdo" is acceptable, but the statement "Wearing your hair like that excites me" is not.

Take Randy, for example. He's a "toucher." When he greets people, he grasps their hands, pats them on the back, and gives them hugs. That's his way of expressing himself, and he has been doing it for years. He's also a kisser. He doesn't kiss his male associates, but when he greets his female colleagues, he often pecks them on the cheek. Randy was shocked when he was called into the human resources office and told that some of the women in his department had complained about his hugging and kissing. In Randy's eyes, these were acts of friendship with no sexual connotation, but to the women who complained, they were unwelcome.

What Is "An Intimidating, Hostile, Work Environment?"

As noted in the legal definition, sexual harassment isn't limited to demands for sexual favors: It also includes conduct that creates an intimidating and hostile work environment.

Ken's team has always been all-male, and now two women have been added to his group. Some of the men resent this "intrusion" and make life unpleasant for the female team members. The men make snide remarks, give the women incorrect information that causes them to make errors in their work, and exclude them from work-related discussions. No actions are taken that can be interpreted as "sexual" in nature, but it still qualifies as sexual harassment. The men have created a hostile work environment for the women.

Tina works in a warehouse. She is offended by the street language some of the men use. When she complains, she is told, "That's the way these guys talk. They talked this way before women worked here, and they're not going to change now. Get used to it."

Men and women alike are offended by this kind of language. Because dirty language can create "an offensive work environment," it can be legal grounds for a complaint.

If you're faced with a similar situation, talk to the people (or person) using the inappropriate language. Point out diplomatically that their behavior is unprofessional and offensive to both women and men. Inform them that such behavior can cause legal problems for them and the company. Tell them that if they continue to use street language they will be subject to disciplinary action.

Dating, Romance, and Marriage on the Job

Cathy was perplexed. Dennis, one of her team members, had gone out a few times with Diane, who worked in another department. It never developed into a romance, but Diane continually bugged Dennis to go out with her again. Diane would go into Dennis' office several times a day to talk with him, even though Dennis didn't welcome her visits. Diane's constant attention interfered with his work. The next time Diane visited Dennis, Cathy called her aside and told her that social visits were not permissible. Diane never returned, but continued to harass Dennis by telephoning him after work.

Is the company off the hook? Not yet. Even though the harassment has ceased on the job, because both Dennis and Diane are employed by the same company, the company has an obligation to stop Diane from bothering Dennis. Cathy should discuss the situation with Diane's manager and, if necessary, with the human resources department. If Diane continues her harassment, she should be appropriately disciplined.

But dating isn't always unwelcome. Many romances that start on the job end up in marriage. So, what effect does it have on your team when two associates become romantically involved? This situation can be a delicate one. Some companies, fearing that closely related people working together will lead to complications, prohibit parents, children, siblings, and spouses from working on the same team or even in positions in which they must interrelate.

Communication Breakdown

Why lose productive workers because of an archaic rule against spouses working at the same company? Most married couples work well together and have enough control over their own lives not to bring their personal problems into the workplace.

Secret Weapons

Companies can protect themselves from charges of sexual harassment by clearly notifying all employees that the behavior will not be tolerated and by establishing and publicizing a procedure for dealing with complaints. This policy should be administered by a senior executive, and all complaints, if true, should be quickly investigated and corrected.

Relationships other than spousal relationships are not covered by law, and companies are left to deal with them at their own discretion. But when it comes to marriage, there are additional complexities. If a company prohibits married couples from working together and two team members marry, which one should leave the team? Some companies base their policy on rank (the lower ranking spouse leaves) or salary (the lower paid spouse leaves). Because it may be more likely for the man to be the higher ranked or higher paid employee, this policy discriminates against women. If this type of policy exists in your company, the best way to deal with it is to let the couple make the determination about which one will leave.

Discrimination based on marital status isn't expressly prohibited by federal law, but it is barred by interpretation of the sex discrimination clauses by the EEOC. Some states do have specific laws prohibiting discrimination based on marital status.

Caution: The Harasser Can Be Anyone

Suppose one of the salespeople who comes into your office makes a point of telling off-color jokes to the female workers. Some of them think he's hilarious, but you notice the look of disgust on the faces of others. Although no complaints have been made, you see that the behavior is creating an offensive work environment. The salesperson doesn't work for your company, but you still have an obligation to do something about it.

The courts have ruled that an employer is responsible for the offensive behavior of all its employees (regardless of whether they're in management) and even non-employees when the employer or its agents (that's you, in this case) know about it *or should have known* about it.

Speak to the person on whom that sales rep calls. Tell him or her to discuss the matter with the sales rep. If the undesirable behavior continues, the company has an obligation to tell the salesperson that it cannot continue doing business with him.

Note that your company is responsible not only when it knows about the offensive behavior but also *when it should have known* about it. This point is a delicate one. How are you supposed to know about everything that might happen? You can't, of course, but if you're observant, you should know a great deal about what transpires.

Ten Steps to Prevent Sexual Harassment Charges

1. Establish a formal policy prohibiting sexual harassment. Clearly indicate all actions that could be construed as harassment and what steps employees should take if they are harassed. Appoint a senior executive to administer the policy.

2. Publicize the policy through bulletins, articles in the company newspaper, regularly scheduled meetings, and training programs.

3. Make it easy for complainants to bring matters to the attention of management. Post notices throughout your offices detailing to whom and how employees should bring up their complaints.

4. Investigate all complaints—no matter how trivial or unjustified they appear to you. Keep written records of all findings (memos, reports of interviews, and statements from the complainant, the person accused, and witnesses).

5. Never terminate or threaten complainants or potential complainants.

6. Don't make rash decisions. Analyze all the facts. Consult your attorney (remember the matter may wind up in court).

7. Take action. If the complaint is justified, correct the situation. Depending on the case, this may include requiring the harasser to apologize, ordering a cessation of the acts that led to the complaint, adjusting the salary, promoting or changing the working conditions of the persons who have suffered, or, in flagrant or repeated offenses, firing the harasser.

8. If the investigation finds the complaint was not justified, explain the decision carefully and diplomatically to the complainant. Keep in mind that if he or she is not satisfied, a charge can still be filed with appropriate government agencies or brought to court.

9. Don't look for easy ways out. Transferring the harasser to another department may solve the immediate problem, but if the harasser repeats the offense in the new assignment, the situation is compounded.

10. If a formal complaint is made to the EEOC or a state equivalent—even if you feel the complaint is groundless—treat it seriously.

Meanings & Gleanings

According to the EEOC, religious practices include not only traditional religious beliefs but also moral and ethical beliefs and any beliefs an individual holds "with the strength of traditional religious views."

Religion in the Workplace

The law requires you to make reasonable accommodation for a person's religious practices unless doing so results in undue hardship on your company.

Sometimes accommodation is easy. Suppose your company is open seven days a week and that members of your team take turns working on Saturdays and Sundays. One of your employees, David, who is Jewish, can never work on Saturdays. Just schedule him for Sunday work. Say you're not open on Sunday but you have other employees who can work Saturdays; then you're still required to excuse David from Saturday assignments. The other employees may resent having to work on Saturday, but the unhappiness of other employees doesn't qualify as "undue hardship."

If your business is small and there aren't enough people qualified to cover the Saturday shift, it may be considered an undue hardship, and you would not have to hire David.

Here are two other religious considerations in the workplace:

Religious holidays: Employees must be given time off to observe their religious holidays, though you're not required to pay them for these days. These holidays are usually considered excused absences and are charged against personal or vacation days.

Proselytizing on company premises: Margaret, a devout member of her denomination, believed that it was her mission to convert people to her religion. She continually pressed her religious beliefs on her co-workers and distributed tracts and other religious literature. At the request of team members, her team leader asked her to refrain from this behavior. She refused, claiming that the religious accommodation law and the First Amendment gave her the right to proselytize. Margaret was wrong. Just as a company can prohibit political campaigning on company premises and during working hours, it can restrict religious behavior that disturbs other people in the workplace.

Manager's Minute

Here we go again. What is "reasonable accommodation"? And what is "undue hardship"? These same words were mentioned in discussing the implementation of the ADA (see Chapter 11). You must make an honest effort to accommodate the affected employee as long as it can be done without having a negative effect on your company.

Other Areas of Concern

Suppose you're upset that some of the young people on your team come to work dressed in clothes that are more appropriate for leisure activities. The women wear shorts and tank tops; the men, shirts open to their navels. What can you do about it?

It's not illegal to require people to obey a *dress code*, as long as the dress code isn't discriminatory. If women were prohibited from wearing shorts, for example, but nothing was done about the men's open shirts, it would not be considered equal treatment under the law. Prohibiting a Muslim woman from dressing as prescribed by her religion or an Orthodox Jew from wearing a yarmulke would also violate the law's religious provisions.

Dress codes may vary within a company depending on the type of work that's done. Dress codes for factory and warehouse workers are different from those of office employees and employees who deal with the public.

Don't overdo it. Even IBM has dropped its requirement that male employees wear dark suits, white shirts, and blue ties and that women wear dark dresses or suits. As long as what an employee wears is in good taste, it should be acceptable.

Another area of concern is smoking: If you want to stop employees from smoking in your work area, can you do it?

Despite the surgeon general's warning and increasing evidence of the dangers of secondhand smoke, no federal law prohibits smoking on the job. Several states and local communities have laws, however, that restrict smoking in commercial buildings.

Even in areas in which no local laws apply to this situation, many companies have either prohibited smoking or restricted it to specific areas.

In some companies that have no company-wide policy, team members determine the smoking policy for their work area. These policies vary from total prohibition to restricted smoking places and times. Some teams apply no restrictions.

Communication Breakdown

Unless the need to speak English is job related, you cannot require employees to speak only English in the workplace. Employees who normally speak a different language and are more comfortable conversing in their native tongue cannot be compelled to speak English among themselves.

The Rules on Employment of Non–U.S. Citizens

You're worried. You continually read about companies that get into trouble for hiring undocumented aliens (no, not Martians—people from foreign countries). You're almost afraid to hire anyone who has a foreign accent.

Not hiring someone because of this fear is illegal. You cannot discriminate against a person because he or she isn't an American. But you must ensure that an applicant is legally allowed to work in this country.

To prevent your company from inadvertently falling afoul of immigration laws, follow these guidelines:

➤ **Have all new employees (not just those you suspect are foreign) fill out an I-9 form.** You can obtain copies from the Immigration and Naturalization Service. This form should be completed *after* a person is hired. When a starting date is agreed on, the employee should be advised that he or she must submit proper documentation before being put on the payroll.

➤ **Have new employees provide documents to prove their identity.** You have to be sure that a new employee isn't using someone else's papers. Acceptable documents include a driver's license with photo, a school ID with photo, and similar papers.

➤ **Have new employees provide documents to prove citizenship.** These documents include a current U.S. passport, certificate of naturalization, birth certificate, or voter registration card.

➤ **Noncitizens must have documents that authorize employment.** The most commonly used authorization is INS Form I-551, commonly called the "green card" (it originally was green, but now it's white). The employee's photograph is laminated to the card. There are other cases—for example, with students who are allowed to work while in school—in which different forms are acceptable.

Meanings & Gleanings

Diversity: A variety of conditions and activities that create an environment where people can achieve their fullest potential, regardless of the many ways they may differ from each other.

Working with a Multicultural Workforce

If your team consists of men and women who come from different cultures, it can lead to misunderstandings and conflicts. As team leader, you cannot ignore this situation. Your job is to make your team a smooth-running, collaborative group. It isn't always easy to change a person's deeply ingrained perceptions. Newcomers to America must be taught American ways, and Americans must learn to understand the attitudes and customs of newly arrived immigrants.

Digital Equipment Corporation (DEC) has set up a program to address this situation. Small groups of employees meet regularly to explore people's assumptions and stereotypes about their own culture and those they have of others. This list shows some of the goals of DEC's program:

➤ To identify and eliminate preconceptions and myths about new ethnic groups in the company.

➤ To overcome the tendency of people to fraternize with people of only their own ethnic group. All DEC employees—Americans and new immigrants—are encouraged to make friends with people from other backgrounds.

➤ To become aware of assumptions that cause differences in the perception of other cultures and to take steps to correct them.

A large company such as DEC has resources you may not have available to you, but with a little imagination and sensitivity, any team leader can adopt a similar program.

Coping with the Language Barrier

"How can I supervise these people when they don't speak English and I don't know their language?" You've heard this complaint over and over again. It's not a new phenomenon. A hundred or more years ago when immigrants from Europe flooded this country, their supervisors were faced with the same problem. The usual approach then—and it still works—was to find employees who did speak the language and use them as interpreters. If the non-English speakers in your company are all from the same country, you can make an effort to learn enough of their language for basic communication. And, of course, many companies today offer English as a Second Language programs for their employees.

If you're worried about your non-English speaking employees' abilities to understand instruction manuals, just have the manuals translated. Or think about using nonverbal tools, such as demonstrations, training films, and graphics, to train people to perform manual operations.

Other Types of Cultural Diversity

Diversity is not limited to integrating persons from other countries into the work force, but recognizing that there are other cultures within the American population that must be accommodated.

We've previously noted that to discriminate against the physically and mentally challenged is illegal, and that such employees often bring valuable talents and skills to the company. But because accommodations must sometimes be made to assist this group, other workers may be resentful. This is another challenge of the diverse work force.

Integrating women into positions traditionally held by men (or vice versa) is another challenge of diversity.

How should organizations cope with these issues?

Decision-makers must learn to accept the reality of diversity. This calls for abandonment of traditional stereotypes about workers—who they are, what they look like, and why they work. Rather than argue over whether to support diversity, direct your energy toward designing work systems that anticipate the varying and unique qualities of a diverse work force.

Second, develop more objective methods of personnel selection and appraisal. Instead of depending on traditional interviews—which often perpetuate biases—use methods that sample the applicant's ability to do the necessary work. Such tests can serve two purposes. First, they would increase your chances of hiring talented individuals who might otherwise be rejected under the subjective approach. In addition, they can protect your organization from legal challenges in instances where a member of some protected group has been rejected.

159

Establishing Diversity Programs in Your Company

Formal diversity programs have been developed in a number of companies, but they tend to be concentrated in larger organizations. According to a survey by the Society for Human Resources Management, 75 percent of Fortune 500 companies have diversity programs that were developed more than five years ago. In comparison, only 36 percent of companies at-large have diversity programs.

The American Banker's Association has published a guidebook for banks that want to develop diversity programs. Although written expressly for banks, the principles can be applied to any industry.

The first step in a sound hiring and selection process, the guidebook recommends, is writing a thorough job description that identifies the knowledge, skills, and abilities needed. Only job functions viewed as essential to the job should be used to screen applicants. A thorough and accurate job description that is well-communicated to the hiring managers and the HR department will help ensure diverse hiring and prevent legal troubles later.

Determining salaries is another crucial step in promoting a diverse workforce. It is important that a documented method of comparing internal job worth exists in order to support salary practices and policies.

The guidebook advises that a diverse applicant pool should be developed, focusing on both outreach as well as equal and consistent treatment of applicants. All incoming candidates should receive the same information. Employment agencies and temporary agencies used by the company should be instructed to provide applicants from all cultures.

The ABA guidebook also includes:

➤ A comprehensive guide to managing the application process and making selections. The guidebook recommends structured interview forms so that all applicants are asked the same series of questions.

➤ Samples of permissible interview questions, interview evaluation forms, and telephone reference-checking forms.

➤ An overview of equal employment laws.

➤ The mailing addresses of outreach sources with large minority populations and publications aimed at minorities.

➤ Instructions for conducting adverse impact analysis on tests and selection procedures.

Copies of the guidebook are free to ABA members and are available to others for $21. Nonmembers can fax requests to (202) 663-7543.

Manager's Minute

Stereotypes are hard to break. San Diego State University has been ordering classroom furniture for over 100 years. Only recently has it awakened to the reality that not all students are right-handed!

Affirmative Action

Under current civil rights laws, you're not required to give women or minorities any preferential treatment in hiring or promotion. Companies with government contracts or organizations that receive federal funds, however, fall under an executive order requiring them to establish formal *affirmative action plans* (AAP).

If your firm has an AAP, it was probably drawn up by a specialist in the legal or human resources department. You don't have to worry about the technical aspects of this plan. All you have to know is the company's goals for staffing your department with various minority groups and women, so you can make every effort to comply with them.

If your department isn't in line with the affirmative action goals of your company, you should make an effort to hire or promote a person from the group in which the deficiency exists. This advice doesn't mean that you must hire unqualified people just because of their minority status. If you have two candidates with relatively equal qualifications, you're expected to give preference to the minority candidate even if he or she needs more support or training to become productive.

Meanings & Gleanings

Companies that have government contracts in excess of $50,000 and more than 50 employees must have a written *affirmative action plan* committed to hiring women and minorities in proportion to their representation in the community in which the firm is located.

Recent Developments in Affirmative Action

California, Texas, and a few other states have passed laws to loosen their affirmative action practices. For example, colleges and universities are no longer required to

Secret Weapons

Affirmative action is required only for African-Americans, Hispanics, Asians and Pacific Islanders, Native Americans, and women.

engage in affirmative action in admission of students. In addition, these laws repeal affirmative action requirements for state and municipal positions and eliminate preferential treatment of minorities in awarding contracts. Acts have been introduced in Congress to change federal affirmative action policies, but have not passed as of this writing.

Note that none of the state laws affect the private sector. The laws and executive orders discussed throughout this chapter still hold and are strictly enforced. Any changes that are made will be widely publicized.

Twelve Ways to Keep Alert to Your EEO Responsibility

Go along with the spirit as well as the letter of the law.

Offer women and minorities opportunities that were previously denied to them.

Open training programs to minorities, women and the physically challenged, and encourage them, by offering counseling and support, to complete these programs.

Discipline should be administered equitably and should be carefully documented.

Be aware of your own biases and work to overcome any influence they may have on your job decisions.

Use everyone's abilities optimally. Don't base your views about a person's abilities on age, sex, or race. Judge people not on what they cannot do, but on what they *can* do.

Set realistic performance standards based on what a job really calls for. Do not specify, for example, that a job calls for heavy lifting when most of the lifting is done mechanically.

Ignore stereotypes and judge people by their individual abilities, strengths, and weaknesses.

Never use racial epithets or slurs–even in jest.

Encourage all people to deal with their co-workers as human beings, whether they're black or white; Hispanic, Asian, or Anglo; men or women; physically challenged or able-bodied. Mold them into a team.

Sex life and job life must be kept separate.

Support your company's equal-employment and affirmative-action programs fully in every aspect of your job.

Follow these suggestions. They add up to good business.

"I Need Time Off to Take Care of My Mother"

Congress passed the Family and Medical Leave Act (FMLA) in 1993, requiring companies with 50 or more employees to provide eligible employees with as much as 12 weeks of unpaid leave in any 12-month period for the following reasons:

➤ The birth or adoption of a child or the placement of a child for foster care.

➤ To care for a spouse, child, or parent with a serious health condition.

➤ The employee's own serious health condition.

To be eligible, the employee must have been employed by the company for at least 12 months and must request this leave at least 30 days before the expected birth or adoption of the child. When this notification isn't possible, such as the onset of a serious illness of a family member, employees are required to provide as much notice as possible.

Both men and women are eligible for leave under this law. If both husband and wife work for the same employer, however, the total amount of leave is limited to 12 weeks for the couple.

The key provisions of the law make these requirements:

➤ The company must provide the employee, after returning from the leave, with the same position or with a position with equivalent pay, benefits, and other conditions of employment.

➤ Health insurance must be continued during the leave period and paid for in the same manner as though the employee were still on the payroll.

Manager's Minute

Secretary of Labor Alexis Herman reported in August 1998 that an estimated 20 million people have benefited from the Family and Medical Leave Act.

As with most laws, variations apply in special circumstances. For example, Dick's mother receives outpatient chemotherapy every Tuesday, and he brings her to the hospital on Tuesday and stays with her on Wednesday while she regains her strength. Although the law primarily calls for continuing periods of leave, special arrangements can be made so that Dick can take off the time he needs. If the type of work Dick does makes this arrangement unfeasible, however, the company has the right to transfer him temporarily to another job with the same pay and benefits that enable him to take the days off.

To obtain the details about how this law may affect you or a team member, check with your human resources department, legal department, or local office of the Wage and Hour Division of the U.S. Department of Labor (listed in the U.S. government pages of most local telephone directories).

Manager's Minute

The emergence of mandated family leave is largely a result of unprecedented changes in the composition of the workforce and the nature of workers' family responsibilities, dramatically altering the traditional relationship between employees' work and personal lives.

Conflict between work and family obligations has become an inevitable aspect of modern work life, often resulting in absenteeism, work interference, job turnover, and other deleterious impacts. While conflict between work and family responsibilities cannot be eliminated, family leave and other work/family policies can make it easier for America's workers to fulfill their responsibilities as parents, family members, and workers.

The Least You Need to Know

➤ Sexual harassment isn't limited to demands for sexual favors. It also includes permitting a work environment that is hostile or offensive to employees because of their gender.

➤ Prevent sexual harassment situations by instituting a strict policy against that type of behavior—and then enforce it.

➤ Companies must make provisions for employees to observe their personal religious practices.

➤ Encourage employees from different cultural backgrounds to get to know each other as people—not as members of an ethnic group.

➤ If your company has an affirmative action plan, you're required to seek out members of protected minority groups and women for hire and promotion.

➤ Be aware that employees may take as much as 12 weeks off (without pay) to care for a family member with no loss of benefits and the guarantee of returning to the same or equivalent job.

Part 4
Choosing Team Members

It's your dream to build a dream team. Team leaders rarely have the opportunity to choose a full team, but from time to time new members are added either as replacements for people who have left or because the team expands.

Choosing a new team member can be one of your most important acts as a team leader. You'll probably have to live with this person for a long time, so choose carefully and systematically, and use all the tools available to help you make the best decision.

The next time you have a vacancy on your team, you have an opportunity to hire someone who will bring you closer to having the team of your dreams. This part of the book provides you with the know-how to do so.

Chapter 13

Job Description

The employee must be willing to work twenty-four hours a day with little or no reward. They will be expected to perform their job on antiquated equipment and in a hostile environment. Their heart, soul, and first born become property of ACME Inc., International in exchange for the company dental plan.

Creating Realistic Job Specs

In This Chapter

➤ Identifying the skills necessary to do a job

➤ Re-evaluating existing jobs

➤ Making a job analysis when you create a new job

➤ Matching job specs to a job description

➤ Pricing a job

Suppose you have an opening in your department. You want to fill that position with a person who has the necessary skills to perform the required duties of the job and who can contribute to the success of your team. Before you can even begin searching for this person, however, you had better have a clear and realistic concept of what you need.

Maybe you're seeking to fill the position of a person who has left your team, and you already have a job description for that job. The easy way is just to use this existing job description, but that's not necessarily the best way. This is your chance to review the description in light of the changes that may have developed since it was originally written. Re-analyze the job. Treat it as though it were a brand new position. In this way, the new job description will reflect the current duties and activities of the job.

Creating a Good Job Description

Job descriptions are important. Even if you know the job requirements as well as you know the back of your hand, you still need a written job description to begin the hiring process. This description serves many useful purposes:

➤ **Hiring.** Develop realistic job specifications that enable you to seek out candidates who can do what a job requires them to do.

➤ **Training.** Determine what knowledge has to be acquired and which skills have to be developed in your training program.

➤ **Reference.** Devise a permanent source of reference concerning job duties for team leaders and members.

➤ **Performance.** Create a list of standards against which performance can be measured so that everyone knows just what is expected in a job. Each person can measure his or her own performance against those standards.

➤ **Appraisal.** When a formal performance appraisal is made (see Chapter 21), the job description becomes a touchstone against which performance can be evaluated.

Critics are concerned that job descriptions stifle creativity and innovation. They fear many people will take these descriptions too literally and be unwilling to do anything not specifically listed.

How often have you asked someone to do something other than their routine work and heard the response, "It's not in my job description"? All job descriptions should include the phrase "and any other duties that are assigned." The inclusion of this phrase doesn't mean that you have a servant who can be ordered to do any job that pops up. It means that you can assign duties that are at least job-related.

ZAP!

Secret Weapons

A job description isn't a rigid circumscription of functions, and it consists of more than just suggested guidelines. You should make provisions so that deviations, additions, and variations are always open for discussion.

Suppose Don finishes typing a document and you ask him to please take it to the purchasing department. He refuses and says, "I'm an executive assistant, not a messenger. Delivering papers isn't in my job description." That's true: It's not specified, but it is a related duty.

On the other hand, if you say, "Don, you're not busy now; please wash the windows," you're out of line. Your request falls under the phrase "other duties," but it isn't a reasonable extension of his regular work.

When Refilling a Position

Meg was a great customer service representative. Before she left your company, she was not only a good worker but also a contributor to your team and a pleasure to work with. You want to hire another Meg, so you study her background. Because Meg had a liberal arts degree, you believe that the person you hire should have a liberal arts degree. Meg had previous experience in the theater, so you think that a theatrical background would be good. Meg learned computer operations on the job, so you intend to train your new employee to use computers.

Stuart was a difficult person to work with—he wasn't a team player. You want someone quite different from Stuart. Because he had a degree in marketing, you don't want any marketing majors. Stuart had been active in politics; no politicians. Because Stuart had IBM experience and you had to train him to use the Macintosh, you definitely don't want anyone with IBM experience.

Certainly, the backgrounds of people who have been successful (or unsuccessful) in performing particular jobs should be a factor, but not the primary factor, in determining which qualities you should seek in the new person you employ.

Meg's liberal arts degree and Stuart's political background aren't necessarily related to what their jobs required. To learn the key requirements, make a thorough job analysis.

When It's a Brand New Position

Suppose you have finally persuaded your boss to authorize the hiring of an additional member of your team. This position is a new one, so what exactly do you want it to cover?

If the new position is for another person who will perform exactly the same duties as other team members, you can use the same job description and specifications used by team members. In our ever-changing business world, however, a team's functions constantly expand, and new functions and responsibilities require different talents and abilities. You have to create a completely new job analysis.

Meanings & Gleanings

When you perform a *job analysis*, you determine the duties, functions, and responsibilities of a job (the *job description*) and the requirements for the successful performance of that job (the *job specifications*).

Making a Job Analysis

The specialists who perform *job analyses* may be industrial engineers, systems analysts, or members of your human resources staff. If your company employs these people, use them as a resource. The best people to make an analysis, however, are those closest to a job—you and your team members. A job analysis should include a written description of the responsibilities that fall within a job (*job description*) and a written description of the skills and background required to perform a job effectively (*job specification*).

169

Four Techniques for Developing a Job Description

To make a realistic job description, follow the guidelines in this list:

1. **Observe.** For jobs that are primarily physical in nature, watching a person perform the job will give you most of the material you need to write the description. If several people are engaged in the same type of work, observe more than one performer.

   Even a good observer, however, may not understand what he or she is observing. Sometimes it involves much more than meets the eye. In jobs that are not primarily manual, however, there is little you can learn from observation alone. Just watching someone sitting at a computer terminal, for example, isn't enough to learn what's being done.

2. **Question the performer.** Ask the people who perform a job to describe the activities they perform. This technique fleshes out what you're observing. You must know enough about the work, of course, to be able to understand what is being said and to be able to ask appropriate questions. It's a good idea to prepare a series of questions in advance.

3. **Question the supervisor or team leader.** If you are the team leader, review in your mind how you view the position, what you believe the performer should be doing, and the standards that are acceptable. If you're analyzing a job other than the ones you supervise, speak to the team leader or supervisor to obtain that person's perspective of the position.

4. **Make it a team project.** When work is performed by a team, job descriptions cover the work of the entire team. The best way to develop a complete job description is to get your entire team into the act.

The job description worksheet below is a helpful tool. Tailor the form you use to the type of job you're analyzing.

ZAP!

Secret Weapons

Don't base your job specifications on your version of an ideal team member. That person probably exists only in your mind. Be realistic. Your specs should reflect the factors the new member should bring to the job that will contribute to the team's successful performance.

Job Description Worksheet

Job title: _____

Reports to: _____ Dept.: _____

Duties performed: _____

_____

_____

Equipment used: _____

_____

Skills used: _____

_____

Leadership responsibility: _____

_____

Responsibility for equipment: _____

_____

Responsibility for money: _____

_____

Other aspects of job: _____

_____

Special working conditions: _____

_____

Performance standards: _____

_____

Analysis made by: _____ Date: _____

The Specs: What You Seek in a Candidate

After you know just what a job entails, you can determine which qualities you seek for the person who will be assigned to do the job.

The job specifications in some situations must be rigidly followed; others may allow for some flexibility. In civil service jobs or in cases in which job specs are part of a union contract, for example, even a slight variation from job specs can have legal implications. In some technical jobs, a specific degree or certification may be mandated by company standards or to meet professional requirements. For example, an accountant making formal audits must be a certified public account (CPA); an engineer who approves structural plans must be licensed as a professional engineer (PE). On the other hand, if there's no compelling reason for the candidate to have a specific qualification, you may deviate from the specs and accept an equivalent type of background.

Communication Breakdown

Don't clone your current team. When you set up specs for a job, ask yourself, "What must the applicant be able to do that I either cannot or do not want to train him or her to do?" Keep in mind that your team will be stronger if it includes people with different but complementary skills (as opposed to a number of people who all have identical strengths, weaknesses, and capabilities).

Most job specifications include the elements in this list:

➤ **Education:** Does a job call for college? Advanced education? Schooling in a special skill?

➤ **Skills:** Must the candidate be skilled in computers? Machinery? Drafting? Statistics? Technical work? Any of the skills necessary to perform a job?

➤ **Work experience:** What are the type and duration of previous experience in related job functions?

➤ **Personal characteristics:** Does a candidate have the necessary skills in communication, interpersonal relations, and patience? Does he or she have the ability to do heavy lifting?

Eliminating Good Prospects for the Wrong Reason

One of the most common problems in determining the specifications for a job is having the requirement of a higher level of qualifications than is really necessary, thus knocking out potentially good candidates for the wrong reason. This problem frequently occurs in these areas:

➤ **Education.** Suppose certain job specs call for a college degree. Is that degree necessary? It often is, but just as often having the degree has no bearing on a person's ability to succeed in a job. Requiring a higher level of education has more disadvantages than advantages. You may attract smart and creative people, but often a job doesn't challenge them, which results in low productivity and high turnover. More important, you may turn away the best possible candidates for a position by putting the emphasis on a less important aspect of the job.

➤ **Duration of experience.** Your job specs may call for 10 years' experience in accounting, but why specify 10 years? No direct correlation exists between the number of years a person has worked in a field and that person's competence.

Lots of people have 10 years on a job but only one year's experience (after they've mastered the basics of the job, they plod along, never growing or learning from their experience). Other people acquire a great deal of skill in a much shorter period.

It's not that years of experience don't count for anything. Often, the only way a person can gain the skills necessary to do a good job, make sound decisions, and make mature judgments is by having extensive experience. Just counting the years, however, isn't the way to determine that ability.

Rather than specify a number of years, set up a list of factors a new employee should bring to a job and how qualified the person should be in each area. By asking an applicant specific questions about each of these factors, you can determine what he or she knows and has accomplished in each area.

➤ **Type of experience.** Another requirement job specs often mandate is that an applicant should have experience in "our industry." Skills and job knowledge often can be acquired only in companies that do similar work. In many jobs, however, a background in other industries is just as valuable and may be even better because the new associate isn't tradition-bound and will bring to a job original and innovative concepts.

➤ **Preferential factors.** Some job specs are essential to perform a job, but other less critical factors could add to a candidate's value to your company. In listing preferential factors, use them as extra assets and don't eliminate good people simply because they don't have those qualifications.

It may be an extra benefit if a candidate already knows how to use a certain type of computer software, for example, but because that knowledge can be picked up on the job, eliminating a person who is otherwise well qualified might be a mistake.

➤ **Intangible factors.** Intangible factors can be as important (or even more important!) than some tangible requirements.

Of course, you want to hire people with high intelligence, creativity, integrity, loyalty, and enthusiasm, and who have a positive attitude. When you list the intangible requirements for a job, however, put them in proper perspective as they relate to a job.

If a job calls for communication skills, specify exactly which communication skills you need: for example, one-to-one communication, the ability to speak to large groups, innovative telephone sales methods, or creative letter writing skills.

Secret Weapons

To ensure that the person you hire can do a job, the job specs should emphasize what you expect the applicant to have accomplished in previous jobs—not just the length of his or her experience.

173

If a job calls for "attention to detail," specify what type of detail work. If a job calls for "the ability to work under pressure," indicate what type of pressure (for example, daily deadlines, occasional deadlines, round-the-clock sessions, difficult working conditions, or a demanding boss).

Specs Are Guidelines—Be Flexible

Job specs can be so rigid that you're unable to find anyone who meets all your requirements. Sometimes you have to make compromises. Reexamine the job specs and set priorities. Which of the specs are nonnegotiable? These requirements are the ones a new team member absolutely must bring to a job. For example, a candidate must have a degree in electrical engineering or else the work she performs cannot be approved by the government; a candidate must be a certified public accountant or he cannot conduct audits; a candidate must be able to do machine work to precise tolerances or the work will not pass inspection.

Communication Breakdown

The intangibles that make for success on a job are just as important as education, skills, and experience. In making your job analysis, be as diligent in determining the intangible factors as you do the tangible factors.

Some of the specs may be important but not critical. For example, although having a CPA degree may be a good credential, an internal auditor doesn't have to be certified; or, although the specs for a job require knowledge of certain software, experience with different but similar software might do almost as well.

Suppose your specs call for sales experience but an applicant has no job experience in selling. As a volunteer, however, she was a top fund raiser for the local community theater. That person may be able to do the job. In seeking to fill a job, a team leader should make every effort to meet the job specs but should also have the authority to use his or her judgment to determine when deviation from the job specs is acceptable.

What Do I Have To Pay To Get the Person I Need?

Another part of job analysis involves determining the pay scale for a job. Most organizations have a formal job classification system in which various factors are weighed to determine the value of a job. These factors include level of responsibility, contribution of a job to a company's bottom line, type of education, and training and experience necessary to perform the job. Notice that the classification applies to a job, not to the person performing a job.

Negotiating the Pay Package

The pricing of a job in smaller organizations is often done haphazardly: You pay what you have to pay in order to hire the person you want. But you must have some guidelines about what a job is worth so that you don't pay more than necessary or offer too little and not attract good applicants. You have to determine the "going rate" for a job you want to fill.

This list shows some of the sources for obtaining information about the salary scales in your community or industry:

➤ **Trade and professional associations.** These groups conduct and publish periodic salary surveys. Members of these associations can discern how their pay scales compare with other companies in their field and in their geographic area. These surveys are best used when you seek salary information for specialists in your industry or profession.

➤ **Chambers of commerce.** Some chambers of commerce publish salary surveys for their locations. Because these surveys include a variety of industries, you can obtain salary information about jobs that exist in a variety of companies, such as computer operators and clerical personnel.

➤ **Employment agencies.** These agencies can inform you about the going rate for any type of position in which they place employees.

➤ **Networking.** Ask people you know who are managers in other companies in your community or industry. They often are willing to share information about going rates.

Once you have a clear understanding of what the job is worth, you are in a position to negotiate the specific starting salary with the candidate. In some cases, there is no negotiation. You make an offer and the candidate takes it or leaves it. However, when the salary is flexible, there may be some give and take.

Most people are offered a moderate increase over their current salary when hired for a new job. Occasionally, a higher increment is warranted for improved credentials, an advanced degree, or a professional license that the candidate has received since starting the previous job.

Sometimes applicants are unrealistic about what they can obtain. It is advisable to let the applicant know the salary range early in the interviewing process. If the candidate is totally out of line, he or she will withdraw or be eliminated before additional interviewing time is wasted. If the candidate is within range and is being seriously considered, the negotiation should take place before a final offer is made.

Throughout the interview, identify what is important to the applicant—for example, opportunity to accomplish his or her goals, advancement, or

Meanings & Gleanings

To attract and keep good employees, your pay scale must be at least as high as the *going rate*, which is the salary paid for similar work in your industry or community.

creative freedom. Show how those things can be attained on the job. In your negotiation, this often will persuade a candidate to accept a lower starting salary. Emphasize not just the salary but the benefits package, the frequency of salary reviews, and opportunities for advancement. Most candidates do not make the decision to accept or decline an offer based on salary alone.

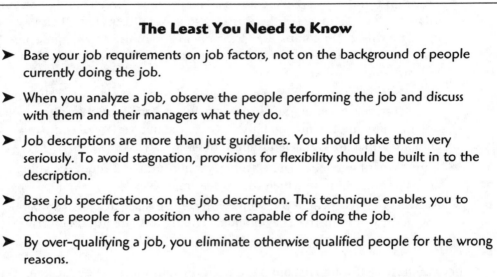

The Least You Need to Know

➤ Base your job requirements on job factors, not on the background of people currently doing the job.

➤ When you analyze a job, observe the people performing the job and discuss with them and their managers what they do.

➤ Job descriptions are more than just guidelines. You should take them very seriously. To avoid stagnation, provisions for flexibility should be built in to the description.

➤ Base job specifications on the job description. This technique enables you to choose people for a position who are capable of doing the job.

➤ By over-qualifying a job, you eliminate otherwise qualified people for the wrong reasons.

➤ Know the going rates for your jobs so that you don't overpay or underpay your associates.

Chapter 14

WELCOME TO THE TEAM!

Choosing Your New Team Member

In This Chapter

➤ Choosing between insiders and new hires

➤ Finding applicants in a tight job market

➤ Studying applications and résumés

➤ Preparing interview questions that provide meaningful information

➤ Conducting an interview

You have a job opening on your team, and you've prepared the job description and job specs. Now you're ready to screen applicants.

The first thing you should do is contact your human resources department. The HR team is composed of experts in recruiting and choosing personnel and usually takes care of most of the initial steps in the hiring procedure. The HR department can provide you with advice that can save you the time and effort involved in the part of the hiring process you do yourself. An important part of their responsibility is that they're aware of all the legal implications involved in this delicate area and can help you avoid problems.

Applicants can come from many sources. People working in other positions in your company may fit your needs—look there first. In addition, you can seek people from outside your organization through a variety of channels.

This chapter explains how to recruit personnel and provides some tips for evaluating application forms and résumés and conducting interviews that will give you meaningful information on which to base your hiring decisions.

Your Best Bet May Be Close By

People who already work for your company may make valuable members of your team. They may work at jobs in which they don't use their full potential, or they may be ready for new challenges. Joining your team would be a move up for them. Even if an opening isn't an immediate promotion, a lateral transfer might enable that person to take a step forward in reaching her career goals.

Taking Advantage of Internal Transfers

Not every transfer is a promotion, but it's often an opportunity for someone to learn, gain experience, and take a step forward in preparing for career advancement.

Seeking to fill a team vacancy from within a company has many advantages:

➤ People who already work in your company know the "lay of the land." They're familiar with your company's rules and regulations, customs and culture, and practices and idiosyncrasies. Hiring these people rather than someone from outside your company saves time in orientation and minimizes the risks of dissatisfaction with your company.

➤ You know more about these people than you can possibly learn about outsiders. You may have worked directly with a certain person or observed him in action. You can get detailed and honest information about a candidate from previous supervisors and company records.

➤ Offering opportunities to current employees boosts morale and serves as an incentive for them to perform at their highest level.

➤ An important side effect is that it creates a positive image of your company in the industry and in your community. This image encourages good people to apply when jobs for outsiders do become available.

Communication Breakdown

The practice of restricting promotions to current employees tends to perpetuate the racial, ethnic, and gender makeup of your staff. Companies whose employees are predominantly white and male and who rarely seek outside personnel have been charged with discrimination against African-Americans, other minorities, and women.

Realizing the Limitations of Promoting Only from Within

Although the advantages of internal promotion usually outweigh the limitations, there are disadvantages to consider:

➤ If you promote only from within, you limit the sources from which to draw candidates and you may be restricted to promoting a person significantly less qualified than someone from outside your company.

➤ People who have worked in other companies bring with them new and different ideas and know-how that can benefit your team.

➤ Outsiders look at your activities with a fresh view, not tainted by over-familiarity.

Searching for Applicants Internally—The Company Job Bank

You can't possibly know everyone in your company who might be qualified for a position on your team. But your human resources (HR) department should.

If a job is a promotion or a position that will give an applicant a raise in pay or more challenging work, look first at your own team. You know these women and men best, and one of them might fit the bill.

If no one on your team is suitable or interested in the position, discuss the opening with someone from your HR department. Go over the job specs with that person. He or she can suggest possible candidates from within your company.

Some companies have formalized this process by using these two methods:

1. **Job banks.** A search of this computerized list of the abilities of all employees should turn up qualified candidates for your screening.

2. **Job postings.** Many companies post the specs for available positions on bulletin boards and sometimes on electronic bulletin boards. Any interested employee can apply. After preliminary screening by the HR department, anyone who meets the basic requirements is sent to you to be interviewed. In addition, by doing this, companies inform women and members of minority groups, who might not have been considered, about the availability of these jobs.

Meanings & Gleanings

Recruiting is the process of seeking candidates to be considered for employment. The *selection* process involves screening applicants to determine their suitability, usually by reviewing résumés and then conducting interviews.

Recruiting and Selection

In addition to searching for candidates within your company, the HR department may help you *recruit* from outside sources. It may advertise the opening, contact employment services, visit colleges (for trainees), or use executive recruiters (often called "headhunters") for higher level positions.

Before the actual recruiting begins, the team leader and the members of the HR team review the job specifications to coordinate the process. As expert as HR people may be in their specialty, however, they cannot do the job alone. A team leader's knowledge of the job and the team's personality is necessary to ensure that the best-qualified candidates are sought out and considered.

Applicants, Applicants, Where Are the Applicants?

"Good help is hard to find" is one of the oldest laments in business and still one of the most valid. Today, more than ever, retaining human talent is essential for fast growing, fast changing companies.

In one recent poll, 53 percent of employees surveyed said they expected to leave their current employer voluntarily within the next five years. In such an environment, the ability to recruit and retain the most qualified workers is essential. Simply running a classified ad or calling an employment agency is no longer enough to attract good employees.

Reaching and retaining today's highly mobile, well-connected workers is a major challenge to human resources staffs and business managers.

To cope with a job market in which there is a shortage of good workers, managers must use the best resources available to them and create new, innovative approaches.

Today's job market has been called the most active in a generation. Unemployment is at one of its lowest points in years, and employee turnover increases when jobs are easy to find. More important, a million or more new jobs have been created over the past few years.

Due to the high level of downsizing in the late 1980s and early 1990s, the attitude of employees toward their employers has changed. Loyalty to companies was eroded when companies showed they were not loyal to their employees. The career-oriented person today thinks in terms of growth wherever opportunity arises—and does not limit herself to the current employer.

Attracting and keeping employees by financial incentive alone does not work. The most desirable employees expect solid compensation, but they also look for intangible benefits, such as growth opportunities, greater flexibility and self-direction, more personal satisfaction and a more "family-friendly" workplace.

Kicking the HR Department to Get on the Ball

If you work for a large organization, chances are that you do not do your own recruiting. You work through the Human Resources or Personnel Department.

Naturally, you're not their only client. Other team leaders and managers are bugging them to fill their jobs. In this job market, they have their hands full.

But that's no excuse, as far as you're concerned. You need to fill those vacancies. Some suggestions:

➤ Make friends with the HR staff. Not just when you need people, but as a regular practice. If you haven't done this up to now, it may be too late for your current needs, but work on it, and next time you have a job to fill, you'll see the difference.

➤ Offer to help them by contacting people you know. For example, you may be a member of a professional association and can tap their resources.

➤ Offer to screen résumés from ads. This saves them time and work, and you will have to look at the résumés anyway sooner or later.

➤ Give them prompt reactions to anybody they refer to you. One of the biggest gripes HR people have about team leaders is their stalling on making decisions.

Secret Weapons

Make friends with the HR staff. Help them help you. When you need that extra push to fill your job vacancies, you'll be one step ahead of other team managers.

Routine Sources for Job Applicants

If you work for a company that does not have a Human Resources or Personnel Department, you may have to dig up candidates on your own.

Even if a job is hard to fill, don't overlook the standard sources for recruiting applicants. These are tried and true methods.

➤ **Help wanted ads.** The most usual source for hiring is to place ads in local newspapers for routine jobs. These ads are read by local residents who are seeking positions. However, if your job is hard to fill and you are willing to relocate people from other areas, your best bet is to advertise in trade or professional journals.

➤ **Private employment agencies.** Most of these agencies have files of applicants who are immediately available and can match them against your job specs, enabling you to fill the job quickly. Because they screen applicants before referring them, you will see only qualified people and avoid wasting time interviewing countless unqualified people.

Contact employment agencies that specialize in your type of work. You can identify these agencies by studying the ads that they place in newspapers and professional journals. If you note that they cover a variety of jobs in your areas of interest, they may know people who fit your needs. Once you have established a relationship with one or two agencies, you will have a ready source of personnel when needed.

Most employment agencies require the employer to pay a fee, which may range from 10 to 20 percent of the annual salary paid to the employee, and even more for technical and management jobs.

➤ **Headhunters.** Executive or technical recruiters differ from employment agencies in that they put their efforts into identifying and going after specific candidates, who are usually currently employed and not actively seeking jobs. These firms usually work on higher paying positions. Some firms charge a flat fee, paid whether they fill the job or not; most take a non-refundable retainer and a percentage of salary if they succeed in filling the job.

➤ **State employment services.** All states have an employment or job service that can recommend applicants for your jobs. You certainly should list your jobs with the local office of this agency. Often state services also provide testing and other screening facilities. Some companies have developed excellent relations with these agencies. Other firms have expressed dissatisfaction because state placement services are primarily concerned with finding jobs for unemployed people. They feel that the better applicants may be currently employed and not registered with these agencies.

➤ **School affiliated employment services.** High school, college, and technical or specialized school employment services are excellent sources for recruiting people with little or no experience. Most do not charge a fee and are anxious to place their graduates. Some schools whose graduates are looking for jobs in industries with a short supply of trained people do charge fees. These schools sometimes have records of alumni who do have work experience.

Manager's Minute

IN SHORT SUPPLY! The 10 fastest growing occupations (1996–2000): 1. Database administrator/computer scientist; 2. Computer engineer; 3. Systems analyst; 4. Personal and home care aide; 5. Physical and corrective therapy aide; 6. Home health aide; 7. Medical assistant; 8. Desktop publishing specialist; 9. Physical therapist; 10. Occupational therapy aide.

Source: Bureau of Labor Statistics

Finding Qualified People for Hard-to-Fill Jobs

Your first move is to tap the resources you have on hand—your current staff. Most people in technical and other specialized work have friends and acquaintances in their own fields. They belong to professional associations, keep up with classmates, and attend conventions. Ask them for referrals. Some companies have formal programs in which rewards are given for referrals that result in a hire. Another source is to contact the placement committees of appropriate professional associations.

The Internet

If your company doesn't have a Web page, get one. This is a particularly effective tool for recruiting computer specialists and other technically trained people. There are also several Web sites that carry classified ads or even match applicants with job openings (for a fee).

Job Fairs

These are sometimes organized by trade associations or private recruiting firms. They tend to specialize in specific types of jobs. Companies may rent a booth at the fair to attract the applicants, provide people with job information, and even conduct preliminary interviews.

Some larger firms conduct their own job fairs. Advance Micro Devices ran such a fair in Austin, Texas. They promoted the fair in radio ads for weeks in advance, then set up a big tent to supply job information to those who wandered in. The fair was "wildly successful," and AMD hired 30 people.

Train People

Another approach is to hire willing and adaptable people and train them in the particular skills required to do the jobs. Some firms seek community college, vocational school, and high school graduates who don't plan to go to college and train them for entry level positions.

Retirees, Part-Time, and Share-Time Workers

Some employers are asking retirees if they would consider working part-time; others are luring mothers of young children back to the work force early by helping with day care. Others arrange for two people to share a job—each person working part-time. This allows for continuity in the work and gets jobs done. These methods, usually used by people who need time for family responsibilities, bring to the company talents that would have been lost if full-time work was demanded.

Importing Foreign Workers

Employers are bringing into the U.S. as many foreign computer specialists and other technicians as they can. But by law only 65,000 special visas can be issued annually to such workers during a government fiscal year, which runs from October 1 to September 30. All visas for fiscal 1998 were snapped up by the first week in May.

Estimates predict that visas for fiscal 1999 will be gone by next February. Bills to increase the quota have been introduced in Congress, but some employers are apprehensive about ever being able to import enough workers and are moving to shift more operations overseas.

Filling Sales Jobs

Another area in which many companies have difficulty in finding good people is in sales. Here are some ideas to help find sales staff:

➤ **Rethink your job specs.** Too many companies limit their search to people with experience selling the same products they sell. Sales reps with successful sales records can often be far better bets. Unless your product is highly technical, product knowledge can be acquired rapidly.

➤ **Ask purchasing agents.** Buyers and purchasing agents often are impressed by sales reps who call on them. Sometimes they learn that one of these people is seeking a change. Suggest that they refer that person to you. Don't limit your requests to people who work for competitors. People who sell other products to that buyer may be good prospects for you.

➤ **Ask your own salespeople.** Personal recommendations from your own employees are a standard employment source. However, this can be expanded. Sales people spend a good deal of time waiting in the anterooms of buyer's offices. They get to meet and chat with other salespeople calling on that buyer. Ask them to look out for people they believe would be a good addition to your staff. You may offer them a bonus if their referrals are hired.

➤ **Salespeople who call on you.** You have an excellent opportunity to size up her personality, approach, and technique when a salesperson makes her presentation to you. Feel out how she perceives her current opportunities. Perhaps she can better meet her long-term goals in your firm.

Manager's Minute

A survey reported in *The Personnel Administrator* (now called *HR*) indicated that the average Human Resources staff member spent less than three minutes in his first reading of a résumé. To avoid rereading it before the interview, highlight the factors you want to explore in the interview.

Résumés: Separating the Wheat from the Chaff

The résumé is the applicant's promotional piece telling you why he or she should be hired. It is not necessarily an objective recap of qualifications.

You may receive hundreds of résumés in response to an ad. It can take hours of your time to read them and make your preliminary judgments. You can save time and uncover hidden problems in résumés by following these guidelines:

➤ Establish some "knock-out factors." These are job requirements that are absolutely essential to performing the job. They include necessary educational qualifications and/or licenses. For example, a degree in electronics, a plumber's certification, or a jet plane pilot's license.

➤ Select key aspects of the job and screen for them. When you have many applicants for a position, you can narrow the field by looking for experience in those key aspects.

➤ Look for gaps in dates. Many people who have had short duration jobs leave them out of their résumé. Some signs to watch for are:

Communication Breakdown

Show some flexibility in your "knock-out factors." Unless a specific degree is needed for legal or professional reasons, a person with no degree but extensive experience in a field may be better qualified than a person with a degree and less experience.

1. Specifying years only rather than month and year. (1995–1998 for one job and 1991–1995 for the previous job.) It may mean only a short period of unemployment between jobs, but it may also mean that a job held for several months between the listed jobs was omitted from the résumé.

185

2. Listing number of years worked instead of dates. This may also be a cover-up for gaps in work history. And it could indicate the applicant's attempt to emphasize older jobs when his or her more recent work experience is not relevant to the job being sought. For example, say the job sought is market analyst. The applicant was a market analyst 10 years ago, but has been working in a different position since. By placing the marketing experience first in the résumé and not specifying dates, the impression is that the marketing job was most recent.

3. Giving more space on a résumé to older positions. This may be due to an applicant simply updating an old résumé instead of creating a new one—which could be a sign of laziness. Or it may just mean that the more recent jobs were of lesser pertinence than previous ones.

Secret Weapons

Use a résumé as a *supplement* to an application, not as a *substitute* for it.

4. Overemphasis on education for experienced applicants. If a person is out of school five or more years, the résumé should primarily cover work experience. What was done in high school or college is secondary to what has been accomplished on the job. For such applicants, information about education should be limited to degrees and specialized programs completed.

None of these are necessarily knock-out factors. They simply suggest further exploration in the interview.

All Candidates Should Complete an Application Form

Except for those people applying for the most routine jobs, most applicants provide résumés of their background and experience. In addition, most companies require all applicants to complete an application form.

You may wonder why an application form is necessary when you have a résumé. You need it! As pointed out above, résumés are an applicant's sales pitch—designed to make you want to hire him or her. A résumé can hide undesirable aspects of a person's background or overplay positive factors. Many résumés don't list every employer—only those the candidate wants you to know about. Others don't give dates of employment, salary history, and other information you may need. An application form provides you with the information *you* need to know, not what the applicant wants you to know.

Because all the information requested on the application form is the same for all applicants, it complies with the equal employment opportunity laws. In addition, it helps you compare applicants' backgrounds when you make your hiring decision. Make sure that all applicants complete the form, even if they provide a detailed résumé.

Be sure to study an application to get a better idea about a candidate's background before you call the person in for an interview.

Like every aspect of the hiring process, an application form must comply with equal employment laws. In today's litigious society, you would think that most companies would be conscious of this situation and have these forms reviewed carefully by legal experts. As a consultant, I have had the opportunity to see countless company application forms. I'm amazed that even now—30 years after the EEO laws went into effect—I still see application forms that ask for age, marital status, number of children, dates of schooling (which can identify age), and other illegal questions.

The sample application form on the next page is typical of those used by many companies. You have to use the form your company provides, of course, but if you plan to revise it, this sample may give you some guidelines. In addition to the questions asked in the sample, companies often add questions that are of particular concern to them. Companies hiring technical and professional people ask about membership in professional societies, awards earned, and papers published. Some companies ask about felony convictions. Remember that the form should meet your needs while complying with appropriate laws. (The terms of employment and other matters mentioned at the end of the employment application are discussed in Chapter 25.)

Communication Breakdown

Make sure your application form meets EEO guidelines. Questions that you assume are acceptable may have illegal connotations. Have your legal department or an attorney who specializes in labor law review your application before you have it printed.

Preparing for an Interview

Too often it happens that you have a pleasant interview with an applicant and learn little more than basic information. An interview shouldn't consist of just a casual conversation: You should be prepared to ask questions that enable you to judge an applicant's qualifications and give you insight into that person's strengths and limitations as they apply to the job.

To ensure that you get the information you want, make a list of pertinent questions *before* you meet with a candidate:

➤ **Review the job description.** Prepare questions that bring out an applicant's background and experience in the functions of that job.

Secret Weapons

You can get much more (and more useful) information by asking open-ended questions. Rather than asking, "Do you know how to use WordPerfect?" ask, "Tell me about your experience in using Word-Perfect."

➤ **Review the job specifications.** Prepare questions to help you evaluate whether an applicant's background and skills conform with what you're seeking.

➤ **Review a person's application (if available) and résumé.** Some of the information you need may be gleaned from these documents. Prepare questions that expand on what's in those documents.

Application for Employment

Date: _____

Name: _____ Social Security number: _____

Address: _____

City, State, ZIP: _____ Phone: _____

Position sought: _____ Salary desired: _____

EDUCATION

Level: _____ School/Location: _____ Course: _____

Number of years: _____ Degree or diploma: _____

College: _____

Other: _____

_____

EMPLOYMENT RECORD

1. Company/Address: _____

   Dates: _____ Salary: _____ Supervisor: _____

   Duties: _____

   _____

   _____

   Reason for leaving: _____

   _____

2. Company/Address: _____

   Dates: _____ Salary: _____ Supervisor: _____

   Duties: _____

   _____

   _____

   Reason for leaving: _____

   _____

---

3. Company/Address:

Dates: _____ Salary: _____ Supervisor: _____

Duties: _____

_____

_____

Reason for leaving: _____

_____

How were you referred to this company? _____

Are you 18 years of age or older? _____

If you're hired, can you provide written evidence that you are authorized to work in the United States? _____

Is there any other name under which you have worked that we would need in order to check your work record? (If so, please provide.) _____

APPLICANT'S STATEMENT:

I understand that the employer follows an "employment at will" policy, in that I or the employer may terminate my employment at any time or for any reason consistent with applicable federal and state laws. This employment-at-will policy cannot be changed verbally or in writing unless authorized specifically by the president or executive vice president of this company. I understand that this application is not a contract of employment. I understand that the federal government prohibits the employment of unauthorized aliens; all persons hired must provide satisfactory proof of employment authorization and identity. Failure to submit such proof will result in denial of employment.

I understand that the employer may investigate my work and personal history and verify all information given on this application, on related papers, and in interviews. I hereby authorize all individuals, schools, and firms named therein, except my current employer (if so noted), to provide any information requested about me and hereby release them from all liability for damage in providing this information.

I certify that all the statements in this form and other information provided by me in applying for this position are true and understand that any falsification or willful omission shall be sufficient cause for dismissal or refusal of employment.

Signed _____

Questions You Should Ask

Structure interviews so that you don't forget to ask important questions. You usually should explore the five areas in this list:

1. **Education.** Does an applicant have the requisite educational requirements or other background that would provide the necessary technical know-how?

2. **Experience.** Inquire about the type and length of pertinent experience. Ask not only "What did you do?" but also "How did you do it?" You can determine from an applicant's answers whether he or she has the type of experience that's necessary for a job.

3. **Accomplishments.** It's important to learn what an applicant has done to make him or her stand out from other qualified candidates.

4. **Skills.** Learn the special skills an applicant can bring to a job.

5. **Personal characteristics.** The job specifications should indicate the personal characteristics necessary for doing a job. During an interview, try to identify, in addition to these characteristics, other personality factors that may affect the applicant's compatibility with you and your team members.

Communication Breakdown

When you use a list of questions, don't stick only to the questions on the list. Listen to the answers—not only to what an applicant says but also, more important, to what he or she does *not* say. Follow up with probing questions to elicit more detailed information.

The following list of interview questions can guide you in preparing the questions you want to ask a job candidate. Questions similar to these, tailored to the job involved, can provide a great deal of meaningful information.

Conducting an Interview

Suppose an interviewer greets an applicant with a curt "What makes you think you can handle this job?" If you're looking for a tough, no-nonsense person who will be exposed to constant harassment and pressure, this approach might work.

But most jobs aren't like that. Even if applicants aren't intimidated by this approach, they're less likely to be forthright in their responses. It becomes a battle of wits, rather than an elucidating discussion about qualifications.

Interview Questions

Work experience

(Add specific questions to determine job knowledge and experience in various aspects of the job for which you are interviewing.)

Describe your current responsibilities and duties.

How do you spend an average day?

How did you change the content of your job from when you started it until now?

Discuss some of the problems you encountered on the job.

What do you consider to be your primary accomplishment in your current job (or previous jobs)?

Qualifications other than work experience (helpful questions for applicants with no direct work experience)

How do you view the job for which you are applying?

What in your background particularly qualifies you to do this job?

If you were to be hired, in which areas could you contribute immediately?

In which areas would you need additional training?

In what way has your education and training prepared you for this job?

Weaknesses

Which aspects of your previous job did you do best?

In which areas did you need help or guidance from your boss?

In which areas have your supervisors complimented you?

Motivation

Why did you choose this career area?

What do you seek in a job?

What's your long-term career objective?

How do you plan to reach this goal?

Of all the aspects of your last job (or jobs), what did you like most? Least?

What kind of position do you see yourself in five years from now?

What are you looking for in this job that you're not getting from your current job?

Stability

What were your reasons for leaving each previous job?

Why are you seeking a job now?

What were your original career goals?

How have these goals changed over the years?

Resourcefulness

Describe some of the more difficult problems you have encountered in your work.

How did you solve those problems?

To whom did you go for counsel when you couldn't handle a problem yourself?

What's your greatest disappointment so far in your life?

In what way did this disappointment change your life?

Working with others

On what teams or committees have you served?

What was your function on this team (or committee)?

What did you contribute to the team's activities?

How much of your work did you do on your own? As part of a team?

Which aspect did you enjoy more? Why?

What did you like best about working on a team? Least?

Secret Weapons

Elicit from applicants information about what they have done in previous jobs (or other areas of their lives) that they're particularly proud of. Past successes are good indicators of future achievements.

Most job applicants are nervous or at least somewhat ill at ease in an interview. To make an interview go smoothly, put applicants at ease. Welcome them with a friendly greeting, a smile and a handshake, and offer a cup of coffee or tea. Introduce yourself and begin the discussion with a non-controversial comment or question based on something from an applicant's background. For example, starting out with the comment, "I noticed that you graduated from Thomas Tech—two of our team members are Thomas grads" ensures an applicant that you're familiar with the school and are favorably inclined toward its alumni.

After you "break the ice," you're ready to move into the crux of an interview and ask the questions you have prepared.

When the Applicant Is Holding Back

Have you ever had the feeling that an applicant is hiding something or is reluctant to talk about a particular aspect of his or her background? These three techniques may help open these closed doors:

1. **Use silence.** Most people cannot tolerate silence. If you don't respond after someone has finished talking, he or she will usually fill in the gap by adding something more. ("I have experience in mass mailing software." [Silence.] "I did it once.")

2. **Make non-directive comments.** Ask open-ended questions, such as, "Tell me about your computer background." An applicant will tell you whatever he or she feels is an appropriate response. Rather than comment on the answer, respond with "Uh-huh" or "Yes" or just nod. This technique encourages applicants to continue talking without giving any hints about what you're seeking to learn. This approach often results in obtaining information about problems, personality factors, attitudes, or weaknesses that might not have been uncovered by direct questions. Conversely, it can bring out additional positive factors and strengths.

3. **Probing questions.** Sometimes applicants can be vague or evasive in answering questions. Probe for more detail, as in this example:

Interviewer: For what type of purchases did you have authority to make final decisions?

Applicant: Well, I know a great deal about valves.

Interviewer: Did you buy the valves?

Applicant: I recommended which valves to buy.

Interviewer: Who actually negotiated the deal?

Applicant: My boss.

When the Applicant Tries to Dominate the Interview

Have you ever interviewed an applicant who tried to take over the interview? Instead of answering the questions asked, he tells you what he wants you to hear. Sometimes an applicant will rephrase your question so he can answer it in a manner favorable to him. For example, you ask: "Tell me about your experience selling to department store buyers?" The response: Department store buyers are not as difficult to deal with as small store owners." The interviewee then expands on his experience in that market.

To overcome this, when the applicant pauses for breath, quickly interrupt by rephrasing the original question. "I see your point, but what experience have you had selling to department store buyers?"

When the Applicant Is Too Nervous

Applicants are often nervous at an interview. Once you help someone overcome her initial nervousness, you may find that you have an excellent candidate. Some suggestions:

Communication Breakdown

After an applicant has answered your question, *wait five seconds before asking your next question.* You'll be amazed at how many people add new information—positive or negative—to their original response.

➤ Don't start with a challenge: "What makes you think you can handle this job?" Put the applicant at ease. If he appears nervous, start with some small talk. Pick something non-threatening from the application and comment on it. Remember the example I gave you earlier in this section: "I see you graduated from Thomas Tech. Several of our people are Thomas grads and they are doing well."

➤ With young applicants out for their first job, be supportive. Comment about their nervousness. Once it is verbalized, it often dissipates. Reinforce it with a comment such as "I can understand why you are nervous. When I applied for my first job, I was more nervous than you are now."

➤ Comment on an accomplishment. "I note that you had a 3.7 GPA. That's commendable." Compliments inspire confidence.

Take Notes—But Not Too Many

One of my most embarrassing moments occurred in my first job as a personnel manager. I interviewed several candidates for a sales position. Two of the candidates had similar backgrounds but quite different personalities. You guessed it—I mixed them up and made the job offer over the telephone to the wrong person. Was I shocked when he walked in the following Monday morning!

It's difficult to remember every person you interview. It's advantageous to record the highlights of an interview and, of course, the decision you made. Taking detailed notes during an interview is neither possible nor desirable; doing so often makes an applicant "freeze up," and, if you're busy writing, you can't fully listen.

Take brief notes during an interview. Write down enough information that you'll be able to remember who each applicant is, what makes one applicant different from another, and how each applicant measures up to the job specs for which she has been interviewed.

When you're evaluating several candidates for the same job, keep good records to help in comparing them. By using a standard interview report form, you can make a comparison more effectively. Often, more than one person interviews an applicant, and if each one reports comments on a standard form, evaluations are easier to interpret.

In the case of investigations by federal or state EEO agencies, good records of an interview can be your most important defense tool. When records are unavailable or inadequate, the hearing officer bases judgment on the company's word against the word of an applicant. Complete and consistent records give your company solid evidence in case of an investigation.

As mentioned in Chapter 4, in the section "Five Tricks to Make You a Better Listener," take brief notes during an interview and write your report immediately afterward. If it helps, use the sample interview summary sheet on the following pages.

Telling the Applicant About the Job

An important part of the interviewing process occurs when you tell applicants about your company and the job. An interviewer is often so ill at ease about asking questions that he or she spends most of an interview describing the duties of the job, the advantages of working in the company, and the benefits the company offers.

There's a time during interviews to divulge this information—*after* you have obtained enough information about an applicant to determine whether he or she is a viable candidate.

Secret Weapons

Don't give applicants a copy of the job description before an interview. Their responses to your questions will be influenced by what they have read.

At the beginning of an interview, briefly indicate the type of job you're seeking to fill. If you give away too many details about a job, a shrewd applicant will tailor the answers to your questions to fit what you have described.

The best way to give information about job duties is to ask questions about an applicant's qualifications in that area before you give information:

Interviewer: How much of your previous job involved copy writing?

Applicant: Most of it. I spent at least two-thirds of my time writing copy.

Interviewer: Great, writing copy is a major part of this job.

Interview Summary Sheet

Applicant: _____ Date: _____

Position applied for: _____ Interviewer: _____

Job factors [1]: _____

Applicant's background [2]: _____ Qualification rating [3]: _____

Duties: _____
_____
_____

Responsibilities: _____
_____
_____

Skills required: _____
_____
_____

Education required [4] (level): _____

   Specific types: _____
_____
_____

   Educational achievement: _____
_____
_____

Other job factors: _____
_____

[1] *Job factors should be listed from job specifications for position applicant applies for.*

[2] *Interviewer should note aspects of applicant's background that apply to each factor in this column.*

[3] *Rate applicant on a scale of 1 to 5 for how closely background fits specifications.*

[4] *Level of education means how much schooling completed; type represents subjects related to job taken; achievement represents grades or standing.*

Personal factors	Comments	Qualification rating
Growth in career		
Accomplishments		
Intangibles		
Appearance		
Motivation		
Resourcefulness		
Stability		
Leadership		
Creativity		
Mental alertness		
Energy level		
Communications skills		
Self-confidence		

Comments

Applicant's strengths: _____

Applicant's limitations: _____

[   ]   Applicant should be hired.

Recommendations for additional training: _____

[   ]   Applicant should NOT be hired.

Reasons: _____

Additional comments: _____

_____

_____

Listening to and Evaluating the Applicant's Questions

Applicants usually have questions about your company and the job. Give them a chance to ask those questions. You should not only answer them but also listen for the type of questions they ask.

Questions about job content, opportunities to use their own initiative, how your team operates, and what types of training and development are offered show positive qualities in an applicant. But if the questions concern primarily vacations, pay raises, or personal benefits, an applicant may not be as job-oriented as you want.

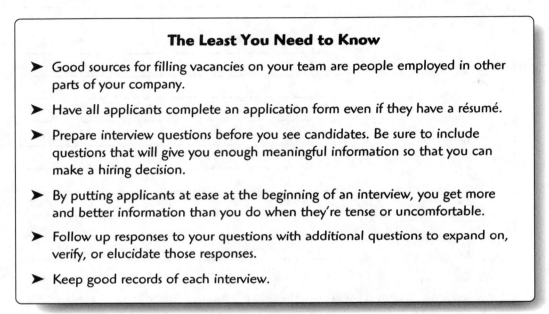

The Least You Need to Know

➤ Good sources for filling vacancies on your team are people employed in other parts of your company.

➤ Have all applicants complete an application form even if they have a résumé.

➤ Prepare interview questions before you see candidates. Be sure to include questions that will give you enough meaningful information so that you can make a hiring decision.

➤ By putting applicants at ease at the beginning of an interview, you get more and better information than you do when they're tense or uncomfortable.

➤ Follow up responses to your questions with additional questions to expand on, verify, or elucidate those responses.

➤ Keep good records of each interview.

Chapter 15

Making the Hiring Decision

In This Chapter

➤ Conducting team interviews

➤ Giving tests and making reference checks

➤ Overcoming roadblocks to making good hiring decisions

➤ Comparing applicants

➤ Making a job offer

An interview is one of the primary tools for choosing new employees, but it's not the only one. An interview is subjective, after all.

To supplement your reaction to applicants, have other managers or team members interview them. Because each person tends to look for different facets of an applicant's background, have several people do the interviewing to uncover much more about a candidate than any one interviewer can find. It's particularly helpful for team members to interview people who may join their team, because their reactions can help you make a better choice. Other techniques for obtaining information about prospective employees are to check their references and, in some cases, have them undergo testing.

This chapter discusses these and other approaches to learning as much as possible about applicants before making your hiring decision.

Two Heads Are Better Than One

Hiring an employee can be the most important decision you make as a manager. The people who comprise your team can make or break your endeavors. No matter how good you may be as an interviewer, it's a good idea to seek the reaction of others before making a final decision.

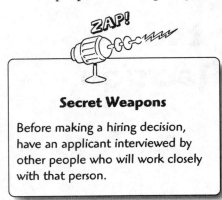

Secret Weapons

Before making a hiring decision, have an applicant interviewed by other people who will work closely with that person.

In larger companies, a member of the human resources (HR) department has preliminary interviews with applicants. Only people who meet basic job requirements are referred to you.

If you're the only person who has interviewed an applicant, it's a good idea to have the applicant interviewed by at least one other person. You may have missed important facts or been overly influenced by one factor or another.

The person (or persons) asked to be the other interviewer should have the appropriate type of job and level of responsibility. To interview for jobs of a technical or specialized nature, a person with expertise in that area is the best choice. If a new employee will work closely with another department, the opinion of the manager of that department will be meaningful. Many companies require finalists to be interviewed by the manager at the next higher level (your boss).

Bringing Your Team Members into the Act

Because the team concept involves every member of a team, the process of choosing members for your team should be a team activity. The danger is that interviewing takes time: If every team member interviews every applicant, no other work gets done.

It's not necessary for every team member to conduct a full interview. Each team member should concentrate on the part of an applicant's background in which she or he has the greatest knowledge. All team members will have the opportunity to size up an applicant and to share their evaluations with the rest of the team.

As mentioned in Chapter 14, by having each interviewer fill out an interview summary sheet, evaluations can be compared more easily.

How Good Are Employment Tests?

Do tests help in choosing employees? Some companies swear by testing; others swear at them. In companies in which tests are used extensively as part of the screening process, the HR department or an independent testing organization does the testing. Except for performance tests (discussed later in this chapter), it's unlikely that you will have to administer tests.

The most frequently used tests in hiring are shown in this list:

➤ **Intelligence tests:** Like the IQ tests used in schools, they measure the ability to learn. They vary from brief, simple exercises (such as Wunderlich tests) that can be administered by people with little training to highly sophisticated tests that must be administered by someone who has a Ph.D. in psychology.

➤ **Aptitude tests:** These are designed to determine the potential of candidates in specific areas, such as mechanical ability, clerical skills, and sales potential. Such tests are helpful in screening inexperienced people to determine whether they have the aptitude in the type of work for which you plan to train them. Most aptitude tests can be administered and scored by following a simple instruction sheet.

➤ **Performance tests:** These measure how well candidates can do the job for which they apply. Examples include operating a lathe, entering data into a computer, writing advertising copy, and proofreading manuscripts. When job performance cannot be tested directly, written or oral tests on job knowledge may be used.

Simply asking an applicant to perform a portion of a job isn't a valid test. You must give the same test in the same manner to all applicants. In a word processing test, for example, you must always use the same material, the same type of computer, and the same timeframe.

➤ **Personality tests:** These are designed to identify personality characteristics. They vary from the *Reader's Digest* quickie questionnaires to highly sophisticated psychological evaluations. A great deal of controversy exists over the value of these types of tests. Supervisors and team leaders are cautioned not to make decisions based on the results of personality tests unless the full implications are made clear to them by experts. A large number of organizations offer personality tests. You can obtain information about tests that have been approved by writing to or calling the American Psychological Association, 750 First St., Washington, DC, 20002. Phone (202) 336-5500.

Communication Breakdown

Sometimes you can't win. If you hire someone whose test score is low and that person fails, management may blame you for not considering the test results. If you have someone whose score is high and he or she succeeds, management often credits the test instead of complimenting you for using good judgment.

Who Uses Employment Tests?

In 1998 the American Management Association administered a survey about workplace testing to nearly 1,100 human resource managers. Because AMA corporate members are mostly mid-sized and large companies, the data does not reflect the policies and practices of the U.S. economy as a whole, where small firms predominate.

In 1998, 48 percent of American employers say they use some form of psychological testing to assess abilities and behaviors for applicants as well as employees. Tests measured cognitive ability, interests/career paths, managerial abilities, personality, and simulated job tasks/physical ability. In 1997, only about 39 percent surveyed used some form of psychological testing.

In particular, use of personality tests is on the rise. Such tests are used by 28 percent of respondents in 1998, compared to 19 percent in 1997. Researchers said the high cost of recruiting—coupled with the high cost for making the wrong choice when hiring or promoting—have helped spur the increase.

Despite the advances in computerized psychological testing, face-to-face interviews or interpersonal exchanges designed to create a psychological profile remain the most frequent types of such tests used (43 percent of respondents test applicants this way).

Nearly 65 percent of employers test applicants' job skills. This includes skill tests such as typing, computing, or specific professional proficiencies (for example, accounting, engineering, or marketing).

Non-Traditional Screening

Companies have been seeking easy ways to identify applicants' personality traits and potential for success. Some study an applicant's horoscope to predict his or her potential. Others retain consultants who promise amazing results by using their magic formulas. Do these methods work? Perhaps, yes; perhaps no. As objective studies are rarely made on these approaches, we must depend on the reports of the users. And as you might expect, reviews are mixed. Companies usually start out enthusiastic about such tests, pointing out early successes. But the majority of such companies tire quickly of these gimmicks.

Face Reading

Recently a television magazine program discussed a new and controversial approach to evaluating personality characteristics—face reading. Originally developed by Mac Fuller, a Texas attorney, as a tool for jury selection, its use has been expanded to personnel selection.

Fuller conducts seminars and has been retained by several large companies to train their HR staffs in this technique. With much anecdotal evidence as proof, Fuller claims that the structure of a person's face reveals his or her thinking style. It can also identify problem-solving preferences, stress level, degree of openness, intimacy requirements, and even the basic truthfulness of the person.

Most psychologists pooh-pooh this approach as quackery and point out there have been no scientific, objective studies made of its effectiveness. You can judge for yourself.

Handwriting Analysis

Not all non-traditional screening techniques fit into the "gimmick" category. Some, like handwriting analysis, have been around for years. Although determining personality characteristics by analyzing handwriting has been used for decades in Europe, it has not been used extensively in the United States.

By studying a sample of the applicant's handwriting, the graphologist can pinpoint strengths and weaknesses of the candidate. Handwriting can also measure specific factors such as attention to detail, persistence, self-esteem, stubbornness, energy, creativity, honesty, and ability to relate to others.

Although there are no official licensing requirements for graphologists, professionalism in this field is maintained by the American Society of Professional Graphologists and training is offered in several colleges.

Secret Weapons

To make reference checks more successful, talk to an applicant's supervisor, not to a member of the HR staff. Prepare good questions. Begin with verification questions. Advance to detailed questions about job duties, and comment on responses. Then ask for opinions about performance, attitudes, and so on.

"Wow! What a Background!" Is It True?

Applicants can tell you anything they want about their experiences. How do you know whether they're telling the truth? A reference check is one of the oldest approaches to verifying a background, but is it reliable? Former employers unfortunately don't always tell the whole truth about candidates. They may be reluctant to make negative statements, either because they don't want to prevent the person from working—as long it's not for them—or they fear that they might be sued. Still, a reference check is virtually your only source of verification.

Unless your company policy requires that reference checks be made by the human resources department, it's better for you, the team leader, to do it. You have more insight into your team's needs and can ask follow-up questions that will help you determine whether the applicant's background fits your needs. Be careful to follow the same guidelines in asking questions of the reference as you do in interviewing applicants. Just as you can't ask an applicant whether she has young children, for example, you can't attempt to get this type of information from the reference.

Getting Useful Information from a Reference

Most reference checks are made by telephone. To make the best of a difficult situation, you must carefully plan the reference check and use diplomacy in conducting it.

The following list provides some tips for making a reference check:

➤ **Call an applicant's immediate supervisor.** Try to avoid speaking to the company's HR staff members. The only information they usually have is what's on file. An immediate supervisor can give you details about exactly how that person worked, in addition to his or her personality factors and other significant traits.

➤ **Begin your conversation with a friendly greeting.** Then ask whether the employer can verify some information about the applicant. Most people don't mind verifying data. Ask a few verification questions about date of employment, job title, and other items from the application.

Communication Breakdown

Never tell an applicant that he or she is hired "subject to a reference check." If the references are good but you choose another candidate, an applicant will assume that you received a poor reference. Also, never tell a person that the reason for rejection is a poor reference. Reference information should be treated as confidential.

➤ **Diplomatically shift to a question that requires a substantive answer,** but not one that calls for opinion. Respond with a comment about the answer, as in this example:

You: Tell me about her duties in dealing with customers.

Supervisor: [Gives details of the applicant's work.]

You: That's very important in the job she is seeking because she'll be on the phone with customers much of the time.

By commenting about what you have learned, you make the interchange a conversation—not an interrogation. You're making telephone friends with the former supervisor. You're building up a relationship that will make him or her more likely to give opinions about an applicant's work performance, attitudes, and other valuable information.

"All I Can Tell You Is That She Worked Here"

If a former employer refuses outright to answer a question, don't push. Point out that you understand any reluctance. Make the comment, "I'm sure that you would want to have as much information as possible about a candidate if you were considering someone." Then ask another question (but don't repeat the same one). After the responses begin coming more freely, you can return to the original question, preferably using different words.

What happens if you believe that the person you're speaking to is holding something back? What if you sense from the person's voice that he or she is hesitating in providing answers or you detect a vagueness that says you're not getting the full story? Here's one way to handle this situation:

"Mr. Controller, I appreciate your taking the time to talk to me about Alice Accountant. The job we have is very important to our firm, and we cannot afford to make a mistake. Are there any special problems we might face if we hire Alice?"

Here's another approach:

"Ivan will need some special training for this job. Can you point out any areas to which we should give particular attention?"

From the answer you receive, you may pick up some information about Ivan's weaknesses.

Manager's Minute

One of the great paradoxes in reference checking is that companies want full information about prospective employees from former employers, but because of their fear of being sued for defamation, when asked for information about their former employees, they give little more than basic information—dates of employment and job title.

Dealing with Poor References

Suppose everything about Carlos seems fine, and in your judgment he's just right for the job. When you call his previous employer, however, you get a bad reference. What do you do?

If you have received good reports from Carlos' other references, it's likely that the poor reference was based on a personality conflict or some other factor unrelated to his work. Contact other people in the company who are familiar with his work and get their input.

Anna's previous boss tells you that she was a sloppy worker. Check it out some more. Anna's ex-boss may have been a perfectionist who isn't satisfied with anyone.

When you contact Pierre's former supervisor, you hear a diatribe about how awful he was. But you notice that he had held that job for eight years. If he had been that bad, how come he worked there for such a long time? Maybe his ex-boss resents his leaving and is taking revenge.

Knowing When to Check References

Check references after you believe that an applicant has a reasonable chance of being hired. If you have more than one finalist, check each one before making a final decision. A reference check may turn up information that suggests a need for additional inquiry. Arrange another interview to explore it.

It's Decision Time

The interviewing is over, and references have been checked. You now have to decide which candidate to hire. Before you make a decision, review the evaluations of all the people who interviewed applicants. Discuss the finalists with your team members and others who may have interviewed them.

Meanings & Gleanings

When you assume an applicant is outstanding in everything because of just one outstanding characteristic, you're applying the *halo effect* (you crown that person with a "halo"). The opposite is the *pitchfork effect,* in which one trait is so poor that you assume that the person is all bad.

One way you can help make a fair comparison of candidates is by making a comparison chart similar to the final selection worksheet that follows.

Final Selection Worksheet				
Job specifications				
	Education	Experience	Intangibles	Other
Applicant 1 Name:				
Applicant 2 Name:				
Applicant 3 Name:				
Applicant 4 Name:				

Avoiding Decision-Making Boo-Boos

In making a hiring decision, avoid letting irrelevant or insignificant factors influence you. These factors include:

➤ **Overemphasizing appearance.** Although neatness and grooming are good indicators of personal work habits, good looks are too often overemphasized in employment. This bias has resulted in companies rejecting well-qualified men and women in favor or their more physically attractive competitors.

➤ **Giving preference to people like you.** You may subconsciously favor people who attended the same school you did, who come from similar ethnic backgrounds, or who travel in the same circles as you.

➤ **Succumbing to the "halo effect."** Because one quality of an applicant is outstanding, you overlook that person's faults or attribute unwarranted assets to him or her. Because Sheila's test score in computer know-how is the highest you've ever seen, for example, you're so impressed that you offer her a job. Only later do you learn that she doesn't qualify in several other key aspects of the job.

In making a final decision, carefully compare each candidate's background against the job specs and against each other. Look at the whole person (you have to live with your choice for a long time).

Making a Job Offer

You've made your decision, and now you're ready to offer the job to the lucky candidate. A few problems remain, however: negotiating salary, getting an applicant's acceptance, and arranging a starting date. In addition, you must notify the people you interviewed and didn't hire.

In most companies, the final offer, including salary, is handled by the HR department. Usually the HR representative discusses directly with the applicant the starting salary, benefits, and other facets of employment. If you're responsible for making the offer in your company, however, it's a good idea to check all the arrangements with your boss and the HR department to avoid misunderstandings.

Communication Breakdown

Don't let your anxiety over losing a desirable candidate tempt you to make an informal offer—promising a higher salary or other condition of employment that hasn't been approved—with the hope that you can persuade management to agree to it. Failure to get this agreement will not only cause the applicant to reject the offer but can also lead to legal action against your company.

Finalizing the Salary Range

Most companies set starting salaries for a job category. You may have a narrow range of flexibility, depending on an applicant's background. But when jobs are difficult to fill and in many higher level positions, starting salaries are negotiable.

In these types of jobs, an applicant is usually interviewed by several people, and you may have several interviews with finalists before making a decision. You should obtain a general idea of each person's salary demands early in this process so that you don't waste time "in" even considering people whose salary requirements are way out of line.

Companies traditionally have used an applicant's salary history as the basis for their offer. Ten or 15 percent higher than a person's current salary is considered a reasonable offer. Because women usually have been paid less than men, however, basing the salary you offer on current earnings isn't always equitable. If the job had been offered to a man and you would have paid a higher rate based on his salary history, you should offer a woman the same rate, even though her earnings record has been lower.

In negotiating salary, keep in mind what you pay currently employed people for doing similar work. Offering a new person considerably more than that amount can cause serious morale problems.

There are exceptions to this rule, of course. Some applicants have capabilities that you believe would be of great value to your company, and to attract these people, you may have to pay considerably more than your current top rate. Some companies create special job categories to accommodate this situation. Others pay only what they must and hope that it won't lead to lower morale.

Some companies believe that they can avoid these types of problems by prohibiting their employees from discussing salary. This "code of silence" is virtually impossible to enforce. People talk—and discussion of who makes how much constitutes great gossip. One of my clients gave an employee a significant raise to keep him from leaving. He and the others in the company who were aware of the raise were sworn to secrecy. His boss told me, "That very afternoon our manager in Los Angeles called to ask whether the rumor about this raise was true. Asked where he picked up this information, he said that it was on his e-mail when he got back from lunch." The grapevine in action again!

Salary alone isn't a total compensation package. It includes vacations, benefits, frequency of salary reviews, and incentive programs. All these items should be clearly explained.

Even when the salary you offer is less than an applicant wants, you may persuade that person to take your offer by pointing out how the job will enable him or her to use creativity, engage in work of special interest, and help reach career goals.

Arranging for Medical Exams

Many companies require applicants to take a medical exam before they can be put on the payroll. You cannot reject an applicant on the basis of a medical exam, however, unless you can show that the reason for the rejection is job-related. If a job calls for heavy lifting, for example, and the candidate has a heart condition that could be aggravated by that task, it's a legitimate reason for rejection. On the other hand, rejecting an applicant, not because of the work, but because it will increase your insurance premiums, isn't acceptable.

Most companies arrange for a medical exam close to a person's starting date. They tell applicants that they are hired subject to passing a physical exam. If this is your policy, caution applicants not to give notice to a current employer until after examination results have been received.

Manager's Minute

The Americans with Disabilities Act (ADA) requires that a medical exam be given only after the decision to hire is made. The exam cannot be used as a reason for rejection unless a person's physical condition is a job-related issue and your company cannot make accommodations for it.

Congratulations—You Made an Offer!

Although most companies make job offers orally (no letter and no written agreement), an oral offer is just as binding as a written one. Some companies supplement an oral offer with a letter of confirmation so that there are no misunderstandings about the terms.

A job offer letter should contain these elements:

➤ Title of job (a copy of the job description should be attached).

➤ Starting date.

➤ Salary, including an explanation of incentive programs.

➤ Benefits (may be in the form of a brochure given to all new employees).

➤ Working hours, location of job, and other working conditions.

➤ If pertinent, deadline for acceptance of offer.

Communication Breakdown

When you make a job offer, the salary should be stated by pay period—not on an annual basis. Rather than specify $30,000 per year, specify $1,250 per half-month. Why? Because some courts have ruled that if you quote a salary on an annual basis, you're guaranteeing the job for one year.

Employment Contracts—Yes or No?

In some situations, the employer and employee sign a formal contract. These contracts are often used with senior management people and key professional, sales, or technical personnel. Although it's rare, some organizations require all salaried employees to sign a contract—often little more than a formalized letter of agreement concerning conditions of employment. In many cases, they're designed for the benefit of the company, and the employee has little room for negotiation.

One of the most controversial areas covered in contracts is the so-called "restrictive covenant," which prohibits employees who leave the company from working for a competitor for a specified period of time. Although these types of contracts have been challenged, they're usually enforceable if they're limited in scope. Prohibiting a person from working for a competitor for a limited period of time, for example, is more likely to be upheld than prohibiting that type of employment forever.

Senior managers and other employees who hold critical positions in a company and applicants who have skills that are in great demand have the clout to negotiate personal contracts with the company. Any contract, whether it's generic or a negotiated special agreement, should be drawn up by a qualified attorney, not by HR or other managers.

When the Applicant Is Unsure About Accepting the Job

You've narrowed the field, and your first choice is Hillary. Early in the interview process, you explored her salary requirements, and your offer is in line. At least that's what you thought. Now Hillary demurs. "If I stay where I am, I'll get a raise in a few months that will bring me above that salary. You'll have to do better."

Secret Weapons

Don't notify unsuccessful applicants until shortly after your new employee starts work. If, for some reason, the chosen candidate changes his or her mind and doesn't start, you can go back to some of the others without having them feel that they were a second choice.

Having received approval of the hire at the salary offered, you have to either reject it, persuade her to take the job by selling her on other advantages, or go back to your boss for approval of the higher rate. What you do depends on many factors. Do you have other viable candidates for the job? If not, how urgent is it to fill the job? Determine whether you can legitimately offer other benefits, such as a salary review in six months, opportunity for special training in an area in which she is particularly interested, or other perks. Think over the situation carefully, and discuss it with your manager. Caution: Don't make commitments you don't have the authority to honor.

If you and your boss agree that Hillary should still be considered for the position, determine how much above your original offer you're willing to pay and what else you can offer. The meeting with Hillary should take place as soon as possible after you and your manager have determined the maximum deal you can offer. With this in mind, you can negotiate with her and try to reach an acceptable arrangement. If this new negotiation doesn't lead to agreement, discontinue the discussion and seek another candidate. Continuing to haggle over terms of employment is frustrating and keeps you from concentrating on your other duties. You're better off using your time and energy to find another candidate.

Countering a Counter Offer

You've knocked yourself out reading résumés, interviewing applicants, and comparing candidates. You make the decision that you'll hire Tom, and he accepts your offer. A week later he calls to tell you that he has changed his mind: When he told his boss that he was leaving, his boss made him a counter offer.

Frustrating? You bet. To minimize the possibility of a counter offer, assume that any currently employed candidate will get one. At the time you make your offer, bring it up and make these points:

➤ You know that he has done a great job in his present company. You also realize that when he notifies his company that he's planning to leave, it will undoubtedly make him a counter offer. Why? Because they need him now.

➤ If his company truly appreciated his work, it wouldn't have waited until he got another job offer to give him a raise. You would have given it to him long ago.

➤ Many people who have accepted counter offers from a current employer find out that, after the pressure is off the company, it will train or hire someone else and let him go.

➤ He will always be looked on as a disloyal person who threatened to leave just to get more money.

➤ When the time for a raise comes around again, guess whose salary has already been "adjusted"?

When these arguments are used, the number of people who accept counter offers decreases significantly.

Rejecting the Also-Rans

Some companies just assume that if applicants don't get an offer, they will realize that they were rejected. It's not only courteous but also good business practice to notify the men and women you have interviewed that the job has been filled.

You don't have to tell applicants why they didn't get the job. Explanations can lead to misunderstandings and even litigation. The most diplomatic approach is just to state that the background of another candidate was closer to your needs.

The Least You Need to Know

➤ When you interview a candidate to join your team, have other team members talk to the candidate.

➤ Tests can be a helpful screening tool, but use them as an aid, not as the chief source, for making your decision.

➤ Whenever possible, check the references of a prospective employee by speaking to the person to whom he or she reported, not to the HR department.

➤ When you compare candidates, consider the whole person, not just one aspect of his or her background.

➤ In making a job offer, make sure that the candidate fully understands the nature of the job, the salary and benefits, and other conditions of employment.

Part 5
Motivating Your Team for Peak Performance

Look at the word motivation. Two other words that begin with the same letters are motion and motor. We call the motors in our cars "internal combustion engines," and each of us has inside us a combusting engine that keeps us in motion.

As a team leader, your job is to provide each of your team members with the fuel that will start their "motors" and keep them going. Of course, not all motors take the same kind of fuel to keep them running; and so it is with people. What motivates one person may not work for another. To be able to help your team move forward, you have to know what kind of fuel to feed to each of your members, how and when to use it, and what reaction you can expect. Tough job? Sure, but it's worth the effort.

As you read the five chapters in this part of the book, you'll pick up some ideas to help you fuel those motors. Remember to keep an open mind—some of the things you think are great motivators may not motivate anyone at all.

Chapter 16

AH, C'MON, WORK HARDER? PLLEEAASSE!

Get a Move On!

In This Chapter

➤ Getting to know your team members

➤ Recognizing your team as a motivational force

➤ Making the transition from boss to team leader

➤ Learning how to lead when you don't work in teams

As team leader, you should meld your team members into a cohesive group and develop their motivation to accomplish the team's goals.

Successful team leaders develop such team spirit by getting to know their team members as individuals. Team members are humans, not robots, each with her own strengths and weaknesses, personal agenda, and style of working. Learning and understanding each team member as an individual are the first steps to building a team.

This chapter will teach you how to build a cohesive team and explores how functioning as a team leader differs from being a boss.

Because many companies aren't organized on a team basis, the chapter also provides suggestions for applying several principles of team management to non-team environments.

Different Strokes for Different Folks

Remember the rocket ship analogy in Chapter 1? You learned that to get a rocket ship off the ground, each of its components must be in A-1 shape, and they must then be coordinated to work interactively. Your team is the rocket ship; its members are the components; you are the rocket engineer.

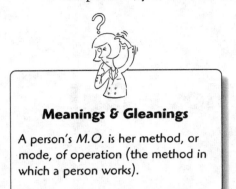

Meanings & Gleanings

A person's *M.O.* is her method, or mode, of operation (the method in which a person works).

Your first job as team leader is to help your associates perform at top capacity—they best way to begin is to learn about each person as an individual.

Maybe you think all you have to know about your associates is the quality of their work. Wrong! Knowing the members of your team requires more than just knowing their job skills—that's an important part, but it's *only* a part of their total make-up. Learn what's important to your team members—their ambitions and goals, their families, their special concerns—in other words, what makes them tick.

Learning Each Team Member's M.O.

If you've ever watched crime shows or read detective novels, you know about the term *M.O.* (*modus operandi*, or method of operation). Detectives can often tell who has committed a crime by his or her M.O., or the manner in which it was committed, because criminals tend to use the same M.O.s in all of their crimes.

M.O.s aren't limited to criminals. We all have M.O.s in the way we do our work and the way we live our lives. Study the way each of your team members operates, and you'll discover his M.O. You might notice that one team member always ponders a subject before commenting on it, and another might reread everything she's worked on several times before starting new work.

Secret Weapons

Encourage your associates to express their ideas, especially when they differ from yours. Their disagreements not only provide you with new ideas but also give you insight into the ways in which they approach problems.

Psychologists don't call them M.O.s; they call them "patterns of behavior." Whatever you call M.O.s, being aware of them helps you understand people and enables you to work with them more effectively.

You don't want to be nosy? Okay, you don't have to *ask* personal questions directly. By observing and listening, you can learn a great deal about your colleagues. Listen when they speak to you: Listen to what they say, and listen to what they *don't* say. Listen when they speak to others. Eavesdropping may not be polite, but you can learn a great deal. Observe how your team members do their work and how they act and react. It doesn't take long to identify their likes and dislikes, their quirks and eccentricities. By listening, you can learn about the things that are important to each of them and the *hot buttons* that can turn them on or off.

Getting to Know Your Team Members

How is listening important in developing productive team members? By observing and listening, you might realize Claudia is a creative person. If you want to excite her about her role in an assignment, you can do so by appealing to her creativity. You notice that Mike is slow when he's learning new things but that, after he learns them, he works quickly and accurately. To allow Mike to do his best, you know you'll need patience.

It's easy to remember these individual characteristics when you supervise a small number of people, but if you're involved with larger groups or have high turnover in your department, it's not so easy. You need help. The following Know-Your-Team Worksheet can help you keep an informal reminder of each of your team members' traits.

Know-Your-Team Worksheet

Member's name: _____

Position: _____ Date employed: _____

Spouse's name: _____

Children's names and ages: _____
_____

Hobbies: _____
_____

Other interests: _____
_____

Schools and colleges: _____
_____

Other pertinent information: _____
_____
_____

Behavioral traits: _____
_____
_____

Hot buttons: _____

Making Your Team Self-Motivating

After team members understand their new roles, you, as their team leader, must ensure that they begin to apply the team system on the job.

Let's look at how Denise did this. As sales manager, her primary role had been to train, motivate, and lead her sales force. Denise discovered that, as in most companies, without the support of the office staff to obtain and maintain sales production, sales were lost and customers dissatisfied.

The salespeople in Denise's company were paid on a commission basis. They worked long and hard to acquire and keep accounts. They were often frustrated, however, when the order department stalled deliveries or when indifferent customer service representatives antagonized customers.

Meanings & Gleanings

One thing in a person's make-up that really gets him or her excited—positively or negatively—is a *hot button*. Find someone's hot button, and you can really get through to them.

Hot Buttons

Denise reorganized the department into five teams, each covering a different sales region. Each team was made up of salespeople, order clerks, and customer service personnel.

Denise followed the TEAM acrostic for successful team development:

Train: All sales and support people were brought in for a weekend training program in which the new system was explained. By using group discussions, case studies, and role-playing, team members were trained to work together.

Enthusiasm: To make any team activity work, team members must not only accept an idea but also greet it enthusiastically. Denise borrowed some sports techniques and had her teams choose names and colors. She announced contests between teams with awards ranging from group dinners to cash bonuses.

Assurance: The teams were assured that they would not be left entirely on their own. Denise promised them that she and other company executives would give them as much informational and financial support as necessary, but stressed that the team members' ideas and concepts were the keys to success.

Measurement: Specific goals were set for each team for the first period. After that, the teams were instructed to set their own goals. Each team would be measured by how close it came to achieving its goals; individuals would be evaluated not only by their own performance but also by how they worked as a team.

The compensation system was changed so that rather than a salesperson alone being rewarded for making a sale, bonuses and raises for all team members would be based on the team's productivity.

At the end of the first year, sales had increased significantly. Rather than stall orders because of minor errors in an order form, order clerks went to the source and corrected the errors immediately. Secretaries and customer service reps went out of their way to help customers, and morale in the department grew immensely.

Making the Transition from Boss to Team Leader

Many traditional supervisors find it difficult to make the transition to team leader. "If I'm going to be held accountable when anything goes wrong, how can I give up control?"

Yes, it's still the team leader's job to ensure that the goals of the team are met, but you can still accomplish this task in a team environment. The key to team control is self-control.

You, the team leader, must keep every member of your team aware of what is expected from him individually and from the team as a whole. Team members should be kept aware at all times of how the team is doing. In this way, they monitor their own activities (Chapter 21 discusses this subject in detail).

Watch Out for These Hurdles

So all you have to do is convert from traditional methods to team concepts and all your troubles are over, right? Of course not. Teams aren't a cure-all for management problems. They have their share of problems.

One common problem occurs when team members don't carry their weight and other members have to work harder to maintain their team's productivity. Team members can often overcome this situation themselves, by working with the weaker person to help him develop the necessary skills. If the reason for poor performance isn't a lack of skill but is instead a lack of motivation, the others may encourage—or in some cases, shame—the slacker into better production. Peer pressure is a powerful tool. If all else fails, the person will have to be removed from the team.

Teams in the workplace have many advantages, but they're not a panacea. People who learn to work together in teams produce more, enjoy their work more, and are less likely to quit for superficial reasons. Teams create a motivational environment and help build the *esprit de corps* that is important to success.

Secret Weapons

To turn a team into a self-motivated unit, create "team spirit" among members by getting everyone on your team involved in every aspect of a job. Team members will then work together to meet goals.

When Your Company Doesn't Use Teams

Your company may not be organized in teams. No matter what the organizational structure, you can use any and all of the techniques in this chapter and in this book to improve your effectiveness as a manager. Just glean the suggested techniques and begin applying them today!

After José returned from an intensive management development weekend at the university, he bubbled with enthusiasm about all the ideas he had learned. He wanted to take immediate action in restructuring his department into teams.

"Whoa," José's boss said. "Take it easy. We're not making any radical changes now." Rather than give up in frustration, José asked himself, "What can I do within the current structure to adapt what I've learned?"

Within the first few weeks, José made the following changes in his management style:

➤ He became more available to the people who reported to him. Rather than brush off their questions and suggestions, he took time to listen, evaluate, and respond to them.

➤ He overcame the temptation to make every decision. When asked for a decision, he threw the decision back to the person requesting it. "What do *you* think should be done?"

➤ Rather than plan the work himself when new assignments were received, he enlisted the participation of his entire team.

➤ He encouraged team members to acquire skills outside their usual work duties. He used cross training and assigned them work that required interaction with others in the group with different types of work.

➤ He conferred with all team members to ensure that they understood what was expected of them on the job and how their performance would be evaluated. Most important, he learned more about their individual goals and aspirations.

➤ He periodically held exciting and productive department meetings.

➤ He visited suppliers and subcontractors and invited them to visit the company and attend meetings.

The payoff didn't take long. Within a few months, productivity increased, quality improved, and cooperation and collaboration among the group members became a way of life. All this—without changing the structure.

Manager's Minute:

"Good management consists of inspiring average people to do the work of superior people."

—John D. Rockefeller

The Least You Need to Know

➤ Learn and remember what's important in the lives of each member of your team.

➤ By identifying your associates' M.O.s and hot buttons, you'll understand them and work more effectively with each one.

➤ Develop team spirit to make your team self-motivated.

➤ The key to team control is self-control. If all team members are aware of what's expected and are informed of what has been accomplished, they'll monitor their own activities.

HEY, YOU! GET TO WORK!

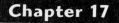

Chapter 17

Money Talks, but Does It Talk Loud Enough?

In This Chapter

➤ Understanding when money does and doesn't motivate

➤ Knowing when money is the scorecard

➤ Determining whether benefits are motivators or satisfiers

➤ Tying money in with performance

Here's a mini-lesson in logic:

A: The more money you earn, the happier you are.

B: The more work you produce, the more money you earn.

Therefore:

C: People will produce more to earn more money and become happier.

Sounds logical, but is it true? Sometimes, but not always. Assume A and B are both true. It should logically follow that C is true, right? Sometimes it is, but often it's not.

Motivators Versus Satisfiers

Remember that the word *motivate* begins with the same three letters as *motion*. Motivation is the incentive to get into motion, or making things move.

A team of behavioral scientists led by Frederick Herzberg studied what people want from their jobs and classified the results in two categories:

➤ **Satisfiers (also called maintenance factors):** Factors people require from a job to justify minimum effort.

These factors include working conditions, money, and benefits. After employees are satisfied, however, just giving them more of the same factors doesn't motivate them to work harder. What most people consider motivators are really just satisfiers.

➤ **Motivators:** Factors that stimulate people to put out more energy, effort, and enthusiasm in their job.

To see how this concept works on the job, suppose you work in a less than adequate facility, in which lighting is poor, ventilation is inadequate, and space is tight. Productivity, of course, is low.

In a few months, your company moves to new quarters, with excellent lighting and air conditioning and lots of space, and productivity shoots up.

Meanings & Gleanings

When managers *motivate*, they stimulate people to exert more effort, energy, and enthusiasm in whatever they're doing. The best motivation is self-motivation. Your job as a team leader is to provide a climate in which self-motivation flourishes.

The company CEO is elated. He says to the board of directors, "I've found the solution to high productivity: If you give people better working conditions, they'll produce more, so I'm going to make the working conditions even better." He hires an interior designer, has new carpet installed, hangs paintings on the walls, and places plants around the office. The employees are delighted. It's a pleasure to work in these surroundings—but productivity doesn't increase at all.

Why not? People seek a level of satisfaction in their job—in this case, reasonably good working conditions. When the working environment was made acceptable, employees were satisfied, and it showed up in their productivity. After the conditions met their level of satisfaction, however, adding enhancements didn't motivate them.

So What Does This Have to Do with Money?

Money, like working conditions, is a satisfier. You might assume that offering more money generates higher productivity. And you're probably right—for most people, but not for everyone. Incentive programs, in which people are given an opportunity to earn more money by producing more, are part of many company compensation plans. They work for some people, but not for others.

The sales department is a good example. Because salespeople usually work on a commission, or incentive, basis, they're in the enviable position of rarely having to ask for a raise. If salespeople want to earn more money, all they have to do is work harder or smarter and make as much money as they want. Therefore, all salespeople are very rich. Right? Wrong!

How come this logic doesn't work? Sales managers have complained about this problem from the beginning of time. They say, "We have an excellent incentive program, and the money is there for our sales staff. All they have to do is reach out—and they don't. Why not?"

You have to delve deep into the human psyche for an answer. We all set personal salary levels, consciously or subconsciously, at which we are satisfied. Until we reach that point, money does motivate us, but after that—no more. *This level varies significantly from person to person.*

Some people set this point very high, and money is a major motivator to them; others are content at lower levels. It doesn't mean that they don't want their annual raise or bonus, but if obtaining the extra money requires special effort or inconvenience, you can forget it.

Suppose Derek is in your production group and that his salary is 60 percent of yours. His wife works, but you know by the nature of her job that it doesn't pay much. Derek drives a 12-year-old car and buys his clothes from thrift shops. The only vacations his family has ever taken are occasional camping trips. You feel sorry for him. But now you can help Derek: You need several workers for a special project to be done over the next six Saturdays at double-time pay. When you ask Derek whether he wants the assignment, he says "No," and you can't understand why. It seems to you that he should be eager to make more money, but he has already reached his level of satisfaction. Taking the Saturday off is more important to him than the opportunity to earn more money.

This example doesn't mean that money doesn't motivate at all. The opportunity to earn money motivates everyone to the point that they are satisfied. Some people, like Derek, are content at lower levels. As long as they can meet their basic needs, other things are more important to them than money. To other people, this point is very high, and they "knock themselves out" to keep making more money.

By learning as much as you can about your associates, you learn about their interests, goals, and lifestyles and the level of income at which they're satisfied. To offer the opportunity to make more money as an incentive to people who don't care about it is futile. You have to find other ways to motivate them.

Secret Weapons

Team leaders rarely have control over the basic satisfiers: working conditions, salary scale, employee benefits, and the like. These factors are set by company policy, but managers do have the opportunity to use the real motivators: job satisfaction, recognition, and the opportunity for team members to achieve successes.

Money as a Scorecard

Barney was unhappy. As vice president of marketing in his company, he earned $250,000 per year in combined salary and bonus but believed that he was underpaid. "Our company had its best year in a decade," he said, "and it was chiefly due to my marketing efforts. I should be paid more."

When Barney was asked about his current quarter-of-a-million-dollar salary, he said, "I don't need the money. But my salary is the score that measures my success."

You don't have to be in the six-figure income bracket to consider your pay a scorecard. A merit raise given to a trainee or a production bonus paid to a factory worker is as much of a boost to that person's ego as is the money.

As discussed in the next several chapters, intangible motivators are extremely effective, and supplementing them with a reward in the form of a raise or bonus adds to their value. It's not only the money itself but also the tangible acknowledgment of success.

When a person is promoted to a higher level position, the increase in pay that goes with the promotion is a recognition of the person's new status. Being in a higher salary classification adds prestige both within and outside a company.

Benefits: Motivators or Satisfiers?

Benefits are important in today's companies. Most companies provide some form of health insurance, life insurance, pension, and other benefits to their employees. In fact, the benefits package is one of the factors that potential employees seek when they evaluate a job offer—but it isn't a motivator. (Have you ever known anyone who worked harder because the company introduced a dental insurance program?)

Benefits are satisfiers. Good benefits attract people to work for a company, and they also keep people from quitting. (Sometimes, the people you wish would quit don't.)

Manager's Minute

A happy team is not necessarily a productive team. Permissiveness and indulgence lead to carelessness and poor work. A team leader's challenge is to develop, with team members, high performance standards that challenge and motivate people.

Raises, Cost of Living Increases, and Other Adjustments

In most companies pay raises are given as part of the performance review system (see Chapter 21); they're rarely given out otherwise. Unless specified in a union or personal contract, companies have no legal obligation to give employees raises at all. The amount of an increase, and how and when it's given, depend on each company's policy.

It is a common practice to give employees who meet minimum performance standards an annual raise based on increases in the cost of living. But in the 1990s, as business became more competitive and inflation stayed relatively low, even this expected annual raise was often discontinued.

When people don't get as high a raise as they expect—or no raise at all—it leads to low morale. It's not easy for team leaders to keep members motivated in the face of disappointing compensation. You can't ignore the situation and hope that it will go away. Encourage any dissatisfied team members to express their concerns. If the reason a member didn't get the raise is poor performance, discuss it and pledge to help him or her improve enough for a raise the next time around. If the reason is a company freeze on pay increases, explain it and point out that it's a temporary situation that should be alleviated soon. (Chapter 19 shows an example of how to handle this situation.)

Old and New Incentive Pay Programs

Since the industrial revolution, companies have used financial incentives as part or all of their compensation programs. It was assumed that people would work harder and faster if they received a direct reward for production. This system was carried forward into the period of "scientific management." Frederic Taylor, the founder of this new movement, and his followers believed that people could be motivated by wages based on productivity, and developed variations on "piecework" to achieve their goals.

In an economy that is moving rapidly away from mass production and manufacturing-based businesses to custom-engineered production and service-type industries, pay per piece has little value. New types of incentive programs have had to be developed. This section looks at some old and new incentive-pay plans.

Secret Weapons

Money is a motivator for some people all of the time; for others, some of the time; and, if combined with other motivators, for everyone all the time.

Piecework

Wages based solely on the number of units produced was the primary pay plan in some industries. The harder you worked, the more money you received. In the early days of scientific management, speed of production was the primary factor in determining wages, and this method worked well. Abuse in the piecework system, however, was rampant. Often, when workers mastered their work and produced more than quotas required, companies reduced the price paid per piece to keep their overall costs down. This practice led to reduced motivation; workers would only do a fixed amount of work, which defeated the purpose of the incentive program.

As work became more complex, paying by the piece was no longer practical. Because of pressure from unions and, later, minimum wage laws, hourly rates replaced piecework rates in most industries.

Manager's Minute

The straight piecework system lives on. In 1995, government agents raided illegal garment factories in which undocumented aliens worked in sweatshops for 12 or more hours a day at piece rates that netted them earnings well below minimum wage.

Quota Pay Plans

Industrial engineers in the age of scientific management (the 1920s and '30s) introduced a variation of piecework. Quotas were established based on time and motion studies, and people who exceeded quotas received extra pay. These types of programs still exist and, properly designed and administered, succeed in motivating some people. Even the best of these programs, however, have problems.

I saw how this system worked during the summers of my college years, when I worked in a factory that used it. Because I was young and energetic and wanted to make money to pay my college expenses, I quickly mastered the work and soon exceeded my quota. One of my co-workers pulled me aside and said, "Hey, you're working too fast. You're making it bad for the rest of us." His implication was that if I didn't slow down, he would break my arm.

Incentive Programs for Salespeople

Most sales jobs are paid on an incentive basis. Salespeople earn a commission or bonus based on their personal sales. This system should motivate people to knock themselves out to make more sales, but, as mentioned, it doesn't always happen. Many salespeople set limits for themselves, and, when they reach that limit, they "take it easy."

Another adverse result of sales incentives is that it encourages salespeople to concentrate on getting new business, often at the expense of neglecting established customers.

Effective sales incentive programs present challenges to the sales reps. They may vary from one period to another. Depending on what the company wants to emphasize at any one time, the incentives may be based on one or more of the following:

➤ Number of new accounts opened

➤ Increase in volume of sales of current accounts

➤ Sales of specific items the company is pushing

➤ Introduction of new markets (for instance, the company has sold primarily to drug stores and now is promoting sales to food outlets)

Stock Options

Stock option programs provide opportunity for employees to benefit from an increase in the company's stock value. They are given "rights" to purchase the stock at a price that is lower than the market price. They do not pay for the "rights." Let's say the stock is currently selling for $25 per share. They are given options to buy the stock at $22 per share. If they exercise the options immediately, they make a $3 per share profit. However, the incentive is to keep the options until the stock rises higher in value. A year later, the stock is selling at $40 per share. They can still purchase it at $22 and sell it immediately for a profit of $18.

The incentive is to help the company grow through their efforts, which will result in higher stock prices.

The downside is that stock price does not necessarily reflect the company's profitability. Other market factors may influence it. If the stock falls below the option price, the rights are worthless.

Stock options usually are not offered to lower-level employees, but often are a major part of executives' compensation packages.

Communication Breakdown

The benefits and incentive-pay area is complex and regulated by federal and state laws. Few companies have the expertise to institute effective programs without professional help. Some of the top consultants in this field are Towers Perrin (245 Park Avenue, New York, NY 10167); Hay Group (229 S. 18th Street, Philadelphia, PA 19103); and Hewitt Associates (40 Highland Avenue, Rowayton, CT 06853).

Hiring Bonuses

If you follow sports, you know all about signing bonuses. The sports pages are always reporting about fabulous amounts of money paid not only to top players, but to promising rookies just out of high school or college.

To attract hard-to-find specialists, such as computer whizzes or financial geniuses, and sometimes just to get people who qualify for high demand positions, companies have paid hundreds, and sometime thousands, of dollars in signing bonuses.

Incentive Plans That Work

In our tough, competitive economy, businesses need incentive plans. Even if money isn't the only, or even the best, way to motivate people, it can play an important role. Money combined with other types of motivation enhances the value of that approach. These programs may be based on exceeding predetermined expectations, rewarding special achievements, or sharing in the company's profits.

Management by Objective (MBO)

Management by objective is used in many companies as both a management tool and an incentive program. Although there are many variations, the basic idea is that managers and associates determine together the objectives and results expected for that period. After a time period is agreed on, associates work with minimum supervision to achieve the specified goals. At the end of the period, the manager and the associates compare what has been accomplished with the objectives that have been set. In some organizations, bonuses are awarded for meeting or exceeding expectations.

When a company is organized on a team basis, MBO is extended to the team. Rather than individual objectives, team objectives are set by the team leader and the entire team, and the team works collaboratively to meet these objectives. Results are measured against expectations at the end of the period, and, if rewards or bonuses are part of the plan, the entire team shares them.

Special Awards for Special Achievements

The Footloose Shoe Store chain has instituted periodic campaigns to emphasize various aspects of its work. One campaign, for example, centered on increasing sales of "add-ons" (accessories for customers who have already bought shoes from the company). The campaign, which lasted four weeks, began with rallies at a banquet hall in each region in which the chain operated. Staff members from all the stores in the region assembled in a party atmosphere, where food, balloons, door prizes, and music set the mood as the program was kicked off.

Footloose announced that prizes would be awarded, including $2,000 to be divided among all the staff members (both sales and support) of the contest-winning store. The sales clerk who made the most personal add-on sales in the region would receive $500, and the sales clerk who made the most add-on sales in each store would receive $100. The campaign was reinforced by weekly reports on the standings of each store and each sales clerk.

The result was not only a significant increase in accessory sales for that period but also an increase in regular sales, attributed to the excitement and enthusiasm generated by the campaign. Another party was held to present awards and recognize winners. Footloose runs three or four campaigns every year (too many parties would lessen the novelty).

Xerox is another company that adds financial reward to recognition. To encourage team partici- pation, special bonuses are given to teams that contribute ideas leading to gains in production, quality, cost savings, or profits.

A company that has instituted a total quality management (TQM) program, in which it puts special emphasis on providing high quality products or services to customers, often augments the pro- gram by offering financial rewards based on reduc- tion of product rejects, measurable improvements in quality, and increased customer satisfaction.

Secret Weapons

Tailor your incentive plan to what the company wants to accomplish. Create innovative programs that will motivate workers to help the com- pany meet its goals.

Profit-Sharing

Companies use many variations of profit-sharing plans—that is, plans that distribute a portion of the company's profits to the employees. Many of these plans are informal. The executive committee or board of directors sets aside at the end of the fiscal year a certain portion of profits to be distributed among employees. Other, more formal, plans follow an established formula.

In many organizations, only managerial employees are included in a profit-sharing plan; in others, all employees who have been with the company for a certain number of years are also included; in still others, the entire workforce gets a piece of the profits. Some profit-sharing plans are mandated by union contracts.

A number of profit-sharing programs are based on employee stock ownership. Various types of stock ownership plans are used, including giving stock as a bonus, giving employees the option to buy company stock at below market rates, and employee stock ownership programs (ESOPs), in which employees own their company.

Another financial incentive approach is *open-book management,* which is revolutioniz- ing the traditional compensation system. Its goal is to get *everyone* in a company to focus on helping to make money.

In the old approach, bosses ran a company and employees did what they were told (or what they could get away with). This system has been replaced by empowered teams that are given all the facts and figures necessary to make decisions; they're rewarded for their successes and accept the risks of failure.

In a June 1995 article in *INC.* magazine, John Case presents these essential differences between an open-book company and a traditional business. In open-book companies:

➤ Every employee has access to numbers that are critical to tracking the company's performance and is given the training and tools to understand them.

➤ Employees learn that, whatever else they do, they must never lose sight of the goal (to move those numbers in the right direction).

➤ Employees have a direct stake in their company's success. If the business is profitable, they share in the profits; if it isn't, there are no profits to share.

There are many variations of open-book management. In some companies employees are given (or can purchase) shares in their company; in others, employees *do* own their company, through employee ownership plans (ESOPs). In still other plans, ownership remains with stockholders, but the books are open and profits shared.

The resulting employee commitment is palpable. Rather than complain and gripe, employees pitch in to solve problems. Rather than evade assignments with the plaintive excuse "It's not my job," employees seek out areas in which they can contribute. They understand the reason that raises are frozen, that some of their actions have curtailed productivity rather than enhanced it, and what steps they can take to save their company and their jobs.

Manager's Minute

According to the U.S. Chamber of Commerce, the fastest growing areas of benefits over the past five years have been day care for working parents and flexible hours.

Perks: The Extras That Add Up

In many companies, employees have been given "freebies"—those little extras that may not seem like much, but often are significant additions to the traditional compensation package.

➤ **Subsidized lunchrooms.** I recently had lunch in the cafeteria of a large insurance company. My bill for a salad, entree, coffee, and dessert was less than half of what I normally pay at a restaurant. This is a great savings for employees.

➤ **Coffee and...** Many companies provide a never empty coffee pot for employees. Often the company offers free doughnuts, bagels, or sweet rolls at break time.

➤ **Child care.** With the great number of families where both parents are working, child care is a major problem. Some companies have child-care facilities right on premises or arrange for child care at nearby facilities and subsidize the cost.

➤ **Transportation.** Vans or buses are made available to employees to bring them to and from work. It's cheaper for the employees to use the company's transportation than to take public transportation or drive themselves.

➤ **Tuition.** Companies often pick up the entire bill for courses taken by employees—even if not specific to their job training. If the company doesn't pay in full, it will usually subsidize the cost of education.

➤ **Scholarships.** Some companies set aside college money for children of employees.

In addition, some executives, salespeople, and specialized staff may be given perks, such as company cars, membership in country clubs, generous expense accounts, subscriptions to technical and professional journals, and membership in professional associations.

The Least You Need to Know

➤ Motivation means getting into motion—getting moving in whatever endeavor you undertake.

➤ Money, benefits, and working conditions are satisfiers. Employees must be satisfied with these aspects of their jobs or else they don't work effectively. After people are satisfied, however, giving them more of the same factors doesn't necessarily motivate them.

➤ Everyone sets a level of income at which he or she is satisfied. Money motivates people up to that point, but after it's reached—no more.

➤ A program of bonuses for productivity combined with other motivational factors is more effective than the bonus by itself.

➤ Profit-sharing plans give team members a vested interest in keeping their company profitable.

➤ Open-book management is a new variation on employee participation in profits. By sharing total information about how a company fares, everyone becomes an integral part of an organizational team.

Chapter 18

Recognition and Praise: Motivators That Work

In This Chapter

➤ Understanding that people are *people*, not cogs in a machine

➤ Recognizing achievement and making praise effective

➤ Putting your praise in writing

➤ Honoring team accomplishments

As pointed out in Chapter 17, many things formerly considered motivators by conventional wisdom are now seen as *satisfiers*. Money, benefits, and working conditions are important in keeping employees satisfied, but they don't motivate people beyond a certain point. Some of the things that do motivate people are:

➤ Recognition of each team member's individuality

➤ Praise for achievements to stimulate continued achievements

➤ Opportunity for growth

➤ Challenge (re-motivating when motivation has been lost)

➤ Job satisfaction—an ideal motivator

This chapter discusses the first two items; Chapter 19 discusses the other three.

People Crave Recognition

Human beings crave recognition. People like to know that others know who they are, what they want, and what they believe. Recognition begins when you learn and use people's names. Of course you know the names of the men and women on your team, but you will be coordinating work with other teams, with internal and external suppliers, subcontractors, and customers. Everyone has a name. Learn them. Use them. It's your first step in recognizing each person's individuality.

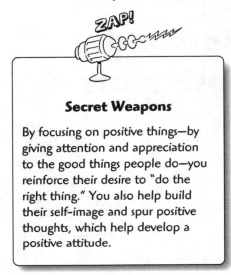

Secret Weapons

By focusing on positive things—by giving attention and appreciation to the good things people do—you reinforce their desire to "do the right thing." You also help build their self-image and spur positive thoughts, which help develop a positive attitude.

In Woody's exit interview after quitting his job with the Building Maintenance Company, he was asked what he liked most and least about the company. Woody responded that, although the salary and benefits were good, he never felt that he was part of the organization. "I always felt that I was looked at as nothing more than a cog in the machine," he said. "During the nine months I worked in the department, I made several suggestions, offered to take on extra projects, and tried to apply creative approaches to some of the work assigned to me. My boss didn't recognize all that I could have contributed."

Providing Positive Reinforcement

An autocratic boss continually criticizes, condemns, complains, and never forgets negative performance. But he or she always takes good performance for granted. Team leaders today are more aware of the value of reinforcing the good things their associates do than of harping on their mistakes and inefficiencies.

When people hear continual criticism, they begin to feel stupid, inferior, and resentful. Although someone may have done something that wasn't satisfactory, your objective is to correct the behavior, not to make the person feel bad.

The famous psychologist B.F. Skinner noted that criticism often reinforces poor behavior (when the only time an offender gets attention is when she is being criticized). He recommended that we minimize our reaction to poor behavior and maximize our appreciation of good behavior.

Rather than bawl out an associate for doing something wrong, quietly tell the person, "You're making some progress in the work, but we still have a long way to go. Let me show you some ways to do it more rapidly." When the work does improve, make a big fuss over it.

Showing That You Care

Just as you have a life outside the company, so does every member of your team. A job is an important part of our lives, but there are many aspects of life that may be of greater importance: health, family, and outside interests, for example. Show sincere interest in a team member's total person.

Virginia, the head teller of a savings-and-loan association in Wichita, Kansas, makes a point of welcoming back associates who have been on vacation or out for several days because of illness. She asks them about their vacation or the state of their health and brings them up-to-date on company news. She makes them feel that she missed them—and it comes across sincerely because she really did miss them.

Jacob, a grandfather, realizes that children are the center of most families. He takes a genuine interest in the activities of his co-workers' children and has even accompanied associates to school events in which their children participate. Some people may consider this situation paternalistic or intrusive, but Jake's true concern comes across as positive interest and has helped meld his team members into a "working family."

Manager's Minute

Some supervisors fear that giving praise indicates softness on their part: "We don't want to coddle our subordinates." Praise is *not* softness—it's a positive approach that reinforces good performance. When you stop thinking of your team members as subordinates and instead think of them as partners working to reach team goals, appropriate praise will become a natural part of your behavior.

Everyone Needs Praise, but What If They Don't Deserve It?

Human beings thrive on praise. Although all of us require praise to help make us feel good about ourselves, you can't praise people indiscriminately: Praise should be reserved for accomplishments that are worthy of special acknowledgment. So, how do you deal with people who never do anything particularly praiseworthy?

Maria faced this situation in her team of word processors. Several marginal operators had the attitude that, as long as they met their quotas, they were doing okay. Praising them for meeting quotas only reinforced their belief that nothing more was expected of them. Criticism of their failure to do more than the quota required was greeted with the response "I'm doing my job."

Maria decided to try positive reinforcement. She gave one of the operators a special assignment for which no production quota had been set. When the job was completed, Maria praised the employee's fine work. She followed this practice with all new assignments and eventually had the opportunity to sincerely praise each of the word processors.

Secret Weapons

People need praise. If employees do nothing that merits praise, assign them projects in which they can demonstrate success and then praise their accomplishments.

Communication Breakdown

Beware of over-praising. When you praise every little thing, you dilute the power of praise. Save it for significant improvements, exceptional accomplishments, and special efforts.

Looking for Praiseworthy Situations

Sometimes you tend to look for things to criticize rather than things to compliment. Because you expect your team to perform well, you concentrate on strengthening areas of weakness. Douglas, a regional supervisor for a California supermarket chain, made regular visits to the eight stores under his jurisdiction. He reported that when he went into a store he looked for *problems*. He criticized store managers for the way products were displayed, for slow-moving checkout lines, and anything else he noticed. "That's my job," he said, "to make sure that everything is being done correctly."

As you can guess, everyone working in the stores dreaded his visits. Douglas's boss acknowledged to him the importance of improving what was wrong but also pointed out that, because the stores exceeded sales volume forecasts and kept costs down, the managers needed to hear compliments on their success. His boss suggested that Douglas seek out good things and express his approbation. Douglas was encouraged to make suggestions for improvements, but not to make them the focus of his visits.

Although it wasn't easy, Douglas followed his boss's advice. Within a few months, store managers looked forward to his visits. They began to share new ideas and seek his counsel about store issues. Clerks and other store staffers soon overcame their fear of the "big boss" and welcomed his comments and suggestions.

Five Tips for Effective Praise

As important as praise is in motivating people, it doesn't always work. Some supervisors praise every minor activity, diminishing the value of praise for real accomplishments. Others deliver praise in such a way that it seems phony. To make your praise more meaningful, follow these suggestions:

1. **Don't overdo it.** Praise is sweet. Candy is sweet too, but the more you eat, the less sweet each piece becomes—and you may get a stomachache. Too much praise reduces the benefit that's derived from each bit of praise; if it's overdone, it loses its value altogether.

2. **Be sincere.** You can't fake sincerity. You must truly believe that what you're praising your associate for is actually commendable. If you don't believe it yourself, neither will your associate.

3. **Be specific about the reason for your praise.** Rather than say, "Great job!" it's much better to say, "The report you submitted on the XYZ matter enabled me to understand more clearly the complexities of the issue."

4. **Ask for your team members' advice.** Nothing is more flattering than to be asked for advice about how to handle a situation. This approach can backfire, though, if you don't *take* the advice. If you have to reject advice, ask people questions about their inadequate answers until *they* see the error of their ways and reissue good advice (refer to Chapter 6).

5. **Publicize praise.** Just as a reprimand should always be given in private, praising should be done (whenever possible) in public. Sometimes the matter for which praise is given is a private issue, but it's more often appropriate to let your entire team in on the praise. If other team members are aware of the praise you give a colleague, it spurs them to work for similar recognition.

   In some cases, praise for significant accomplishments is extremely public, such as when it's given at meetings or company events.

The Mary Kay cosmetics company is known for its policy of giving recognition to associates who have accomplished outstanding performance. In addition to receiving awards and plaques, award winners are feted at company conventions and publicized in the company magazine. Attending a Mary Kay convention is similar to attending a victory celebration: Winners are called to the stage and presented with their awards to the cheers and applause of an audience. Award winners report that recognition from senior executives and acclaim from peers is as rewarding as the award itself.

Manager's Minute

"When I must criticize somebody, I do it orally; when I praise somebody, I put it in writing."

—Lee Iacocca

Give Them Something They Can Keep

Telling people that you appreciate what they've done is a great idea, but *writing* it is even more effective. The aura of oral praise fades away; a letter or even a brief note endures.

You don't have to spend much money. It doesn't take much time. This section looks at how writing the praise has worked for some team leaders.

Writing Thank-You Cards

At the A&G Merchandising Company in Wilmington, Delaware, team leaders are given packets of "thank-you" cards on which the words *Thank You* are printed in beautiful script on the front flap and the inside of the card is left blank. Whenever someone does something worthy of special recognition, that person's team leader writes a note on one of the cards detailing the special accomplishment and congratulating the employee for achieving it. The recipients cherish the cards and show them to friends and family.

Something to Hang on the Wall

No matter what type of award you give employees—large or small (cash, merchandise, tickets to a show or sports event, or a trip to a resort)—it's worth spending a few more dollars to include a certificate or plaque. Employees love to hang these mementos in their cubicles or offices, over their workbenches, or in their homes. The cash gets spent, the merchandise wears out, the trip becomes a long-past memory, but a certificate or plaque is a permanent reminder of the recognition.

Success Files—The Scorecard

Hillary, the sales manager of a large real estate office in Florida, makes a practice of sending letters of appreciation to sales staffers who do something special—selling a property that has been difficult to move, obtaining sales rights to a profitable building, or taking creative steps to make a sale.

With the first of these letters that Hillary sends to a salesperson, she encloses a file folder labeled "Success File" with this suggestion: "File the enclosed letter in this folder. Add to it any other commendatory letters you receive from me, from other managers, from clients, or from anyone else. As time goes on, you may experience failures or disappointments. There may be times when you don't feel good about yourself. When this happens, reread these letters. They're the proof that you're a success, that you have capability, that you are a special person. You did it before; you can do it again!"

The recipients of Hillary's letters repeatedly tell her how rereading the letters helps them overcome sales slumps, periods of depression, and general disenchantment when things aren't going well. It "reprograms" their psyche by reinforcing their self-esteem and enables them to face problems with new strength and confidence.

Creating Recognition Programs That Work

Any form of sincere recognition can be effective—some for short periods of time; others, much longer. Recognition programs that affect the entire organization are usually developed and administered by the human resources department. You participate in implementing the programs in your team. But even if there's no company-wide program, with a little imagination and initiative, you can create a variation just for your own team. This section discusses a few of these techniques.

Employee of the Month

Choosing an associate every month for special recognition is probably the most popular form of formal recognition. The method of choosing employees and deciding which rewards and recognition to offer vary from company to company. This list shows some of the methods used to run an employee-of-the-month program:

➤ **Selection.** In most companies, each team leader or department head nominates candidates for an award. A committee weighs the contributions of each candidate and chooses the winner. In some organizations, peers make nominations in each department; increasingly, all employees are encouraged to make a nomination by writing a note or filling out a form. The committee makes its choice by comparing the nominees against a list of criteria and against each other.

➤ **Award.** Awards vary from company to company. The most frequently awarded prizes are cash, a day off with pay, or merchandise.

➤ **Recognition.** Almost all companies with employee-of-the-month programs have a permanent, prominently displayed plaque on which the winner's name is engraved. In some companies a photo of the winner is also displayed during the month. In addition, individual certificates or plaques are given to monthly winners.

Meanings & Gleanings

ABCD awards are given for performance that's truly Above and Beyond the Call of Duty. This type of special recognition pays off in continued efforts to achieve superior performance.

Awards often are presented at luncheons to which all nominees for that month are invited. The winner is interviewed for an article in the company newsletter, and press releases are sent to local newspapers, radio, and TV stations.

As with anything else, there are drawbacks to the employee-of-the-month program. Here are a few:

➤ **Resentment.** Some people may believe that they were more suited for the award than the winner and resent not having been chosen. Resentment and envy are difficult to overcome, but there will always be unhappy losers.

➤ **Overexposure.** After a while any monthly program can become overdone—it's difficult to maintain excitement and enthusiasm month after month.

➤ **Lack of Team Recognition.** When people work in teams, individual efforts are subordinate to team efforts. When recognition belongs to a team, no single member of that team should be singled out for recognition.

Team Recognition

When individual commendation is undesirable, companies institute team recognition programs. In Xerox's successful program, individuals receive awards for special achievement, but, to encourage teamwork, recognition is also given to teams. These awards include honors to teams that perform outstanding work and special recognition to teams for "Excellence in Customer Satisfaction."

Another way Xerox recognizes teams is by holding an annual Teamwork Day. On the first Teamwork Day, held in 1983 in a company cafeteria in Webster, New York, the objective was to teach managers the results of planning quality-circle activities and fostering a truly competitive team spirit. Thirty teams showed off projects that year and received *no rewards or cash*, just thank-yous. A combination of word-of-mouth and a company newspaper article helped ensure the participation of 60 teams the following year and an audience of 500 visitors.

Meanings & Gleanings

An *internal customer* is a member of your team or another team to whom you provide materials, information, or services. An *internal supplier* is another person in your organization who provides you with materials, information, or services. You may be a "customer" in some aspects of your work and a "supplier" in others.

In the third year of Teamwork Day, hundreds of teams wanted to participate, but there was room for only 200 (1,000 people attended the exhibits). In the fourth year the company rented the convention center in Rochester, New York, and 5,000 people attended. In its fifth year, the program expanded internationally; teamwork fairs were held in Rochester, Dallas, London, Amsterdam, and elsewhere. Teamwork Day is now a highly anticipated annual event.

Peer Recognition

In the total quality management movement (TQM), the commitment to work toward continuing improvement of quality has made every member of a team more aware of the importance of customer satisfaction. One way companies increase this awareness is by considering other employees with whom they interact as *internal customers* or *internal suppliers*.

Encourage your associates to recognize any special achievements of their internal suppliers and customers that enabled them to work with you more effectively.

Supervisors, managers, and team leaders aren't the only people who see the special efforts their associates make. All team members and co-workers are exposed daily to each other's efforts. Enabling them to recognize the work of peers not only brings to the forefront any accomplishments that may not have been recognized by managers but also makes both the nominator and the nominee feel that they are part of an integrated, interrelated, and caring organization.

Minicircuit Labs, which has plants in Brooklyn, New York, and Hialeah, Florida, encourages this concept by providing all its members with "You Made My Day" forms (see the following figure).

Secret Weapons

When companies are organized on a team basis, a program of recognizing team accomplishments should be judiciously incorporated into any formal recognition programs.

You Made My Day!

Date: _____

To: _____   Dept.: _____

From: _____   Dept.: _____

What you did: _____

_____

What it meant to me: _____

_____

Signed: _____

Copy to Human Resources
Copy to team leader

Special Awards for Special Achievements

To win one of Mary Kay's highest and most coveted awards—those famous pink Cadillacs—at its award celebrations, its salespeople must meet a series of challenges and criteria (see the section "Five Tips for Effective Praise," earlier in this chapter). It's not easy to win the award, but every year more Mary Kay associates "make the grade."

Mary Kay doesn't *give* the cars away, however—it *lends* them for one year. Anyone who wants to keep a car or upgrade to the next year's model must continue to meet the standards. What an incentive to keep up the good work! As a result, relatively few winners have to give up their cars.

In some organizations special awards are given not as part of a formal program, but on a manager's initiative. During the pre-Thanksgiving rush at Stew Leonard's food market in Norwalk, Connecticut, several office personnel noticed the long, creeping lines at checkout counters and—with no prompting from management—left their regular work duties to help cashiers bag the groceries, which helped speed up the lines.

Stew, the owner of the market, resolved to do something special for the employees who helped out. After the holiday rush was over, he bought for each of the employees a beautifully knitted shirt with the embroidered inscription "Stew Leonard ABCD Award." The inscription stands for "*a*bove and *b*eyond the *c*all of *d*uty." By giving special recognition to associates who do more than their jobs require, he not only gave credit where credit was due but also let everyone—the associates and their co-workers and supervisors, in addition to customers—know that he appreciated the extra effort.

Motivating Off-Site Employees

Motivating telecommuters, independent sub-contractors, and others who do most of their work away from the central facility, while keeping them from feeling like outsiders is a challenge for managers. Here are a few suggestions:

➤ Schedule meetings either monthly or every other month with all employees working on a project. If the people are scattered all over the country, regional meetings at a convenient location would be more feasible. This enables them to get to know each other and to discuss ideas face-to-face. It also gives people a feeling of community and a closer relationship to the company. They don't feel left out.

➤ Encourage managers to telephone off-site people—frequent but brief calls to touch base and occasional conference calls to the entire project team.

➤ People working off-site should be invited periodically to come to the home office to meet with staff. The personal contacts between on-site and off-site employees builds up feelings of belonging.

➤ Managers should make periodic visits to the locations where off-site people work.

➤ Send a weekly newsletter to all off-site people, telling them about the latest developments in the company. Make it newsy and include human interest stories about employees.

In addition to, or instead of, a newsletter, provide a Web site, updated daily to keep everybody current on company activities. Add some humor. Make it a site they'd want to read every day.

The Least You Need to Know

➤ By showing sincere interest in each of your associates, you establish a climate that's conducive to cooperation and team spirit.

➤ Provide positive reinforcement by seeking out and praising accomplishments instead of concentrating on faults that need correction.

➤ Encourage team members to show appreciation for their co-workers through peer recognition programs.

➤ To make praise truly sincere, specify the reason for the praise in the praise itself.

➤ Put your appreciation in writing. Brief notes, letters of commendation, and certificates of achievement give long-term value to the act of praising.

➤ Create ongoing programs to recognize the achievements of both individuals and teams. Find original ways to keep these programs exciting and rewarding.

➤ Don't ignore your off-site employees. Recognize that they are an integral part of your team.

Keep 'Em Moving

Almost everyone reacts positively to recognition and praise. But these are not the only ways to motivate people. When you work with a team, it's essential that you, as the team leader, identify how each person on the team reacts to various types of motivation. It's easy to fall into the trap of assuming that what motivates you or what has been successful in motivating other people in the past will work for everyone.

This chapter looks at some other motivators that work—for some people, not all. It also explores problems that develop in motivating a team when companies downsize, freeze wages, or change policies.

Opportunity—for What?

You're ambitious. You knock yourself out to get ahead, so you assume that everyone is ambitious. Not so!

When I was an officer in the U.S. Army, I told one of the privates in my unit that I was recommending him for promotion to corporal. Instead of the elation I expected, he objected: "No, sir, I don't want all that responsibility. All I want to be is one of the boys." I couldn't understand his reaction.

During the years I've been in the business world, I've heard similar reactions from men and women who are perfectly content to just "have a job." They do what they have to do and no more. Their real interests lie somewhere outside their work. Before you decide to offer a promotion to a team member, learn that person's real goals. Discuss the ramifications of the promotion in terms of the additional time and effort that may be required. Unless you're sure that he or she will welcome this type of opportunity, to offer advancement is a waste of breath.

Secret Weapons

Help develop career opportunities for your team members by recognizing each member's talents; helping to develop these abilities by coaching and training; and giving them assignments in which they can utilize their special skills and gain recognition for their achievements.

Alicia was desolate. When her boss was transferred, she expected to be promoted to his job, but the company promoted someone else. She complained, "I've been in the department longer than anyone else and have never missed a day's work. My performance reviews are always good. I should have gotten the promotion."

Why was Alicia passed over? Seniority, good attendance, and satisfactory work are important, but they're not the only or even the primary reasons for promotion. Management knew that Alicia was perfectly happy to do her work, but not one bit more. To her, it seemed, advancement was something to which she was entitled, not something toward which she had to work.

Encouraging People to Aim for Advancement

Suppose your organization has excellent opportunities for advancement. You believe that some of your team members have the potential to move up to those jobs, but they seem perfectly content to do no more than what they have to do. You don't want all that talent to be wasted. Here are some guidelines for motivating these folks to change their attitude:

➤ Find out what really turns them on. They may be satisfying their needs outside of work.

➤ Show how working toward advancement might help them meet their outside goals. For example, Christine is a winter skier and summer surfer. To pursue these sports, she needs money, and higher level jobs pay higher salaries. Or what about

Ken, whose life centers around his children? Working toward a higher level job will let him afford the type of education he wants to provide his kids.

➤ Some people are status conscious. Point out how advancement increases prestige not only in the company but also in the community.

➤ Creative people can be encouraged to work for advancement by showing how higher level positions give them the chance to use their own initiative and institute some of their creative ideas.

Communication Breakdown

Don't project your ambitions on others. Their desires may be much different from yours. To motivate an individual, you must know that person's goals and what he or she seeks from a job.

Dealing with People Who Want to Advance When There's No Opportunity

When ambitious people are frustrated by lack of opportunity for career advancement, it's tough to keep them motivated. They often quit or request a transfer to a department that offers better opportunities. If the chances for promotion are blocked because of a temporary economic situation or short-term internal problem, make sure that these factors are clear to everyone and that opportunities become available in the future.

If it's unlikely that advancement will occur in a reasonable period, you have to expect that ambitious people won't be content. Do your best to motivate them in other ways:

➤ Make special assignments to enable them to stretch their minds.

➤ Get them deeply involved in team projects so that their satisfaction in seeing the team's achievements replaces their personal desires.

➤ If you can, set up a compensation system that rewards them financially.

Some companies use a two-track compensation program so that people can be given financial reward and status without being promoted. One track is in management (the traditional promotional ladder); employees on the other track receive the equivalent pay and rank, but are non-managerial. A technical company's tracks may look like this:

Managerial	Technical
Section leader	Engineering leader
Department chief	Principal engineer
Project manager	Project engineer
Engineering manager	Chief engineer

Motivating the Unmotivated

You have to accept that some people just can't be motivated (short of putting a stick of dynamite under their chairs). With the right approach, many men and women who seem to be complacent and unmovable might be spurred toward improved performance.

Meanings & Gleanings

Long-term employees who have gone as far as they can and are not likely to be fired because of their tenure may become *coasters* until they retire.

Some employees have been with their organization for many years. They've gone as far as they can go—and they know it. They also know that it's unlikely they'll ever be fired as long as they meet minimum performance standards, because most companies don't fire long-term employees except under dire circumstances. People with the attitude "I'll do as little as I can get away with" are called *coasters*.

Coasting isn't limited to "old-timers." People of all ages, unfortunately, fall into this category. They meet your minimum standards, but make no effort to do more.

It's difficult to motivate people who really don't want to be motivated, and many managers and team leaders don't even try. They just look at these people as crosses they have to bear.

Learning Not to Give Up

One often-successful approach to motivating coasters is giving them challenges—assignments or projects they can really "sink their teeth into."

Realistically, not everyone gets excited by challenges. Some people, faced with a challenge, turn away from it—it's too much trouble. But for those who enjoy a challenging assignment, it can be a powerful motivator. Here are some guidelines:

➤ **Make the coaster a mentor to a new team member.** Many "old-timers" are flattered when asked to pass on their know-how and experience to the next generation. To ensure that they train newcomers properly, they hone their own skills and brush up on the latest developments in their field. Serious mentors do more than just train—they set good examples for their new associates.

➤ **Assign special projects.** Before the Associated Merchandise Company introduces a new product, it conducts a test market in key cities, a task it usually subcontracts to a market research firm. In testing its latest product, Associated tried a new approach: Rather than subcontract the job, it chose six men and women who had good marketing backgrounds but were now coasting. The six employees were relieved from their regular duties for four weeks. After a week of special training, each was sent to a test site to run the project. The challenge of a special assignment, enhanced by the success of the test, gave the coasters new enthusiasm that carried over into their regular work.

➤ **Plan future projects.** Coasters often feel left out. "I'll be retiring in a few years, so why worry about what the company will do then?" Their attitude is exacerbated by the fact that their managers have already given up on them. By bringing coasters into the process of planning projects along with younger employees, you let them know that they are valued team members and that they can bring to the group the value of their experience. An added benefit is that the coasters will learn from other members.

Secret Weapons

The downside of challenge as a motivator is that after a challenging assignment ends, the excitement it generates gradually fades. After a task is no longer a challenge, it's no longer a motivator either. You have to keep presenting new challenges.

Using the Best Motivator of All

If you enjoy your work, if it provides job satisfaction, if you can't wait to go to work every morning and hate to leave each evening, there's no need for any other type of motivation, right?

Is this a pipe dream? Although many new jobs being created in growth industries have the ingredients that lead to enjoyment and satisfaction, a large number of people have jobs that are routine, dull, and sometimes tedious. It's difficult, if not impossible, to generate excitement about these jobs.

One way to make dull jobs more "worker friendly" is to redesign these jobs. Rather than look at a job as a series of tasks that must be performed, study it as a total process. Make the job less routine by enlarging the scope of the job. Focus on what has to be accomplished rather than on the steps leading to its accomplishment by redesigning the manner in which the job is performed. This section presents some examples.

Enriching the Job

When Jennifer was hired to head the claims processing department at Liability Insurance Company, she inherited a department with low morale, high turnover, and disgruntled employees. The claims processing operation was an "assembly line" in which each clerk checked a section of the form and sent it to other clerks, each of whom checked another section. If errors were found, the form was sent to a specialist for handling. Efficient? Maybe, but it made the work dull and not very challenging.

Jennifer reorganized the process. She eliminated the assembly line and retrained each clerk to check the entire form, correct any errors, and personally deal with problems.

Although operations slowed down during the break-in period, it paid off in a highly motivated team of workers who found gratification in working through the entire process and seeing it completed satisfactorily.

When team members are trained to perform all aspects of the jobs their team handles, you can not only assign any part of the work to any member (which gives a team leader much more flexibility), but also, because members do different work at different times, break the boredom of routine.

Communication Breakdown

Don't assume that just because an employee is close to retirement he or she is a coaster. Many older people remain committed to their jobs and continue to give them their best effort as long as they're part of the team.

Involving Everyone in Planning

There are many types of work for which production quotas are established. Word processing operators are given the number of letters they must complete each day; production workers are given hourly quotas; salespeople must meet monthly standards. Management usually sets these quotas, but most workers don't like having quotas imposed on them. If management wants to raise quotas, employees are resentful and resistant.

Have your team members participate in setting quotas for their own jobs. You might think that they'll set low quotas that are easy to meet, and it may happen. That's why the process is *participatory*—you haven't stepped out of the picture completely. You're one of the participants. Your role is to ensure that realistic goals are set. In most cases, however, team members do set reasonable quotas, and because it's *their* goal, they accept it and work to achieve it.

Manager's Minute

"No one likes to feel that he or she is being sold something or told to do something. We much prefer to feel we are buying of our own accord or acting on our own ideas. We like to be consulted about our wishes, our wants, our thoughts."

—Dale Carnegie

Another example of participation in planning is the experience of Ford Motor Company, in its development of the Taurus. Ford didn't follow the usual industry practice of having a group of specialists design the car. Workers representing every type of job that would be involved in building the car were brought in to work with designers during the planning stage. The suggestions culled from workers' experience on the production line brought forth ideas that might never have occurred to the specialists. When the Taurus was brought to the factory floor, workers looked on it as *their* car. The result: The Taurus became the most trouble-free and profitable car Ford has introduced in recent years—because the company's workers were involved.

Some Motivators to Remember

This section lists some of the best techniques (in my experience) for motivating people to commit themselves to superior performance:

➤ Encourage participation by setting goals and determining how to reach them.

➤ Keep team members aware of how their job relates to others.

➤ Provide the tools and training necessary to succeed.

➤ Pay at least the going rate for jobs that are performed.

➤ Provide good, safe working conditions.

➤ Give clear directions that are easily understood and accepted.

➤ Know people's abilities and give them assignments based on their ability to handle those assignments.

➤ Allow team members to make decisions related to their jobs.

➤ Be accessible. Listen actively and empathetically.

➤ Give credit and praise for a job well done.

➤ Give prompt and direct answers to questions.

➤ Treat team members fairly and with respect and consideration.

➤ Help out with work problems.

➤ Encourage employees to acquire additional knowledge and skills.

➤ Show interest and concern for people as individuals.

➤ Learn employees' M.O.s and deal with them accordingly.

➤ Make each person an integral part of the team.

➤ Keep people challenged and excited by their work.

➤ Consider your team members' ideas and suggestions.

Meanings & Gleanings

Some companies, in their drive to cut costs or increase profits, eliminate total job categories. This process is usually called *downsizing*. Some companies prefer the terms "rightsizing" or "destaffing" or corrupt the term "re-engineering" (see the definition in the glossary) to make it sound less threatening.

➤ Keep people informed about how they're doing on the job.

➤ Encourage team members to do their best and then support their efforts.

Avoiding Negative Motivation

Remember K.I.T.A.? Chapter 2 debunked the myth that to get people to work you have to kick them in the you-know-what.

Threatening to fire people if they don't work is sometimes effective, at least temporarily. When jobs are scarce and people know that they won't have a job if they get fired, they *do* work. But how much work do they do? Some folks work just enough to keep from getting fired and not one bit more. This fear isn't real motivation; *real* motivation spurs people to produce more than just what's necessary to keep their jobs.

Fear of being fired becomes less of a motivator as the job market again expands. If comparable jobs are available in more amenable environments, why work for a martinet?

Some people do respond to negative motivation. Maybe they've been raised by intimidating parents or have worked under tyrannical bosses for so long that it's the only way of life they understand. Good leaders must recognize each person's individualities and adapt to them.

Motivating People Under Unfavorable Circumstances

Things don't always go well. Businesses go into slumps. Companies downsize and eliminate jobs. Large companies swallow smaller ones. How can morale be maintained and staff members motivated when they see their economic world toppling down around them? It's not easy, but, as you'll learn in this section, there are ways to do it.

Manager's Minute

"If you aren't fired with enthusiasm, you'll be fired with enthusiasm."

—Vince Lombardi

When the Company Downsizes

When business is slow, companies reduce costs by laying off employees. Layoffs have always been an element of the job world, particularly among blue collar industries. When business picks up, workers are likely to be rehired.

Downsizing differs from traditional layoffs in that total job categories are eliminated: There's little chance that people who have held these jobs will ever be rehired. Downsized positions are increasingly white collar and managerial jobs.

Elliot left his boss' office in shock. He had been told that the company was downsizing and that he would have to cut his team from 20 people to 15. He had worked hard to build a highly motivated team. Not only would he lose five good members but also the remaining employees would feel insecure, stressed, and unmotivated.

After the trauma of the layoffs subsided, Elliot took these steps to begin the rebuilding process:

➤ Reassured team members that management had completed the downsizing process and that their jobs were secure.

➤ Set up a series of meetings to restructure the team so that all work would be covered.

➤ Assigned projects to sub-teams to implement the new structure with minimum loss of productivity in ongoing activities.

➤ Personally counseled team members who showed signs of unusual stress.

Within a short time, Elliot's team again functioned at optimum capacity.

When Your Company Is Merged or Acquired

It seems that every time you pick up a newspaper you read about another merger or acquisition. Chase Manhattan's acquisition of Chemical Bank is the largest bank merger ever, but it resulted in the loss of thousands of jobs. Disney bought Capitol City/ABC, and more jobs were lost as the offices of its headquarters were consolidated. Your company could be next.

The people most likely to survive an acquisition are those who work for the acquiring company, but even that's not a sure thing. Federated Department Stores bought Macy's and closed several of its own stores.

Whenever a merger or acquisition occurs, employees of both groups are certain to be insecure and concerned. As a team leader, little ol' you can do nothing until the dust settles, which often takes months or even years.

The following suggestions can give your team a better chance of survival:

➤ **Work harder, work smarter.** When Associated Finance acquired Guardian Loan, all of Guardian's employees were concerned. They were sure that the larger company would eliminate their jobs. Alberta, Guardian's credit manager, thought differently. She told her team, "Our credit people are the best in the business. One reason they bought us was our excellent record in this area. They need us. It will take at least six months before Associated can make any changes here. Let's show them that we are essential to their success." And they did. When the reorganization finally took place, Associated merged several departments with its own, but the credit department was left intact.

➤ **Be prepared to do things differently.** Companies that acquire others install their own systems and procedures. Accept them without complaints. Neither you nor your associates should ever say, "We never used to do it that way." Work their way. If it requires you to learn new technology, learn it as soon as possible.

➤ **Be patient.** After you master the new company's methods and win the confidence of the new management team, they will listen to your ideas for improvements and innovations.

> **ZAP!**
>
> **Secret Weapons**
>
> When you deal with survivors of downsizing, mergers, or reorganizations, don't assume that things are the same as before. Take overt action to help your team members cope with their fears and stresses. Get your entire team involved in productive activities that not only keep them from brooding but also actively engage their minds and bodies.

When the Pressure Is On

Regardless of whether a company has downsized or reorganized because of an acquisition or another reason, you usually wind up with fewer people having to accomplish more work.

Suppose that a team of six people has been reduced to four but that the amount of work hasn't decreased. Work previously done at a leisurely pace must now be rushed. People who went home at 5 P.M. now work regularly until 7 or 8. Everyone feels the pressure. Morale is at a low.

How to motivate people who work longer hours and under constant pressure is the primary challenge managers face, and there are no easy answers. Some managers counter complaints by telling team members that they're lucky to have a job. This answer isn't a good one, though. As mentioned, negative motivation has limited value.

By encouraging your team to find shortcuts to better production, to eliminate unnecessary paperwork, and to come up with creative innovations, you can help them reduce some of the added burden.

Some companies have instituted stress reduction programs to help people cope with downsizing and reorganization. Let team members know that, as business improves, temporary and, eventually, permanent staff members will be added to ease the workload.

Manager's Minute

A 1995 survey of managerial and professional personnel by the U.S. Chamber of Commerce showed that the 40-hour work week is dead. Most respondents said that they work nine-hour days, another hour or more at home, and at least two hours on weekends.

When Wages Freeze

Suppose your company hasn't raised anyone's wages for three years. Your team members are unhappy and resist all your efforts to get them to produce more. You repeatedly hear the complaint, "Why should I knock myself out when they won't pay me more?"

Sanjay, a chief engineer at a chemical company, was tired of hearing this complaint. He had tried hard, but unsuccessfully, to get management to lift the freeze. At one of his team meetings he addressed the issue: "I know you haven't had a raise in three years. Neither have I, nor has my boss. You all know that business has been down during this time. After it improves, the freeze will end. Business is up this year, but not enough. Let's get to work so that we can do our part to make this a profitable company again."

This technique is one way to help team members understand the problem—that it's one that can and will be overcome. (Of course it doesn't help if people read in the newspaper that the company CEO has just taken a $1 million bonus.)

The Least You Need to Know

➤ Not everyone seeks advancement, but for those who do, it's a great motivator.

➤ If opportunity for advancement is limited in your organization, you can motivate people by giving them assignments that enable them to stretch their minds, be creative, or take leadership roles in team activities.

➤ You can often "remotivate" coasters by giving them new challenges.

➤ The best motivator of all is to enrich the job so that people can obtain real satisfaction from their work.

➤ Survivors of downsizing are often worried and insecure. They need reassurance. Get them involved in productive projects that stimulate them and enable them to experience success.

➤ If your company is acquired by another, your chances of survival can be improved if you and your team make yourselves too valuable to drop.

Chapter 20

Empowerment— Today's Buzzword

If you've been around management circles for any length of time, you've been exposed to buzzwords. *Everyone* uses these terms and phrases. You go to trade association meetings where these terms are the main topic of discussion. They pop up in casual conversations among business people, and they're featured in every business publication.

Over the years, terms such as "scientific management," "industrial engineering," "sensitivity training," "management grid," and "management by objective" have come and gone.

The concepts these terms represented weren't fireworks that lit up the industrial sky for a short time and disappeared forever. We all learned something from each concept that, after the use of the buzzword faded, remained as part of the practice of management.

Here's a buzzword for the millenium: *empowerment*. It's not easy to empower people: Some leaders don't want to give up their power, and some team members don't want to take the responsibility that goes with power. This chapter looks at how empowerment works in practice and how it can make you a more effective team leader.

Whether the concept remains as a major force in management thinking or eventually fades away, it has already contributed a great deal to individual and team performance and productivity.

Meanings & Gleanings

Empowerment means sharing your power with the people over whom you have power. Team members are given the authority to make decisions that previously were reserved for managers.

Who's Got the Power?

Who has the power in a company? Who makes the decisions that govern how a company, a department, or a team operates? In most companies, power is in the hands of management. In a typical hierarchy, the power flows downward from the CEO through the layers of management. Each layer has power over the one beneath it. For example, you have power over the people you supervise.

Here's how the traditional power structure works: Your boss gives you an assignment. You look it over, determine how it should be done, and assign various components of the job to your team members. Then you follow it through until it's completed.

Empowerment changes this process. You share with your team the power to make decisions about an assignment. Rather than tell team members what each of them will do, you work together to plan and execute the entire project.

The concept of empowerment isn't entirely new. For years companies have engaged in a variation called "participative management." Empowerment carries participation one step further. Team members not only participate in decision making but also are authorized to make decisions on their own without seeking approval from higher level managers.

The installation of a new sprinkler system at the Woodbury Golf Club was the biggest job that All-Star Landscaping had ever received. Bill, the owner-manager, had just attended a management seminar on empowerment and thought that this project was a good chance to put into practice what he had learned in the course.

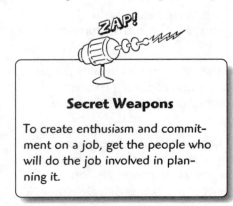

Secret Weapons

To create enthusiasm and commitment on a job, get the people who will do the job involved in planning it.

A few weeks before the job was to begin, Bill invited his team members to his home for a breakfast meeting to discuss the job. He outlined the project and asked for ideas about how to proceed. One associate suggested that, in their regular landscaping work at the club, they could identify the best locations for the sprinkler heads and save the time and cost of a special survey. Another volunteered to examine the current system to determine which parts, if any, could be incorporated into the new system.

At their next meeting, the team planned the entire job and agreed on who would complete each part. When the work began, the team went to work full of enthusiasm because they had been completely involved in the planning.

During the installation, as problems arose, the team members were empowered to make decisions to correct them without having to get Bill's approval every time.

Bill reported that if he had done all the preparatory work himself and had just assigned the work to his team members and required them to come to him to solve every problem, it would have taken longer and cost more, and the workers involved would have looked at it as just another job.

The Three Pluses of Empowerment

As Bill learned from his first experience in empowerment, much can be gained from it. The three major benefits of empowerment are described in this section.

Ideas

You've heard the expression "two heads are better than one." Perhaps 10 heads are even better. People who work on a job know a great deal more about what's going on in their working environment than many managers realize. They see things that are done inefficiently, and they have ideas for improvement. By eliciting their input about new projects and assignments, you're likely to pick up ideas that may not have occurred to you.

Rachel, Baldwin Insurance Agency's office manager, empowered her staff to design and institute a new filing system. Some of the best suggestions came from a high school student who worked part-time. The young woman demonstrated that some of the practices they had followed for years and had assumed were the best methods could be made easier.

Synergism

As noted, when a team generates ideas, a suggestion made by one participant can trigger ideas from another that he would never have come up with alone. This process leads to an abundance of ideas from an empowered team.

This process of *synergism* isn't limited to generating ideas, however. Synergism, defined as "two or more units (people, in this case) working together to achieve a greater effect than individuals can do by themselves," is exactly what happens in an empowered team.

Meanings & Gleanings

Ownership is the feeling of being a full partner in the development and implementation of a project and being committed to its successful achievement.

If each of Bill's landscapers had worked alone to perform a specific phase of the sprinkler installation, the job would have been completed, but it would have taken longer and errors probably would have occurred that had to be corrected later. By working as a team, each person knew what the others were doing and, if help was needed, could pitch in.

When all members of an empowered team are engaged in the same type of work, each person should be trained to do all aspects of that work. As noted, some teams are multifunctional—they consist of people from different disciplines. Although each member of a team made up of marketing, engineering, and finance specialists cannot be expected to do the jobs of their colleagues in other areas of expertise, their total involvement in the planning process lets them know exactly what each team member is doing. The results are a coordinated effort and goals that are easier to achieve.

Ownership

When people participate in planning a project, they identify with the project. Because *their* ideas are being implemented, they're committed to its success.

Gail looked at her job as routine and dull. She did what she had to do and no more. When her boss informed the department that the company was changing its structure to team empowerment, Gail was skeptical. "It's just another gimmick to get us to work harder," she thought.

When the first project under the new system was introduced, Gail sat quietly and listened. Instead of being told what had to be done, the group was asked how they thought the project should be approached. Gail was alert and interested. After a while she timidly raised her hand and made a suggestion that everyone thought was a good idea. By the time the meeting ended, Gail and her associates were excited about the job and were eager to get to work and make it a success.

Three Problems of Empowerment

Empowerment can be a great way to motivate people to accomplish superior work, but it doesn't always work. This section looks at some of the major problem areas.

"I Won't Give Up My Power"

Men and women who have worked hard to be promoted to managerial positions often believe that empowering their team members will lower their own positions. A couple of the reasons that they may feel this way are:

➤ **Status.** Whether you work as a traditional manager or as the leader of an empowered team, you don't lose your status by sharing power with the team. It's a difference not in rank or position, but in methodology. Rather than "boss," you teach, inspire, and motivate your team. Being the leader of an empowered team is a position high in status.

➤ **Control.** Some managers ask the question, "I'm still responsible for this department—how can I give up my power without losing control?" You don't have to lose control when you share power. You're a member of a team. You're in the midst of every activity and know how each team project is progressing. You are aware of this, and so is *every member* of your team. Control becomes team control. As team leader, you guide your team to meet performance standards (see Chapter 21).

Communication Breakdown

Not everyone is thrilled to be empowered. Sometimes you have to sell them on the idea.

"I Don't Want to Be Empowered"

Wendy was perplexed. She thought that her team members would be excited and enthusiastic about learning of their company's move to empowered teams. Instead, she realized that several people were upset. They had these reactions:

"I'm not paid to make decisions—that's your job."

"Just tell me what to do, and I'll do it."

"I work hard enough as it is. I don't want more responsibility."

Your first job as team leader of a newly empowered team involves converting people who think this way into enthusiastic supporters of the new method of working. Here are some suggestions that may help you do this:

➤ **Figure out why people don't want to stretch their brains.** Employees are often happy doing routine work in a routine way. Find the true reason that they feel this way. Perhaps they don't believe that they have the ability to do more than routine work. Sometimes you have to work with team members to build up their self-confidence.

➤ **Make team members understand their new roles.** Take the time in the beginning to explain the true meaning of empowerment. Time spent in good orientation pays off in better team efforts.

➤ **Train your team members to generate ideas.** Show videos about team participation; teach team members to brainstorm. Have members of another team that has been successful in empowered activities describe how empowerment has worked for their team.

➤ **Get under way slowly.** Choose assignments or projects that easily lend themselves to participatory effort in the beginning. Gradually progress to the point at which team members tackle all projects collaboratively.

Secret Weapons

Empower people who deal with customer problems to deal with them without the usual delays and red tape that result from the need to seek approval from above. At Nordstrom's department stores, any sales clerk can make exchanges, give refunds, or provide special service. At AT&T Universal Credit Company, requests for credit limit increases are handled by the person receiving the call.

"If Everybody's Empowered, Who Needs a Leader?"

Some managers fear that their company will have no need for them after empowerment becomes the way of organizational life. If everyone is involved in what managers traditionally do, what role is left for managers?

In some companies, the job of the team leader has been redesigned. Traditional teams are replaced by "self-directed" teams that have no permanent team leader (see Chapter 24); the team chooses a project leader (or two or more leaders) for each project. Few companies now have totally self-directed teams, however. Because most teams work on multiple projects, a modified version may be used in which a permanent team leader serves the important purpose of coordinating all team activities and providing training and support.

Making Empowerment Work for You

Empowerment isn't a panacea for curing all management problems. Rather, it enhances collaborative efforts by giving every member of a team the power to get things done.

In General Motors' Saturn division, any assembly line worker can push the button that stops the line if she sees something that needs correction (a power most companies reserve for managers).

One GM employee reported on television that he "pushed that button once," after he realized that a part had not been inserted properly on a chassis. The correction took just a few seconds, but the employee said that it made him feel good that he had the power to stop the line and that he was able to help maintain the quality of GM's cars.

Jerry Junkins, the CEO of Texas Instruments, believes that the number one strength of his organization is its 1,900 empowered teams.

Major companies such as General Electric, Kodak, and Federal Express have reported that instituting empowered teams has made them able to not only keep up but also move ahead in their tough, competitive industries. Thousands of smaller companies relate similar experiences.

Manager's Minute

Many helpful programs are available for empowerment training: The Franklin-Covey Leadership Center (3507 N. University Avenue, Provo, UT 84604 (800) 331-7716); Dun & Bradstreet Business Education Services (711 Third Avenue, New York, NY 10017 (800) 999-1237); and Dale Carnegie Training (1475 Franklin Avenue, Garden City, NY 11550 (516) 248-5100).

To help your empowerment program succeed, follow these guidelines:

➤ The program must have the full support of top management. Empowerment works most effectively when a company's CEO empowers its senior management group, which, in turn, passes that empowerment down through the organization.

➤ Team members and team leaders should be trained in the techniques of empowerment. Because many companies assume that the transition to empowerment is more difficult for team members than for team leaders, they concentrate their training on team members. Because the program is collaborative, supervisors (now team leaders) and employees (now team members) should be trained together by consultants or others who are knowledgeable in this type of work.

➤ All team members should be given full information about team projects; support to acquire necessary skills and techniques; freedom to interact with the team leader and any team member to accomplish the team's goals; and encouragement to use their initiative in planning and implementing projects.

➤ Counseling should be available to assist people who have difficulty adjusting to the new techniques.

➤ Training should be ongoing. Many organizations have excellent training programs for orienting and starting up an empowered team program; after the program is under way,

Secret Weapons

Titles may change, and functions may be altered, but there will always be a role for people who can guide, counsel, and motivate their co-workers. Empowerment doesn't mean giving up power—it means *sharing* it. It doesn't mean that you abdicate responsibility either; instead, you create a climate in which all team members are as excited about the job as you are.

however, they assume that it will work smoothly. As teams mature, many initial problems are overcome, but new problems do occur. Hold reinforcement training meetings periodically to discuss and resolve complexities that develop.

➤ In self-directed teams, every team member may be required to coach and facilitate certain projects or parts of projects. These members should have the opportunity to take the same leadership training programs that are given to permanent team leaders.

In theory, everyone can be trained to be a leader, but in practice, it doesn't always work. Some people aren't emotionally suited for leadership roles; they just aren't motivated to assume these types of duties. These people will not or cannot change their patterns of behavior from dogmatism to participation. Allowing them to remain in leadership positions is destructive—they must be removed. The team leader is the fulcrum on which a team revolves. Highly motivated, well-trained, committed team leaders are essential to the success of empowered teams.

The Least You Need to Know

➤ Empowerment is the sharing of power to make decisions in planning and implementing a job with the people who will perform that job.

➤ Empowerment fosters synergism. By interacting and collaborating, team members produce more and better work than they can as individuals.

➤ Empowerment fosters ownership. People involved in determining how a project will be accomplished are committed to its success.

➤ When you empower your team, you don't have to lose control. Empowered teams work with you to ensure that performance standards are met.

➤ Some team members may not want to be empowered. Win them over with a well-planned orientation, and, if necessary, augment it with individual counseling.

➤ Team leaders and members alike should be thoroughly trained in the way empowerment will change the way they work. This training should be conducted by experts in empowerment and should be reinforced with periodic refresher meetings.

Part 6
Dealing with Employee Problems on the Job

You have a good team in place, and all its members are carrying their weight—well, maybe not everyone. You know that some of your co-workers can do better. They're meeting their performance standards, but just barely. Performance review time is approaching, so here's your chance to shape them up. There's Burt, who seems to be on the verge of burnout; Ellen, who is so sensitive you're afraid to correct her errors; Stacey, who's always finding something to gripe about; and then there's that new programmer, whom you suspect has a drinking problem. To keep your team functioning effectively, you need to counsel and help them.

So, you shape up your team, but your company decides to outsource some of your team's work to consultants and subcontractors. Now you're concerned about melding the scattered members of your team into the total operation.

This part of the book provides tips and techniques to help you overcome the challenges of maintaining a top performing team.

Chapter 21

Evaluating Team Members' Performance

In This Chapter

➤ Setting performance standards

➤ Completing a formal performance appraisal

➤ Deciding whether to measure by traits or by results

➤ Conducting effective appraisal interviews

➤ When your performance is evaluated

"How am I doing?" you ask your boss. Just as you want to know what your bosses think of your work, your team members are concerned about your opinion of their work. Most companies have periodic (usually annual) employee appraisals, but team leaders shouldn't wait for this formal review. Between appraisal sessions, you should talk to your team members regularly about their performance and make it an ongoing part of your coaching.

This chapter discusses how to set performance standards that are meaningful to team members and describes some of the techniques for measuring performance. You'll also learn how to conduct a formal appraisal interview.

Setting Performance Standards

All employees should know just what's expected of them on the job. Many companies develop and incorporate *performance standards* at the time they create a job description. In other companies, a job evolves as standards are established.

Meanings & Gleanings

Performance standards define the results that are expected from a person performing a job. For performance standards to be meaningful, all people doing that job should know and accept these standards. Team participation in the establishment of performance standards is one way to ensure this understanding.

In routine jobs, the key factors of performance standards involve quantity (how much should be produced per hour or per day) and quality (what level of quality is acceptable). As jobs become more complex, these standards aren't an adequate way to measure performance. Ideas and innovations that are conceived in creative jobs cannot be quantified, and quality may be difficult to measure. This situation doesn't mean that you can't have performance standards for these jobs, but it does require a different approach, such as the results-oriented evaluation system described later in this chapter.

Establishing Criteria for Performance Standards

Performance standards are usually based on the experiences of satisfactory workers who have done that type of work over a length of time. Whether the standards cover quality or quantity of the work, or other aspects of the job, they should meet these criteria:

➤ **Specific.** Every person doing a job should know exactly what she is expected to do.

➤ **Measurable.** The company should have a touchstone against which performance can be measured. Measuring performance is easy when a standard is quantifiable; it's more difficult (but not impossible) when it isn't quantifiable. When a numerical measurement isn't feasible, some of the criteria may include timely completion of assignments, introduction of new concepts, or contribution to team activities.

➤ **Realistic.** Unless standards are attainable, people consider them unfair and resist working toward them.

Let Them Evaluate Their Own Performance

When all team members know what's expected of them and against which standards they'll be measured, self-evaluation becomes almost automatic. Members don't have to wait for their team leader to tell them that they're below standard or behind schedule—they see that for themselves and can take corrective action immediately.

Self-evaluation makes a team leader's job easier. Like a good coach, he helps keep the team aware of the standards and provides support and encouragement to stay on target.

Manager's Minute

W. Edwards Deming, the father of the quality movement, was strongly opposed to performance reviews. He believed that, in most companies, performance was equated with quantity at the sacrifice of quality. This was the case for a long time, but quality standards today are given equal or greater weight in evaluations.

Conducting Formal Performance Appraisals

Even if team members know the performance standards and can measure their own performance, and if team leaders reinforce this process with ongoing discussions about performance, there's still a need for formal appraisals. Most formal appraisals are conducted annually. Many team leaders add an informal appraisal semi-annually or quarterly as a means of helping team members be aware of their progress.

This list describes some of the reasons that formal appraisals are important:

➤ They provide a framework for discussing a team member's overall work record. The team leader can use this meeting to recognize an employee for past successes and provide suggestions for even greater contributions.

➤ They become more objective and enable team leaders to compare all members of the team against the same criteria.

➤ They provide helpful data for determining what type of additional training team members need.

➤ In many companies, they're the primary factor in determining salary increases and bonuses.

➤ Their formality causes them to be taken more seriously than informal comments about performance.

➤ They can be used as a vehicle for goal setting, career planning, and personal growth.

Secret Weapons

When you rate your team members, don't be overly influenced by their most recent behavior. Employees know that it's rating time, and they'll be as good as a kid just before Christmas. Keep a running log of their behavior during the entire year.

Examining the Downside of Formal Appraisals

Formal appraisals have some inherent problems, a few of which are:

➤ They can be stressful for both leaders and team members.

➤ They make some team leaders so uncomfortable about making associates unhappy that the leaders overrate their performance.

➤ Many are inadequate, cumbersome, or poorly designed, which creates more problems than solutions.

➤ In some appraisals, good workers are underrated because their team leaders are afraid that team members might become competitors.

Manager's Minute

At Dun & Bradstreet seminars, supervisors were asked what they thought were the worst aspects of their jobs. The worst was having to fire people; a close second was conducting formal appraisal interviews.

A properly managed performance appraisal can be a highly stimulating experience for both team member and team leader. To make it most effective, don't treat it as a confrontation. Treat it instead as a meaningful two-way interchange that leads to an employee's commitment to reach out for improvement and set and implement goals for the coming year that will lead to a more productive and satisfying work experience.

Choosing the Best System for You

Your company may have in place an appraisal system that you are obligated to use. It may be helpful, however, to use aspects of other appraisal methods in addition to the method formally requested by your company. In addition, many companies use an appraisal system that combines aspects of all the methods described here, so these aren't "pure" types.

Check the Box: The Trait-Based System

You've been rated by them. You've used them to rate others. The most common evaluation system is the "trait" format, in which a series of traits are listed in the left margin, and each is measured against a scale from unsatisfactory to excellent (see the following figure):

Trait-based Appraisal Worksheet					
	Excellent (5 points)	Very Good (4 points)	Average (3 points)	Needs Improvement (2 points)	Unsatisfactory (1 point)
Quantity of work					
Job knowledge					
Dependability					
Ability to take instruction					
Initiative					
Creativity					
Cooperation					

This system seems on the surface to be simple to administer and easy to understand, but it's loaded with problems:

➤ **A central tendency.** Rather than carefully evaluate each trait, it's much easier to rate a trait as average or close to average (the central rating).

➤ **The "halo effect."** Some managers believe that one trait is so impressive they rate all traits highly. Its opposite is the "pitchfork effect" (see Chapter 15).

➤ **Personal biases.** Managers are human, and humans have personal biases for and against other people. These biases can influence any type of rating, but the trait system is particularly vulnerable.

➤ **Latest behavior.** It's easy to remember what employees have done during the past few months, but managers tend to forget what they did in the first part of a rating period.

Some companies encourage the use of the bell curve in rating employees. The bell curve concept is based on the assumption that in a large population most people will fall in the average (middle) category, a smaller number in each of the poorer-than-average and better-than-average categories, and a still smaller number in the highest and lowest categories.

The trouble with the use of the bell curve in employee evaluations is that small groups are unlikely to have this type of distribution—and it may work unfairly against top and bottom level workers.

Suppose Carla is a genius who works in a department in which everyone is a genius. Carla is the lowest level genius in the group, however. In a bell curve for that group, she would be rated as "poor." In any other group, she probably would be rated "superior." Or suppose that Harold's work is barely satisfactory but that his entire group is performing below average. Compared with the other employees, he's the best. If you use a bell curve, you have to rate him "superior."

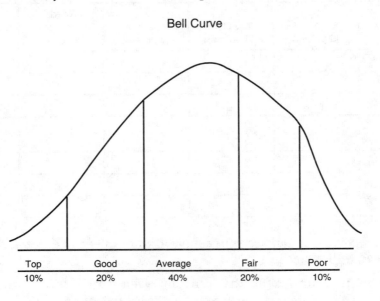

Bell Curve

Top	Good	Average	Fair	Poor
10%	20%	40%	20%	10%

Making the Trait-Based System More Effective

The best way to overcome deficiencies in the trait system is to replace them with a results-oriented system (described later in this chapter). If your company does use the trait method, here are some suggestions to help make it more equitable:

➤ **Clarify standards.** Every manager and team leader should be carefully informed about the meaning of each category and the definition of each trait. Understanding quantity and quality is relatively easy. But what is dependability? How do you measure initiative, creativity, and other intangibles?

By using discussions, role-playing, and case studies, you can develop standards that everyone understands and uses.

➤ **Establish criteria for ratings.** It's easy to identify superior and unsatisfactory employees, but it's tougher to differentiate among people in the middle three categories.

➤ **Keep a running log of member performance throughout the year.** You don't have to record average performance, but do note anything special that each member has accomplished or failed to accomplish. Some notes on the positive side may say, for example, "Exceeded quota by

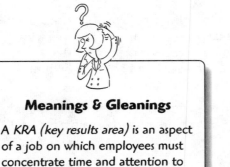

Meanings & Gleanings

A *KRA (key results area)* is an aspect of a job on which employees must concentrate time and attention to ensure that they achieve the goals for that job.

20 percent," "Completed project two days before deadline," or "Made a suggestion that cut by a third the time required for a job." Notes on the negative side may say, "Had to redo report because of major errors" or "Was reprimanded for extending lunch hour three days this month."

➤ Make an effort to be aware of your personal biases and to overcome them.

➤ Have specific examples of exceptional and unsatisfactory performance and behavior to back up your evaluation.

Measuring Results: A More Meaningful System

Rather than rate team members on the basis of an opinion about their various traits, in this appraisal system the people who do the rating focus on the attainment of specific results. Results-based ratings can be used in any situation in which results are measurable. This system is obviously easier to use when quantifiable factors are involved (such as sales volume or production units), but it's also useful in such intangible areas as attaining specific goals in management development, reaching personal goals, and making collaborative efforts.

In a results-oriented evaluation system, the people who do the evaluating don't have to rely on their judgment of abstract traits, but instead can focus on what was expected from team members and how closely they met these expectations. The expectations are agreed on at the beginning of a period and measured at the end of that period. At that time, new goals are developed to be measured at the end of the following period.

Here's how this system works:

➤ For every job, the team leader and the people doing the job agree on the *KRAs (key results areas)* for that job. Employees must accomplish results in these areas to meet the team's goals.

➤ The team leader and the team member establish the results that are expected from the team member in each of the KRAs.

➤ During a formal review, the results an employee attained in each of the KRAs are measured against what was expected.

➤ A numerical scale is used in some organizations to rate employees on how closely they come to reaching their goals. In others, no grades are given. Instead, a narrative report is compiled to summarize what has been accomplished and to comment on its significance.

➤ Some companies request that team members submit monthly progress reports compiled in the same format as the annual review. This technique enables both the team member and the leader to monitor progress. By studying the monthly reports, the annual review is more easily compiled and discussed.

Following is a sample form for a results-oriented evaluation.

Results-Oriented Evaluation

Team member: _____

Job: <u>Tax accountant</u>   Date: _____

Results expected   **Results achieved**

Key Results Area 1   Prepare federal, state, and local tax
                                              returns on a timely basis.

_____   _____

_____   _____

_____   _____

Key Results Area 2   Advise management of changes in and
                                              administrative interpretations of tax laws.

_____   _____

_____   _____

_____   _____

Key Results Area 3   Study management policies and report on
                                              their tax ramifications.

_____   _____

_____   _____

_____   _____

Pros and Cons of Appraisal by Results

Although results-oriented evaluations can be more meaningful than trait systems, they're not free of problems:

➤ **Set reasonable goals.** Unless you and the team member take an objective view of what he or she should accomplish, you may set unrealistic expectations. The danger is that you may set standards so low employees attain them with little effort, or that you set them so high employees have little chance of attaining them.

➤ **Not all goals are equal in importance.** You should consider the value of the expectation in comparison to the overall goals of the team and the company.

➤ **Intangible goals are more difficult to measure.** Even intangible factors, however, have tangible phases that can be identified. For example, rather than indicate that a goal is to "improve employee morale," specify it in terms that are measurable, such as "reduce turnover by X percent" or "decrease the number of grievances by Y percent." Rather than state a goal as "Develop a new health insurance plan," break it into phases, such as "Complete study of proposed plans by October 31" or "Submit recommendations by December 15."

Meanings & Gleanings

In a *joint leader/associate* evaluation, a team member evaluates his or her own performance, and the team leader also evaluates it. The final report results from a collaborative discussion between the team leader and the team member.

Collaborative Evaluation

To make the results-oriented format even more meaningful, use the *joint leader/associate* model. If performance evaluations are based on the arbitrary opinion of a supervisor, they serve only part of the real value that reviews can provide. Such a model provides a formal evaluation for the purpose of raises or promotions and enables you to tell employees how to improve performance, but it doesn't involve team members in the process.

A joint review can do this more effectively. The joint leader/associate review is particularly useful for evaluating creative jobs such as research and development or jobs in the arts. Team members and their leaders collaborate on the standards that are expected, build in the flexibility to accommodate the special circumstances under which they are working, and agree on the criteria that will be used in evaluating the work.

The team member and team leader then complete the evaluation form. The KRAs and the "results expected" items are agreed on in advance (usually during the preceding review). The team member and the leader independently indicate the "results achieved."

Many companies that don't use joint evaluations ask employees to evaluate their own performance before meeting with their team leader. They complete a copy of the appraisal form. At the meeting, similarities and differences in the ratings are discussed, and adjustments in the ratings resulting from the discussions are reflected in the formal evaluation that's filed with the human

Communication Breakdown

If a team member gives himself or herself a significantly higher rating than you do, be particularly sensitive in the discussion so that it doesn't degenerate into a confrontation. Use specific examples rather than statements of opinion to make your points.

resources department. If the employee still disagrees with the evaluation after the discussion, in some companies a rebuttal may be written, which is filed along with the team leader's report.

At the appraisal interview (described later in this chapter), the team leader and the team member discuss the comments on the form. During this session, the appraisal begins to move from a report card to a plan of action for growth and teamwork.

Benefits of the Collaborative Review

A collaborative review of performance has the following advantages:

➤ Gives team members the opportunity to make a formal appraisal of their own work in a systematic manner.

➤ Allows for a thorough discussion between the team leader and the team member about their different perceptions of expectations and results achieved.

➤ Enables a team leader to see areas in which he or she may have failed in developing a team member's potential.

➤ Helps the team member and the team leader identify problem areas that might easily be overlooked on a day-to-day basis.

➤ Pinpoints areas in which employees need improvement and in which they need additional training.

➤ Gives an opportunity to discuss areas in which a team member can become even more valuable to her team.

➤ Provides a base on which realistic goals for the next period can be discussed and mutually agreed on.

➤ Helps team members measure performance and progress against their own career goals and serves as a guide in determining the appropriate steps to move forward.

The Nuts and Bolts of the Appraisal Interview

Regardless of whether you have evaluated employees by the trait method or the results method and whether they have made a self-evaluation, the most important facet of the appraisal process is the face-to-face discussion of the evaluation.

To make this interview most valuable, you should carefully plan it and systematically carry it out.

Prepare and Plan Your Approach

Before sitting down with a team member to discuss a performance appraisal, study the evaluation. Make a list of all aspects you want to discuss—not just those that need improvement but also those in which the employee did good work. Study previous appraisals, and note improvements that have been made since the preceding one. Prepare the questions you want to ask about past actions, steps to be taken for improvement, future goals, and how the team member plans to reach them.

Reflect on your experiences in dealing with this person. Have there been any special behavioral problems? Any problems that have affected his work? Any strong, positive assets you want to nurture? Any special points you want to discuss?

Discussing Performance with Team Member

After you have made a team member feel at ease, point out the reasons for the appraisal meeting. Say something like this: "As you know, each year we review what has been accomplished during the preceding year and discuss what we can do together in the following year."

Point out the areas of the job in which team members have met standards, and particularly the areas in which they have excelled. By giving specific examples of these achievements, you let team members know you're aware of their positive qualities.

Because salary adjustment is usually based on overall performance, team members should be made aware that your praise of one or a few accomplishments isn't a guarantee of a raise. You might say, "The way you handled the *XYZ* account shows that you're making great progress. Keep up the good work." By saying it this way, you show that you're aware of the progress, but that there's still a ways to go. Rather than interpret the praise as "Wow, I'm good—this means a big raise," the reaction is, "I'm doing fine, but I'm not there yet."

Encourage team members to comment. Listen attentively, then discuss the aspects of performance or behavior that didn't meet standards. Be specific. It's much more effective to give a few examples where expectations haven't been met than to just say, "Your work isn't up to snuff." Ask what team members plan to do to meet standards and what help they want you to provide.

If employees' problems aren't related to performance, but rather to behavior, provide examples: "During the past year, I've spoken to you several times about your tardiness. You're a good worker, and your opportunities in this company would be much greater if you could only get here on time." Try to obtain a commitment and a plan of action to overcome this fault.

Meanings & Gleanings

The word *interview* is derived from *inter* (which means "between") and *view* (which means "look"). An interview is a "look" at a situation "between" the parties involved. An appraisal interview isn't the leader telling the team member, "This is what you did well, and that is what you did poorly"—it's a two-way discussion about performance.

Making Criticism Constructive

Many managers find it difficult to give criticism. Here are some guidelines to help deal with this sensitive area:

➤ Begin with a positive approach by asking the team member to assess the successes achieved and the steps taken to achieve those successes.

➤ Encourage her to talk about projects that didn't succeed and what caused the failure.

➤ Ask what might have been done to avoid the mistakes made.

➤ Contribute your suggestions about how the matter could have been done more effectively.

➤ Ask what training or help you can provide.

➤ Agree on the steps the associate will take to ensure better performance on future assignments.

Soliciting Team Members' Comments

Throughout interviews, encourage team members to comment on or make suggestions about every aspect of the review. Of course, they may have excuses or alibis. Listen empathetically—you may learn about some factors that have inhibited optimum performance. There may be factors within the company that keep an employee from performing adequately. For example, you may find out that someone has an older-model computer that has started "crashing" several times a day ever since the company upgraded software. You may not have been aware that this recurring problem was affecting the person's job performance. With this new information, you can take steps to correct the situation by budgeting for a computer upgrade. By giving the person the opportunity to express his or her reasons or arguments, you can take steps to correct the situation.

Even if a team member's excuses are superficial and self-serving, allowing them to be voiced clears the air. Then you both can be prepared to face real situations and come up with viable ideas.

Reviewing Last Year's Goals and Setting Next Year's

If the preceding year's goals were met, congratulate the team member. Talk about the steps that were taken to meet goals and what was learned from this experience. If not all the goals were met, discuss any problems and the steps that might now be taken to overcome them.

An appraisal interview isn't just a review of the past—it's also a plan for the future. Ask the question, "What do you want to accomplish during the next 12 months?" The answer might include production goals, quality improvement, behavioral changes, and plans for advancement.

In addition to goals directly related to work, team members' future plans may include personal career development plans (such as obtaining additional training on the job or in school), participation in trade or professional societies, and other off-job activities that can enhance a career. Be supportive of these types of goals, and point out what your company can do to help, such as providing tuition reimbursement. But don't make promises for advancement or career growth you can't deliver.

Have team members write down each of their goals, and indicate next to them what they plan to do to achieve them. Give one copy to the team member, and keep one with the performance appraisal form. You can use it as part of the appraisal interview the following year.

Conclude with a Summary and an Action Plan

At the end of an interview, ask the team member to summarize the discussion. Make sure that the person fully understands the positive and negative aspects of her performance and behavior, plans and goals for the next review period, and any other pertinent matters. Keep a written record of these points.

In many companies, team members who disagree with an evaluation are given the opportunity to write a rebuttal to be attached to the appraisal. When salary adjustments are based on ratings, some organizations provide a procedure for appealing a review.

End the interview on a positive note, by saying, "Overall, you've made good progress this year. I'm confident that you'll continue to do good work."

Recording the Review

In most companies the appraisal form is sent to the human resources department to be placed in the employee's personnel file. Some companies require that a copy be sent to the next level of management—the person to whom the team leader reports.

Even if it's not a formal practice in your company, it's a good idea to give a copy of the appraisal to the team member. It serves as a reminder of what was discussed at the appraisal interview and can be referred to during the year. And, as mentioned, if it includes goals the employee and you have agreed on for the year, the employee can reread it from time to time to keep motivated.

Ten Points to Remember When Reviewing Performance

1. Know exactly what you want to achieve. Let your employees know what is expected of them.
2. Keep a record of employee performance from which to cite specific examples.
3. Discuss the written evaluation with the team member.
4. Listen to team member's comments, then ask questions to stimulate thought.
5. Focus on the individual. Do not compare him with other members of the team.
6. Show that you care about employees' performance and their careers.

7. Reinforce good behavior. Be specific in your criticism. Give examples from their performance record. Ask them how they can do even better. Add your own suggestions.

8. Focus on the behavior, not on the person.

9. Don't be afraid to give honest criticism. Most employees want to know where they stand and how to improve.

10. Help team members to set personal goals that are congruent with the goals of the team—and the company—and to develop a plan of action to reach those goals.

The 360° Assessment

Multilevel assessments have become an increasingly popular approach, used to identify how a manager is viewed by his or her bosses, peers, subordinates, and even outsiders (for example, vendors and customers). Usually referred to as 360° assessments, such reviews have been adopted by companies like AT&T, IBM, and other Fortune 500 corporations.

People do not see themselves as others see them. We perceive our actions as rational, our ideas as solid, our decisions as meaningful. Traditionally, performance is evaluated only by one's own manager. This does give us insight into how our work is perceived by that person, but she is not the only person with whom we interact.

Even more complex is the evaluation of senior managers, who frequently are not evaluated at all. When these executives are assessed by peers and subordinates, they may learn things about their management style that they were not aware of. Many are shocked to find out how people perceive them and, as a result, take steps to change their management styles.

Despite the advantages of multilevel assessments, there are also potential drawbacks. Feedback can hurt. Evaluators aren't always nice or positive. Some people see their role as assessor as an opportunity to criticize others' behavior on the job.

Another flaw concerns conflicting opinions. Who decides who is right? Or what if an appraisal is biased? If the evaluator does not like the person being evaluated, the responses might be skewed negatively; if the assessee is a friend, the evaluation might be skewed positively. Often, people rating senior executives fear it is dangerous to be completely truthful.

In order to ensure that the 360° assessment has a better chance of producing a change, it is recommended that:

➤ The appraisal be anonymous and confidential.

➤ To have sufficient knowledge of the person being rated, the appraisers should have worked with the appraisee for at least six months.

➤ Appraisers should give written comments as well as numerical ratings. This enables their evaluations to be more specific and meaningful.

➤ To avoid "survey fatigue," don't use 360° assessments on too many employees at one time.

Turning the Tables: When Your Boss Reviews Your Performance

Performance reviews aren't limited to you assessing your staff. Your own performance is also evaluated by your boss. Now it's you sitting in the hot seat.

Even though you may have undergone many such reviews in your career, it's always a bit disquieting to be in that spot. You feel like a kid sitting in the school principal's office. You may even feel jittery and ill at ease, even though you have a good relationship with your boss. Maybe you're scared, especially if you and your boss have a shaky relationship.

Most people have these kinds of reactions even when they know they have done good work. It is human nature to fear such an important meeting. So much depends on it: your immediate future; whether or not you'll get a raise; the opinion your boss has of your potential. And for sure the boss will have something negative to say.

Here are some tips to help you handle this situation:

➤ **Review your own performance.** Whether or not your company requires employees to make self-evaluations, do it. Take a blank copy of the review form in this chapter and fill it out. This will allow you to think about your performance in the same way your boss does.

➤ **List your accomplishments.** Include all the special things you did over the past year to contribute to the success of the department. Give specifics, such as how much you exceeded quotas, the amount of money one of your suggestions saved the company, tough problems you solved, and so on.

➤ **Consider your deficiencies.** None of us is perfect. You probably did some things that did not work out and have areas in which you know you can do better. Your supervisor is likely to bring this up at the review. Instead of thinking up excuses, point out what you have already done or what you plan to do to improve your skills in those areas.

➤ **At the interview, listen attentively.** Do not interrupt except to ask clarifying questions. Under no circumstances should you disagree or try to rebut a point. Let the supervisor finish before you make any comments.

➤ **Be constructive.** Now is the chance to make your rebuttal. If you have carefully prepared a list of accomplishments and are cognizant of your deficiencies, you are ready to make your points. Start by thanking your supervisor for his or her support over the past year, then say: "I understand what you have told me and I appreciate your frankness. However, there are certain accomplishments of which I am particularly proud and for which you complimented me at the time, which you may not have taken into consideration in the review." Then enumerate the items. If the supervisor focused on some of your deficiencies, don't make excuses for them. Instead, talk about what you are doing to overcome them. Suggest that before the evaluation is made final, these be considered.

➤ **Set goals for the future.** If you had set goals for this year at last year's review, discuss how close you came to reaching them. If, during the year, they changed, discuss the circumstances. Now, discuss your goals for the ensuing year. Get your boss's agreement that these are worthwhile goals and then commit yourself to attain them.

The Least You Need to Know

➤ For every job, set performance standards that are clearly understood and accepted by those who will perform the job.

➤ When team members know what is expected of them, they can monitor their own performance on an ongoing basis.

➤ If you use the trait method to evaluate your staff members, be careful to avoid the dangers of central tendency, the halo and pitchfork effects, personal biases, and an emphasis on most recent behavior.

➤ Results-oriented evaluations measure actual performance against predetermined expectations.

➤ A joint leader/associate evaluation enables both parties to evaluate performance and agree on what can be done to reinforce strengths and build up weaknesses.

➤ An evaluation interview should be an interchange between you and your team member in which you openly discuss accomplishments, areas for improvement, and goals established for the next review period.

➤ Don't fear the performance review. It can be a beneficial and worthwhile experience. You can make it even more valuable to yourself by going into the review prepared to handle it in a constructive manner.

Chapter 22

HELLLO!
EARTH TO FRED!

Dealing with Problem Employees

In This Chapter

➤ Helping people who don't like themselves

➤ Dealing with sensitive, temperamental, and negative team members

➤ Avoiding stress and burnout

➤ Confronting alcohol and drug abuse problems

➤ When the problems are not with your staff, but with peers

➤ Dealing with the boss's relatives

➤ Violence in the workplace

Your team is made up of people—human beings—who bring to their jobs skills, intelligence, and creativity. But people also have idiosyncrasies, attitudes, moods, and problems—and they bring those things to the job. One of the great challenges of being a leader lies in recognizing and dealing with these types of problems so that your department will run smoothly.

Some of the more common problems that leaders must deal with are discussed in this chapter. Among them are helping build up team members' self-confidence so that they'll become better contributors to your team's efforts, overcoming negative thinking, and dealing with sensitive and temperamental people.

You'll also learn how to cope with members who are under stress and those who burn out. In addition, this chapter explores what can be done if team members have AIDS or are facing alcohol and drug abuse.

Meanings & Gleanings

Self-esteem refers to the way you feel about yourself—it's based on the perceptions you have about yourself. If you think of yourself as a success, you will be a success; if you think of yourself as second rate, you will always be second rate—unless you change your self-perception. And it *can* be done.

Building Up Low Self-Esteem

Most people recognize the importance of self-esteem. In one Gallup-Newsweek poll, 89 percent of respondents said that self-esteem was the primary factor that motivated them to work harder to succeed. Sixty-three percent said that spending time and effort to develop self-esteem was a worthwhile endeavor.

Consider the phrase "developing self-esteem." Many people who have had a low opinion of themselves have been able to overcome it by making a commitment to make a change. Sometimes they seek professional help, but often they do it through self-determination: They rewrite the script on which they base their life. As a team leader, you're in a position to help such people develop self-esteem.

People with low self-esteem show it in the way they talk about themselves. They're more likely to complain about their failures than to brag about successes. They rarely express opinions that differ from those of other team members, and when they do, they preface it with an apology. When pressed to express their thoughts or ideas, they start their answers with, "I'm not sure about this" or "I'm probably wrong, but...." They never volunteer to lead a discussion, and they take charge of a project only when the leader assigns it and then they express doubts about their ability to do it properly.

A person's low self-esteem (or worse, self-loathing) unfortunately may have deep psychological roots that stem from childhood. Parents may instill this trait in their children by being overdemanding (for example, if Jason gets a test score of 90 percent and his parents berate him for not getting 100 percent, or if Sarah is a talented pianist but her parents deride her playing because she's not a child prodigy).

Jason and Sarah are likely to write scripts for themselves as failures, doomed always to be inadequate. People whose scripts are based on parental belittlement need professional assistance to overcome it.

As a manager, you can help by focusing on successes, not on failures. Most people don't loathe themselves, but they may have temporary self-esteem slumps and need bolstering. If they don't deal with those slumps, more serious consequences can occur. Most people don't need professional care; they can do it themselves.

Focusing on Success, Not on Failure

Loss of self-esteem stems from failure. All of us have failures and successes in our jobs and in our lives. By focusing on failure, self-esteem deteriorates. Concentrate instead on the successes you have achieved.

One technique involves keeping a success log (see Chapter 18). Enter in this log any accomplishments you're especially proud of—things for which you've been commended. These things prove that you've succeeded in the past and serve as your assurance that you can succeed again.

Esteem-Building Suggestions

In addition to maintaining success logs, you can help team members build self-esteem in other ways:

➤ Give them positive reinforcement for every achievement, and praise for progress made in their work. Equally important, be positive when they come up with a good idea or make meaningful contributions to team discussions and activities. People with low self-esteem need to be continually reminded that you, the team leader, respect them and have confidence in them.

➤ Give them assignments you know they can handle, and provide added training, coaching, and support to ensure that they'll succeed. The taste of success is a surefire way to build self-esteem.

➤ Suggest that they take courses designed to build self-confidence, such as the Dale Carnegie Course or assertiveness training programs. Provide them with inspirational tapes or books.

If, despite these efforts, a person doesn't become more self-confident, professional help may be necessary. Suggest that he see a counselor in your employee assistance program (see Chapter 23).

Secret Weapons

Keep a success log for your team. Enter in it the special achievements of each of your team members and of your team as a whole. Encourage each team member to keep a personal success log. When things don't go well or when you and your team members are feeling low, have everyone reread the log.

Dealing with Sensitive Sam, Temperamental Terry, Negative Nell, and Others

You undoubtedly have some of these people on your team. Every team leader does. They can make your life miserable or make it an ever-changing challenge. You can't ignore these folks—you have to deal with them, so this section gives you some suggestions.

Sensing the Over-Sensitive

No one likes to be criticized, but most people can accept constructive criticism. Some people resent any criticism, though. Whenever you make even the slightest criticism of their work, they pout and get defensive and accuse you of picking on them.

Be gentle with them. Be diplomatic. Begin by praising the parts of assignments that they have done well. Then make some suggestions about how they can do better in unsatisfactory areas.

Kathy's fear of being criticized made her overly cautious in all areas of her work. Rather than risk a slight error, she checks, double-checks, and then rechecks everything she does. This process may minimize her exposure to criticism, but it's so time-consuming that it slows down her entire team. Worse, she stalls in making decisions, claiming that she needs more information. Even after she gets the information, she passes the buck to someone else.

If members of your team behave as Kathy does, follow these guidelines to help them overcome their fears:

➤ Assure them that, because of their excellent knowledge in their field, their work is usually correct the first time and doesn't have to be checked repeatedly.

Communication Breakdown

Don't praise sensitive people *only* as a prelude to criticism. They may have low self-esteem and, therefore, need a great deal of positive reinforcement.

➤ Point out that occasional errors are normal and that they can be caught and corrected later without reflecting on the ability of the person who made the errors.

➤ If you agree that team members need more information before making a decision, guide them toward resources to help them obtain it. If you feel that they have adequate information, insist that they make prompt decisions.

➤ If team members ask you what to do, tell them that it's their decision and to make it quickly.

In most cases, overly sensitive people have the expertise and do make good decisions. They may need your reassurance to help convert their thinking into action.

Tampering with Temper Tantrums

Terry is a good worker, but from time to time he loses his temper and hollers and screams at his co-workers and even at you. He calms down quickly, but his behavior affects the work of your entire team, and it takes a while to get back to normal performance. You've spoken to Terry about his temper several times, but it hasn't helped.

It isn't easy to work in an environment in which people holler and scream, particularly if you're the target. Because the victims of a tirade may be unable to work at full capacity for several hours afterward, this situation cannot be tolerated.

Here are some suggestions for dealing with someone who has temper tantrums:

➤ After the person calms down, have a heart-to-heart talk. Point out that you understand that it's not always easy for someone to control her temper but that such tantrums aren't acceptable in the workplace.

➤ If another outburst occurs, send the person out of the room until he or she can calm down. Let the person know that the next offense will lead to disciplinary action.

➤ Recommend the old adage, "Count to 10 before opening your mouth."

➤ If you have an employee assistance program (see Chapter 23), suggest that the team member see one of its counselors.

Secret Weapons

If the person you're criticizing begins to cry or throw a tantrum, walk out! Say you'll return after he or she calms down. Wait 10 minutes, then try again. Assure the person that this isn't a personal attack but a means of correcting a situation. *Note:* Don't conduct these types of meetings in your office. It's not a good idea to leave an upset person alone in your office—use a conference room instead.

Negating Negativity

Almost every organization has a Negative Nell or Ned. Whenever you're for something, they're against it. They always have a reason that what you want to accomplish just can't be done. They can tear down your team with pessimism.

The reasons for a team member's negativity vary. It may stem from some real or perceived past mistreatment by your company. If that's the case, look into the matter. If the person has justifiable reasons for being negative, try to persuade him that the past is past and to look to the future. If misconceptions are involved, try to clear them up.

Communication Breakdown

In dealing with negative people, acknowledge their arguments and persuade them to work with you to overcome their perceived problems so that the project can move along. Make the person part of the solution rather than an additional problem.

Negativity is often rooted in long-term personality factors that are beyond the ability of any team leader to overcome. In that case, professional help is necessary.

Let's look at some of the problems negative people cause:

➤ **Resistance to change.** Even people with a positive attitude are reluctant to change. It's comfortable to keep doing things the way they've always done them. Positive thinking people can be persuaded to change by presenting logical arguments. Negative people resist change just for the sake of resisting. No argument ever helps. They often do everything they can to sabotage a situation so that the new methods won't work and they can say, "I told you so."

➤ **Impact on team morale.** Just as one rotten apple can spoil a whole barrel, one negative person can destroy the entire team's morale. Because the negativism spreads from one person to another, it's tough to maintain team spirit under these circumstances.

When you present new ideas to negative people, get them to express their objections openly. Tell them, "You bring up some good points, and I appreciate them. As we move into this new program, let's carefully watch for those problems. We must give this new concept a try. Work with me on it, and together we'll iron out the kinks."

Negative Personalities

Opal exudes negativity. It's not what she says—it's how she acts. She takes any suggestion as a personal affront and takes on any new assignment with such reluctance and annoyance that she turns everyone off.

People such as Opal often don't realize how they come across to others. They probably act this way in their personal lives as well as on the job. They're the type of people who don't get along with their families, have few friends, and are forever the dissenters. Have a heart-to-heart talk with these people to let them know how their attitude affects your team's morale. Amazingly, many negative thinking people have no idea that their behavior is disruptive to others. You might suggest that they enroll in a personal improvement program.

Playing "Gotcha"

Have you ever worked with an associate whose greatest joy in life is to catch other people—especially you—making an error?

People who play this game are trying to show their superiority. Because they usually have no original ideas or constructive suggestions, they get their kicks from catching other people's errors, particularly their boss's. They try to embarrass you and make you uncomfortable Don't give them that satisfaction. Make a joke about it ("What a blooper!"), or smile and say "Thanks for calling it to my attention before it caused real problems." If Gotchamongers see that you're not riled by their game, they'll stop and try to get their kicks elsewhere.

Working with Unhappy People

There's likely to be at least one unhappy person on your team. We all experience periods when things go wrong at home or on the job—and it affects the way we do our work and how we interact with other team members. Team leaders should be alert to this likelihood and take the time to chat with the person. Giving a person the opportunity to talk about a problem often alleviates the tension. Even if the problem isn't solved, it clears the air and enables the team member to function normally.

Some people, however, will always be unhappy about something. They often aren't satisfied with work assignments. Even when you comply with their requests and accommodate their complaints, they're not satisfied. They display their unhappiness by being negative. If someone's request for a change in scheduling a vacation is denied, for example, that person may get angry and let it show both overtly and subtly in his attitude.

You can never make everyone happy. Rebuilding the morale of people who believe that they've been treated unfairly takes tact and patience. Team leaders can avoid some unfair situations by making sure—at the time a decision is made—to explain the reasons behind the decision. In the vacation example, you could explain that your company sets up the vacation schedule months in advance and that two other team members are taking their vacations at the same time. Then make it clear that your team can't spare more than one member on vacation at a time. You may even suggest that the unhappy person try to find another team member who will trade vacation time.

If this technique doesn't satisfy your team member, have a heart-to-heart talk with the person. Point out how constant griping and a negative attitude affect other team members. Make reassurances that the person is a valuable member of your team and that it's not always possible to get everything we want. Encourage the person to be mature—to accept disappointments and go on with life.

Meanings & Gleanings

Dr. Hans Selye defines *distress,* or *bad stress,* as the chronic state of anxiety caused by unremitting pressures of job, personal, or societal problems.

Addressing Stress and Burnout

All jobs have their share of stress. If they didn't, they would quickly become boring. It's when *stress* becomes *distress* that problems occur. The stress may show up in the way employees' behavior has changed. People who had always been patient become impatient. Calm people may become tense. Team members who have always been cooperative rebel. All these signs show up when people are under stress. Team members under stress may show physical symptoms or complain that they have trouble falling asleep or in sleeping through the night. They're often tired all the time—even if they do get a good rest. They may have stomach pains, a fast heartbeat, or frequent headaches.

"I'm So Tired I Can't Think Straight!"

Physical fatigue can be cured by rest, but most people are more likely to be mentally not physically fatigued on the job. If your team members work with computers or in other mentally strenuous jobs, remind them that physical exercise can alleviate fatigue and stress. Suggest that they take a lunch-time walk, go swimming or jogging, or participate in a sport after work. Some companies have exercise rooms in which employees can use a stationary bike or a weight machine during their lunch hour. People who have a regular regimen are less likely to become mentally fatigued.

Burnout

People are not light bulbs. A light bulb shines brightly and suddenly—poof! It burns out. People burn out slowly and often imperceptibly. Although some burnouts result in physical breakdowns such as a heart attack or ulcers, most are psychological. Team members lose enthusiasm, energy, and motivation, and it shows up in many ways. They hate their job, can't stand co-workers, distrust the team leader, and dread coming to work each morning.

Burnout can be caused by too much stress, but that's not the only cause. It can also be a result of frustration: Promises made weren't kept or an employee was passed over for an expected promotion or salary increase. Some leaders and managers burn out because of the pressures of having to make decisions that, if made poorly, can cause catastrophic problems. Others just burn out from having to work excessively long hours or do unrewarding work.

Often the only means of helping someone recover from burnout is to suggest professional help (see Chapter 23). There are some things you can do, however, to help put a burned-out team member on the road to recovery:

Communication Breakdown

If a team member is constantly fatigued from work, suggest that she see a physician for a thorough medical examination and for suggestions to relieve fatigue and stress.

➤ **Be a supportive person.** Demonstrate your sincere interest by encouraging the person to talk about and assess her concerns and put them into perspective.

➤ **Consider changing job functions.** Assigning different activities and responsibilities or transferring the person to another team changes the climate in which she works and provides new outlets that may stimulate motivation.

➤ **Give the team member an opportunity to acquire new skills.** This not only helps him focus on learning rather than on the matters that led to the burnout but also makes the person more valuable to your company.

If, despite your efforts, he doesn't progress, strongly suggest professional counseling.

Plowing into Pressure

When pressure on a job becomes so great that you feel like you're going to break down, follow these suggestions:

➤ **Take a break.** If possible, get away from your workplace—get out of the building. If you work in a city, take a walk around the block. If you work in an industrial park, walk around the parking lot. If the weather is bad, walk around inside the building. In 10 or 15 minutes, you'll feel the stress dissolve and be able to face your job with renewed energy.

➤ **Exercise.** If you work in a crowded office, it's obviously not expedient to get up in the middle of the room and do jumping jacks or push-ups, but you can choose from several relaxation exercises without being obtrusive. Books and videotapes are available to show you how. If your company has an exercise room, get on the treadmill for five minutes (not enough to work up a sweat, but enough to relax your mind).

➤ **Change your pace.** Most people work on more than one project at a time. If the pressures are too great on your current project, stop for a while and work on another one. When you return to your original assignment, it will go much more smoothly.

When There's Too Darn Much Work to Do

Your team has survived downsizing and reorganization. You now have fewer members, and each of them is working longer and harder. Your boss is piling more and more work on you, and your team just can't handle it. Because there's a limit to any group's time and energy, you decide that you have to speak to your boss.

Before you approach your manager, thoroughly analyze the jobs your team is doing. Indicate how much time team members devote to each project, and determine each project's importance to the accomplishment of your team's goals. Reexamine your boss's priorities. Decide with your team what they can do to work smarter rather than harder.

If you still feel after this analysis that your team has more work than it can handle effectively, meet with your boss to review its results and try to reorder your team's priorities. Your boss may agree to defer certain time-consuming jobs because others are more important; reassign some jobs to other groups; or authorize additional personnel.

Secret Weapons

Learn to say "no." When you're asked to take on a special assignment that won't help you meet your goals, decline diplomatically. Explain that you realize it's an important project but that you're already involved with several high-priority assignments and, as much as you want to help, you just can't.

Don't let other teams push your team around. Sometimes pressure comes from other teams or departments with whom you're collaborating. You and the leader of the other team should try to work out a schedule that alleviates the pressure. If you can't agree, take it up with the manager who supervises both teams.

Sometimes the pressure results from you or members of the team volunteering for special projects. Learn to say "no." Keep team members aware of your team's priorities, and point out that it's not an indicator of laziness or unwillingness to cooperate if they reject requests to volunteer for special projects outside the team's activities.

Managing Stress

Although some physicians treat stress with tranquilizers and other medication, unless you're under extreme pressure, you can take other steps to help manage your own stress:

➤ **Keep in tiptop shape.** Watch your diet, and engage in a regular exercise program.

➤ **Learn to relax.** Participate in deep meditation or programmed relaxation exercises. Be sure to reserve time to spend alone.

➤ **Learn to love yourself.** People with high self-esteem are less likely to be adversely affected by pressure from others.

➤ **Explore your spirituality.** Whatever your religion, spiritual experience can guide you toward peace of mind.

➤ **Keep learning.** The experience of ongoing learning keeps you alert, open-minded, and stimulated.

➤ **Develop a support team.** Avoid major stress by having friends and family members available to back you up when things don't go well.

➤ **Accept only commitments that are important to you.** Politely turn down other projects that drain your time and energy.

➤ **Seek new ways of using your creativity.** By rethinking the way you perform routine tasks, you make them less boring and stressful. By developing creative approaches to new assignments, you make them less stressful to handle.

➤ **Welcome changes.** Consider them new challenges rather than threats to the status quo.

➤ **Replace negative images in your mind with positive ones.**

Some Jobs Are Boring—Most Can Become Boring

Some jobs are basically boring, but any job can become boring when you do it over and over again, day after day, year after year. In many companies, jobs are enriched to minimize boredom. By adding new functions and combining several simple tasks into a more challenging total activity, jobs can be made less boring.

To prevent your team members' jobs from becoming boring:

➤ Reexamine all routine work that your team performs. Encourage all people who perform the work to suggest ways of making it more interesting.

➤ People performing routine work often get into a rut. They start out every day performing aspect 1, and then go to aspect 2 and 3, and so on. Unless it's essential that work be done in a predetermined order, suggest that they change the pattern. Start one day with aspect 6, and then go to 3 or 7 or 1. Breaking the routine alleviates boredom.

➤ Cross train team members to do a variety of jobs so that they can move from one type of work to another and be less likely to become bored.

Communication Breakdown

If you send drunk people home, don't let them drive. If they get into an accident, you or your company may share liability. Don't ask another employee to drive the person home. Call a taxi.

Dealing with Alcohol and Drug Problems

Suppose one of your team members seems to have an alcohol problem. You've never seen the person drink or come to work drunk, but you often smell alcohol on the person's breath. He is frequently absent, especially on Mondays.

You can't ignore this situation. Speak to the team member about it, and prepare to hear all sorts of denials: "Me, drink? Only socially." Or, "Alcohol breath? It's cough medicine."

Rather than talk about a drinking problem, talk about job performance, absence from work, and other job-related matters. Inform the person that if the situation continues, you'll have to take disciplinary action.

If your team member continues this behavior pattern, bring up your concern about the drinking and suggest—or insist on—counseling.

Discussing Alcohol Problems

It isn't easy to discuss with a team member such a sensitive and personal matter as an alcohol problem. The U.S. Department of Health and Human Services suggests the following approach, in its pamphlet "Supervisor's Guide on Alcohol Abuse":

➤ **Don't apologize for discussing the matter.** Make it clear that job performance is involved.

➤ **Encourage your team member to explain why work performance, behavior, or attendance is deteriorating.** This approach may provide an opportunity to discuss the use of alcohol.

➤ **Don't discuss a person's right to drink or make a moral issue of it.** Alcoholism is a disease that, left untreated, can lead to many more serious illnesses.

➤ **Don't suggest that your team member use moderation or change drinking habits.** According to Alcoholics Anonymous, alcoholics cannot change their drinking habits without help. It's up to them to make the decision to stop drinking and take steps to get that help.

➤ **Don't be distracted by excuses for drinking.** The problem as far as you're concerned is the drinking itself—and how it affects work, behavior, and attendance on the job.

➤ **Remember that alcoholics, like any other sick people, should be given the opportunity for treatment and rehabilitation.**

➤ **Emphasize that your primary concern is the team member's work performance.** Point out that if the person's behavior doesn't improve, you'll have to take disciplinary action, including suspension or discharge.

➤ **Point out that the decision to seek assistance is the team member's responsibility.**

If your company has an employee assistance program (see Chapter 23), describe it and strongly recommend that it be used.

> **ZAP!**
>
> **Secret Weapons**
>
> To prevent any misunderstandings or ambiguities, every company should have a formal policy prohibiting drinking on company premises or during working hours. This policy should be in writing and reviewed periodically with all employees. Restrictions should specifically include beer and wine in addition to "hard" liquor.

Preventing Drinking and Drug Use on the Job

In most companies, showing up at work drunk or drinking on the job is a punishable offense. But it's not always easy to prove that a person is drunk. Appearing to be drunk isn't enough. Even a police officer cannot arrest a suspect for driving while intoxicated, unless he or she substantiates the claim with a breath or blood test.

If one of your employees seems to be drunk, your safest course is to send the person to your medical department for testing. If that's not possible, don't allow the person to work—send her home. The next day, discuss the situation and point out that if it occurs again, you'll take disciplinary action. Also, make sure to suggest counseling.

Although drug use on the job has increased, it isn't nearly as common as drinking. Treat drug users in the same way you deal with drinkers. Because drug use (and particularly the sale of drugs) is illegal, however, you should consult your attorney about the best ways to handle this situation.

Testing for the use of drugs is becoming an increasingly routine practice in many companies. A 1993 survey of more than 3,500 companies showed that 48 percent test job applicants and 43 percent periodically test employees. Although some companies do conduct random drug tests, most of them test employees only when they suspect drug use.

The ADA (Americans with Disabilities Act) includes alcoholism and drug addiction as disabilities (see Chapter 11).

HIV/AIDS in the Workplace

Despite all the articles and TV programs that make clear that HIV is spread primarily through semen and blood, many people still have an unreasonable fear of even casual contact with a person who has the virus.

When it becomes known that an employee of a company has HIV or AIDS, many co-workers refuse to work with that person. If the person with AIDS is on your team or works in conjunction with it, this attitude can disrupt your team's activities.

To avoid these situations, companies have instituted programs to inform employees of the true facts about the virus and the disease. HIV/AIDS-awareness programs include videos, pamphlets, articles in the company newspaper, and talks to employees by doctors.

Manager's Minute

You can obtain literature about HIV/AIDS and information about awareness programs from your local health department or from the CDC National AIDS Clearing House at (800) 458-5231.

"It's Not My Staff—It's My Peers"

You get along fine with your boss. You and your team members have a great relationship. But you keep running into conflicts and problems with one or more of your peers—other team leaders or staff managers. Why?

There could be dozens of reasons. First look into yourself. Is it you or them who cause the problem? It's not easy to be introspective, but try to be honest with yourself. If you don't get along with many people, it may be something that you are doing or thinking that causes it. You may be stubborn and insist on doing things your way. You may come across as arrogant or domineering and you are not aware of it. So evaluate yourself. Ask friends or associates to help you with this.

On the other hand, if you get along fine with most people but have problems with one or a few, the difficulties are more likely their fault. Look for the cause if you can. Maybe they're the kind of people who can't get along with anyone. Maybe their goals and agenda differ from yours. Here are a couple of explanations:

➤ **Competition:** The other person may look upon you as a competitor for advancement in the company and consciously or subconsciously fears cooperating with you.

➤ **Jealousy:** He resents your position or accomplishments.

There is not much you can do about your peers' personality problems. These people need professional help. They rarely succeed in their jobs and unless they are experts in a hard-to-replace technical job, they won't be around for long.

As for problems stemming from competition or jealousy, you can deal with them diplomatically. Remember you need to gain the cooperation of even competitive or jealous people to accomplish any project in which both of you are collaborating.

Don't Command Them—Sell Them Instead

Follow the principles of good salesmanship when you deal with peers who are reluctant to cooperate.

1. **Gain their attention.** When presenting an idea they may resist, make a comment that will get them to sit up and take notice. Everybody likes compliments. So compliment them on something they accomplished that you truly admired. You now have their attention.

2. **Ask questions.** Find out what excites the other person about the situation that is involved. Instead of presenting your idea, ask questions. Listen to their responses. Most people are so anxious to "sell" their ideas that they do not fully listen to what the "buyer" really wants. Do not presuppose that his interests are identical to yours. You may want to emphasize the cost savings your idea will engender, but your colleague may be much more excited about the creative potential it provides. You won't know this unless you listen.

3. **Present evidence.** Develop considerable evidence to back up the ideas you want to sell. Once you learn what the other person really wants, you can tailor your evidence to that person's desires.

4. **Be prepared to deal with objections.** If you have had previous dealings with that person, you may anticipate what objections may be raised and be ready to counter them. Your questions will uncover others. Learning the objections is the best way to know where the real problems lie.

5. **Close the sale.** Get the other person to agree to a plan of action that you both feel will get the job done. Ask her to summarize it so you are sure that there is a clear understanding.

Dealing with the Boss's Relatives

Have you ever worked for a company in which the boss placed his relatives in key positions? Well, sometimes these men and women are real contributors, but often they are incompetent or worse. Some business owners do feel an obligation to hire relatives, even when they know they are incompetent, but smart managers place them in positions where they can do minimal harm.

I've seen dim-witted daughters, brazen brothers, nutty nephews, crazy cousins, and incompetent in-laws in positions that they handled poorly and, even worse, that led them to derail the good work of competent staff members.

Meanings & Gleanings

The Einstein Theory of Advancement: Relativity. If you're a relative of the boss, you get the promotion.

In one company, the boss's brother had only one agenda—to keep costs down. He had veto power over all purchases and never approved anything that wasn't, in his opinion, absolutely necessary. If a clerk wanted a pencil, he had to show that the stub of the one he was using was less than two inches long. To obtain approval of major expenditures, people always had to go over his head to the boss.

In another company, the boss's daughter held a variety of jobs. She not only messed up the jobs but would cry on her daddy's shoulder if her supervisors criticized her. Rather than lose some of his top producers, the boss transferred her to another department—where, of course, the same thing occurred.

What can you do when faced with this nepotism? Here are some suggestions.

➤ **Make an honest effort to smooth the relationship.** Be diplomatic. Be patient. Try to persuade the relative to see things your way. Let her think that what you want is really her idea.

➤ **If that fails, have a heart-to-heart talk with the boss.** Let her know what the specific problems are and suggest solutions that are in the best interest of the company.

➤ **Find ways to bypass the relative.** For example, in dealing with the penny pinching brother, sell the boss on the value of your idea before you even bring it up to the brother.

➤ **Be prepared to defend your stand.** The boss may favor relatives, but the success of the business comes first. Have the pertinent facts and figures to back you up.

➤ **Last resort: Draw the line** (not to be used unless you are confident that you'll win). Point out that unless the relative ceases to interfere, you cannot do the job you have been assigned to do. This may be interpreted as an ultimatum, and it may force you to quit if not accepted. But, if the boss is objective about it, you may win your point.

Workplace Violence—A Growing Menace

Workplace violence is the second leading cause of death in the workplace. Three people in America are murdered on the job every working day. Although the rate of homicides has decreased in recent years, the rate of violent assaults has increased. Reasons that workplace violence occurs include:

➤ **Economic.** Corporate downsizing and layoffs cause unrest in the company.

➤ **Societal.** Drugs, alcohol, availability of guns, fractured families.

➤ **Psychological.** Personal breakdowns of individuals due to serious problems in their lives.

➤ **Organizational culture.** Over-stressed work force; pressure of the job.

➤ **Workplace climate.** Some workplace environments have the seeds of violence built into them—just waiting for a chance to explode. Some of these are:

    ➤ Authoritarian management style

    ➤ Unpredictable supervisory methods

    ➤ Undervalued work and dignity of people

    ➤ High degree of secrecy (not sharing information)

    ➤ Disproportionate discipline

    ➤ Bias against and favoritism toward some employees

    ➤ Strained labor/management relations

In recent years, post offices have drawn much public scrutiny for seeming to breed workplace violence. The actual incidence of such violent acts at post offices, however, is well below average. As a matter of fact, the U.S. Postal Service has taken special steps to provide a safe working environment for its employees.

A six-step procedure, emulated by many private sector companies, has been established to strategize prevention of violence in the postal service:

➤ **Selection.** Hire the right people for the right job in the first place. By carefully selecting and placing new employees, you greatly minimize the risk of their ever becoming discontent.

➤ **Security.** Ensure appropriate safeguards for people and property.

➤ **Communication of policy.** The policies of appropriate behavior on the job should be clearly established and communicated to all employees at all levels of the organization. Employees should fully understand what constitutes acceptable and unacceptable behavior. And management should reinforce its policy: All employees should be aware of the penalties of violation.

➤ **Environment and culture.** Create a work environment and maintain a climate that is perceived as fair and free of unlawful and inappropriate behaviors.

➤ **Establishment of resources.** Ensure that managers, supervisors, and employees are aware of the available resources to assist them in dealing with the problems of work and daily living. Employee assistance programs should be set up and be easily accessible to all employees.

Secret Weapons

Prevent trouble by rapid redress of disputes:

Resolve

Employment

Disputes

Reach

Equitable

Solutions

Swiftly

➤ **Separation.** When separation is necessary, the process should be handled professionally. Managers should assess the possibility of inappropriate behavior or potential violence and confer with specially trained people to figure out how to handle the situation.

Before a worker is ever handed a pink slip, the service makes sure the employee receives a threat assessment interview to assess any inappropriate behavior and/or potentially violent circumstances. A union representative is called in to outline the reasons termination is necessary. Often, they will agree and will explain to the worker why they will not represent them in a protest of the firing.

In addition, company-paid career counseling sessions can go a long way in creating goodwill and a peaceful parting. Follow-up security by an outside firm can also be helpful.

To implement this strategy, workplace violence awareness programs have been instituted for Postal Service managers, supervisors, and union leaders. In these programs, they are taught to use the skills and techniques that foster professional interactions with employees.

The Least You Need to Know

➤ Build up team members' self-esteem by helping them to focus on their successes—not on their failures.

➤ When you discuss a team member's work and she is sensitive, be gentle, tactful, and positive.

➤ When you present new concepts to negative people, let them express their reservations and then get them to help develop solutions.

➤ Help your team (and yourself) alleviate mental fatigue by following a regimen of physical activity before, after, and even during working hours.

➤ When team members are overcome by the pressures of the job, suggest that they take a walk, do relaxation exercises, or shift to a different project. The tension will ease, their minds will clear, and they'll work more effectively.

➤ If an employee has an alcohol or drug abuse problem, don't ignore it. Discuss how it affects that person's work and the work of your entire team. Suggest counseling (if necessary, insist on it).

➤ The best way to deal with problems with peers is to use diplomacy and salesmanship to persuade the person to your way of thinking.

➤ To minimize the risks of violence in the workplace, develop a program to sensitize supervisors and workers to identify and deal with potential problems.

Chapter 23

The Manager as a Counselor

In This Chapter

➤ Knowing when counseling is appropriate

➤ Handling gripes, complaints, and grievances

➤ Resolving conflicts

➤ Understanding the counseling process

➤ Working with employee assistance programs

It takes the coordinated effort of all team members to keep your team operating at optimum capacity. It takes only one member of the team who isn't functioning effectively to prevent your team from achieving its objectives. As coach of the team, you must identify problems in their early stages and correct the situation before it mushrooms into a major problem. Your tool: Counseling.

Counseling is a means of helping troubled associates overcome barriers to good performance. By careful listening, open discussion, and sound advice, a counselor helps identify problems, clarify misunderstandings, and plan solutions.

When a team leader "counsels" an associate, it's more analogous to a coach of an athletic team counseling a player than to a psychotherapist counseling a patient. Professional counseling should be done by trained specialists, and, as you will learn in this chapter, sometimes referrals to these specialists are necessary.

Handling Gripes and Grievances

Sometimes you see a problem; sometimes you don't. You find out only when someone complains. A complaint may be your first hint of an impending problem, a reminder of an ongoing situation that hasn't been attended to, or it may just be one of your associates letting off steam. But you don't know until you check it out. This section addresses how you can best work through gripes and grievances with your team members.

Communication Breakdown

As tempting as it may be to threaten to fire uncooperative team members, don't do it unless you really can carry it out. Most union contracts make the process for firing employees complex. Sometimes company policies, EEO implications, or other factors restrict these actions.

Dealing with Chronic Complainers

You know your team members. Some of them are always complaining. They gripe about the temperature in the room. They gripe about the work they're assigned. They gripe about everything you tell them. You've heard these same complaints over and over again.

These types of people work in every company. They get their kicks from complaining. Sometimes they do have legitimate complaints, of course, so you can't just automatically ignore them. You have to listen—and that can be time-consuming and annoying.

One way to minimize this kind of griping is to pay more attention to the people who complain. The reason for the complaints is often their desire to be the center of attention. By talking to them, asking their opinions, and praising their good work, you satisfy their need for attention and give them less reason to gripe.

Checking Out Complaints

Most complaints are signals to you that shouldn't be ignored. Even if a complaint seems to have no validity, check it out anyway. You don't always have all the information, and you may discover facets of the situation you weren't aware of.

Follow these steps to find out what's going on:

1. **Listen.** Even if a complaint seems to be unfounded, in the mind of the complainant it's a serious matter.

2. **Investigate.** Take nothing for granted. Look at the record, and talk to others who know about the situation.

Meanings & Gleanings

A *gripe* is an informal complaint. A *grievance* is a formal complaint, usually based on the violation of a union contract or formal company policy.

3. **Report back.** If the gripe is unfounded, explain your reasoning to the complainant. If it *is* substantiated, explain what you will do to correct it.

4. **Take action.** Do what must be done to correct the problem.

What Happens When You Don't Have the Authority to Correct a Problem

Suppose a complainer is correct: Your investigation verifies that the complaint is justified, but you can't do anything about it. Find out who can. Bring the situation to the attention of your boss or whoever can adjust it.

Diana was frustrated. When she described to her boss, Charles, a problem her team members were having, he promised to rectify it but never did.

Diana's reminders were rebuffed. She was concerned about not only having to continue to work with this unsatisfactory situation but also losing the respect of her team members. She discussed the situation with Elizabeth, a manager who had been her mentor earlier in her career.

Elizabeth's advice: "Let Charles know how important it is to your team to have someone listen to their complaints and consider them seriously. Remind Charles that you deal with every problem over which you have authority, but that this one is out of your jurisdiction. Point out that you screen all complaints and don't pass on the ones that aren't justified. If there's a reason that action has not or cannot be taken, you want to know so that you can pass on the information to your team. Tell him that they're reasonable people who understand that they can't get everything they want, but that they expect that their complaints will be taken seriously. Then let your associates know what action you're taking and what results from it."

Filing Formal Grievances

When a company has a union contract, the procedures for handling grievances are clearly outlined. Companies that don't have union agreements often set up their own procedures for dealing with employee grievances.

Here's a typical four-step approach:

1. The person making the complaint discusses it with his or her immediate supervisor or team leader. Every attempt to resolve the problem should be made at this level.

2. If no settlement is reached, the individual should be given an opportunity to bring the problem to the next level of management without fear of reprisal.

Communication Breakdown

If no complaints are called to the management's attention, it doesn't necessarily mean that there aren't any. It may mean that communication is blocked. If no one attends to grievances and gripes, they fester in the minds of the aggrieved and burst out sooner or later in low morale. Keep those channels open.

3. If the complaint is still unresolved, it may go to the general manager or a specially appointed manager (often the human resources director). An agreement is usually reached during this stage.

4. Although arbitration is rare in a non-union environment, management in some companies provides for a mutually agreed upon third party to be available if the company and the aggrieved person cannot work out their problem.

As the immediate supervisor or team leader, you play the key role in this process. You should make every effort to resolve grievances without having to go beyond step 1. Grievance procedures take time and energy that would be better spent doing your team's primary work. To help you deal with a grievance systematically, use the following sample grievance worksheet.

Grievance Worksheet

Complainant: _____ Date: _____

Team leader: _____

Grievance: _____
_____
_____
_____

Report of investigation: _____
_____
_____
_____

If justified, action taken: _____
_____
_____

If not justified, reason: _____
_____
_____

Date reported to complainant: _____

Complainant's comments: _____
_____
_____

Team leader's comments: _____
_____
_____

Preventing Grievances

Dealing with grievances is time-consuming and takes you away from more productive work. This section provides some suggestions for preventing grievances from developing on your team:

➤ Regularly let all team members know how they're doing. People want feedback on not only their failures but also their successes.

➤ Encourage team members to participate in all aspects of planning and performing the team's work.

➤ Listen to team members' ideas.

➤ Make only promises that you know you can keep.

➤ Be alert to minor irritations and trivial problems so that you can correct them before they become serious dissatisfactions.

➤ Resolve problems as soon as possible.

Resolving Conflicts Within Your Team

Two types of conflicts occur when people work together. One is tangible (a disagreement about a project, for example), and the other is intangible (two people just don't like each other, for example, and can't get along). In this section, you'll learn some techniques for managing both types of conflicts.

Suppose you give an assignment to two of your team members, Ken and Barbie. They discuss the project and cannot agree about how it should be pursued. They both come back to you, their team leader, to resolve the problem.

You can use one of two approaches: arbitrate or mediate.

> **Meanings & Gleanings**
>
> In *arbitration*, both parties present their side of a problem and an arbitrator decides what should be done. In *mediation*, both parties present their side of a problem and a mediator works with them to reach a mutually satisfactory solution.

Mediating Disagreements

Mediation is the preferred approach because it's more likely to result in a win-win compromise. The most negative effect of using mediation is that it's time-consuming (and you often don't have much time to solve a problem).

Suppose you have chosen to mediate the disagreement between Ken and Barbie. To make a mediated conflict resolution work, all parties involved must be fully aware of the procedure to be followed. *Unless all parties have a clear understanding of the approach, it cannot succeed.*

First, Barbie tells how she views the situation. You might think that the next step is for Ken to state his side—but it isn't. Instead, Ken is asked to state Barbie's view as he understands it.

The reason for this step is that when the first party explains his view to the other party, the other person typically only partly listens. That person may be thinking about what she plans to say and how to rebut the argument. By being aware of having to repeat the first person's views, that person becomes aware of having to listen carefully.

By having the second person repeat the first person's side of the story, any areas of misunderstanding can be clarified before the second person presents her views. It's amazing how often conflicts are caused by these types of misunderstandings. The same process is then followed with the second person stating her views.

During this discussion, you (as the mediator) take notes. After each person presents his views, you review your notes with the participants. You might say, "As I view this, you both agree on 80 percent of the project. Now let's list the areas in which you disagree." Most disputes have many more areas of agreement than disagreement. By identifying these areas, you can focus on matters that must be resolved and tackle them one at a time.

Because you don't have an unlimited amount of time, you must set a time limit on these meetings. Suppose you've set aside two hours for the first meeting. At the end of the specified time, you still have several more items to discuss. Set up another meeting for that purpose. Suggest that the participants meet in the interim without you to work on some of the problems. Often, after a climate of compromise is established, a large number of issues can be resolved without your presence.

Now the next meeting is scheduled for one hour, and more problems are resolved. If the project must get under way, this may be all the time you have. If some unresolved problems still exist, you have to change your role from mediator to arbitrator and make the decisions.

Secret Weapons

In explaining why you made a decision, treat your associates as adults. It's childish to say, "I'm the boss, and this is what I've decided." Let team members know the reason behind decisions, and clarify misunderstandings before implementing a decision.

Time to Arbitrate

The following five steps can help you arbitrate a conflict, if you choose to deal with it in that way:

1. **Get the facts.** Listen carefully to both sides. Investigate on your own to get additional information. Don't limit yourself to "hard facts." Learn about underlying feelings and emotions.

2. **Evaluate the facts.**

3. **Study the alternatives.** Are the solutions suggested by the two parties the only possible choices? Can compromises be made? Is a different resolution possible?

4. **Make a decision.**

5. **Notify the two parties of your decision.** Make sure that they fully understand it. If necessary, "sell" it to them so that they will agree and be committed to implementing it.

When Team Members Can't Get Along

If two people on your team dislike each other so much that it affects their work, you have to do something about it. First find out why the two people dislike each other. This type of animosity often stems from a past bitter conflict. In the rough and tumble of competition for advancement in many organizations, some people stab others in the back to gain an advantage. It's unlikely that you'll ever be able to get them to work together in harmony, however, because a deep-seated antagonism taints their every contact with each other.

If at all possible, transfer one or both parties to different departments that have little contact with each other. That option isn't always feasible; because there may not be any other departments in which they can use their skills, you have to take steps to overcome this situation.

Speak to each person. If your attempts to persuade them to cooperate fail, lay down the law: "If this team is to succeed, all its members must work together. What happened in the past is past. Write it off. I'm not asking you to like each other. I don't care if you never associate with each other off the job. I'm demanding that you work together to meet our goals." If necessary, follow up this directive with disciplinary action.

Often the reason for the dislike isn't based on any specific factor. It happens to all of us: You meet a person and something about him or her turns you off and you immediately dislike that person.

Suppose you introduce your new team member, Jack, to Rachel. Rachel's first reaction is, "I don't like him," and it carries over into their working relationship.

Psychologists say that this reaction occurs because something about this person subconsciously reminds the other of some unpleasant past experience. Something about Jack (his haircut, the manner in which he speaks, a mole on his left cheek) reminds Rachel of a third grade bully who made life miserable for her that year—and she hates him. These factors, called *minimal cues*, trigger long forgotten subconscious memories that still influence our reactions to people.

Communication Breakdown

Don't give advice about serious personal matters. You're not a trained psychologist. Listen! Help put the problem into perspective. Provide or suggest sources for additional information. Help associates clarify a situation and come to their own conclusions.

When you notice that team members have an unexplainable dislike for other members, tell them about minimal cues. Help them understand that their reactions are normal, but that it's important not to let these reactions influence their attitudes toward other people. Awareness of the psychology underlying this feeling will help overcome a person's irrational attitude.

"I'm Not Ann Landers"

Counseling about employee performance was discussed in Chapter 21, and counseling about gripes and grievances was covered earlier in this chapter. Another area in which supervisors counsel their associates concerns personal matters that may affect employees' work.

All of us have personal problems. We worry about our health, about our families, and about money. We always have something to worry about. People carry their worries with them into the workplace, and worries do affect their work.

You may be reluctant to pry into an associate's personal life—and many people resent prying. Sometimes, however, it's necessary. It's much easier if you and your team members have good personal relationships and if you've always shown interest in the members as individuals. Counseling is a natural follow-through on your usual interest.

If you have this type of relationship, begin the discussion by commenting about job-related matters. Ask a question about the project that's involved, for example. It may lead into a discussion of the problems the person is having with the project, which may be caused by personal matters.

Be an empathetic listener. Your role as counselor is to give team members an opportunity to unload their problems. Encourage them by asking questions. Don't criticize, argue a point, or make a judgment. Act as a sounding board to help release the pressures that are causing the problem. Help the person clarify the situation so that the solution will be easier to reach.

Counseling isn't a cure-all. There are many areas in which you just can't help. When a problem is one you can help by just talking it out, your intervention can be useful. Don't lose patience or give up too easily. Often, more than one session is necessary to build a sense of trust and to get a team member to open up.

ZAP!

Secret Weapons

When you have to work with someone you dislike, make an effort to find something you *can* like about the person: job skills, sense of humor, or a personality trait, for example. Focus on the good point(s). You'll soon forget the intangible factor that generated your dislike.

Knowing What to Do When Talking Doesn't Help

When job problems are caused by alcoholism or drug addiction, there's little you can do other than encourage or even insist on appropriate programs (refer to Chapter 22).

When the real cause stems from deep-seated emotional factors, professional help is necessary.

You may be reluctant or even embarrassed to suggest that a team member see a professional counselor. Many people take umbrage at this suggestion: "Do you think I'm nuts?" Point out that going to a professional counselor is now as accepted as going to a medical doctor. Young people are exposed to counseling beginning in elementary school. The most frequently given advice offered by Ann Landers, Dear Abby, and other advice columnists is to seek counseling when faced with serious problems.

Not all problems that require professional assistance are psychological. They may be caused by a medical condition or serious financial troubles. Often they're marital or family situations.

If your company has an EAP (employee assistance program), making a referral to it immediately relieves you of the burden of suggesting specific counseling (see the following section). If not, your human resources department may help provide referrals. You may find it helpful to research the available sources of help in your community:

Communication Breakdown

When you refer someone for professional help, avoid using the terms "psychiatrist," "psychologist," or "therapist"—they have negative connotations to most people. Tell a troubled person that she might benefit from seeing a counselor who specializes in a particular area. Back up your advice by explaining how counseling has helped other people.

➤ **Medical doctors:** If a company doesn't have its own medical department or an employee doesn't have a primary care physician, local hospitals or medical societies can provide a list of qualified physicians.

➤ **Psychiatrists:** These M.D.s deal with serious psychological disorders.

➤ **Psychologists or psychotherapists:** These specialists usually have a degree in psychology or social work and handle most of the usual emotional problems people face.

➤ **Marriage counselors and family therapists:** These professionals deal with marital problems, difficulties with children, and related matters. Obtain from your local family service association or mental health association the names of qualified psychologists, psychiatrists, or marriage and family therapists in your area.

➤ **Financial counselors:** These people help others work out payment plans with creditors, develop budgets, and live within their income. Your bank or credit union can provide referrals.

Employee Assistance Programs (EAPs)

An employee assistance program, or EAP, is a company-sponsored counseling service. Many companies have instituted these programs to help employees deal with personal problems that interfere with productivity. The counselors aren't company employees, but instead are outside experts retained on an as-needed basis. Initiating the use of the EAP can be done in two ways, which are discussed in this section.

Sometimes an employee takes the initiative in contacting the company's EAP. The company informs its employees about the program through e-mail, bulletins, announcements in the company newspaper, meetings, and letters to their homes. Often a hotline telephone number is provided.

Gerty believes that she needs help. Constant squabbling with her teenage daughter has made her tense, angry, and frustrated. In a brief telephone interview with her company's EAP, the screening counselor identifies Gerty's problem and refers her to a family counselor. Gerty makes her own appointment on her own time (not during working hours—EAPs are not an excuse for taking time off the job). Because the entire procedure is confidential, no report is made to the company about the counseling (in most cases, not even the names of people who undertake counseling are divulged).

Another way to start the process is by having a supervisor take the initiative to contact the EAP. Suppose the work performance of one of your top performers has recently declined. You often see him sitting idly at his desk, his thoughts obviously far from his job. You ask him what's going on, but he shrugs off your question by saying, "I'm okay—just tired."

After several conversations, he finally tells you about a family problem, and you suggest that he contact your company's EAP.

Even though you've made the referral and the employee has followed through, don't expect progress reports. From now on, the matter is handled confidentially. Your feedback comes from seeing improvement in the employee's work as the counseling helps with the problem.

Manager's Minute

EAPs aren't new. They began in the 1940s as alcohol rehabilitation programs. People who couldn't perform their job duties because of a drinking problem were usually fired. Companies that often had invested large amounts of money in developing employees' skills started these programs to protect their large investments.

Employee assistance programs are expensive to maintain, but organizations that have used them for several years report that they pay off. EAPs salvage skilled and experienced workers who, without help, may leave a company.

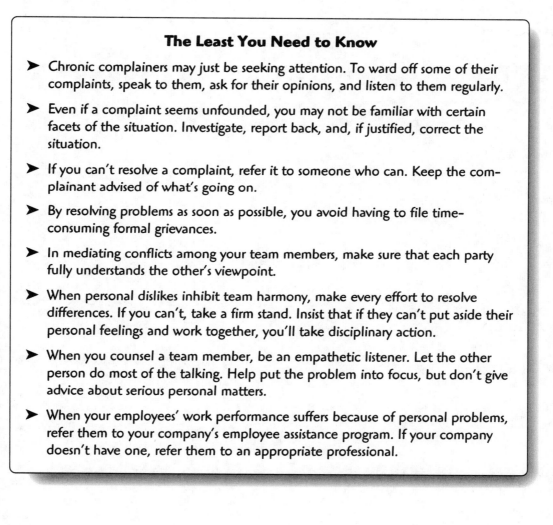

The Least You Need to Know

➤ Chronic complainers may just be seeking attention. To ward off some of their complaints, speak to them, ask for their opinions, and listen to them regularly.

➤ Even if a complaint seems unfounded, you may not be familiar with certain facets of the situation. Investigate, report back, and, if justified, correct the situation.

➤ If you can't resolve a complaint, refer it to someone who can. Keep the complainant advised of what's going on.

➤ By resolving problems as soon as possible, you avoid having to file time-consuming formal grievances.

➤ In mediating conflicts among your team members, make sure that each party fully understands the other's viewpoint.

➤ When personal dislikes inhibit team harmony, make every effort to resolve differences. If you can't, take a firm stand. Insist that if they can't put aside their personal feelings and work together, you'll take disciplinary action.

➤ When you counsel a team member, be an empathetic listener. Let the other person do most of the talking. Help put the problem into focus, but don't give advice about serious personal matters.

➤ When your employees' work performance suffers because of personal problems, refer them to your company's employee assistance program. If your company doesn't have one, refer them to an appropriate professional.

YABLONSKY, HIT
THE SHOWERS!
I'M SENDING IN
MARY

Chapter 24

The Changing Shape of the Playing Field

> **In This Chapter**
>
> ➤ The scattered workforce
>
> ➤ Outsourcing: the workplace of the future
>
> ➤ Self-directed teams
>
> ➤ Changes in work schedules: flextime, job sharing
>
> ➤ The flexible workforce—using temps

A Look into the Company of the Next Century

In the late 18th and early 19th centuries, as a result of the industrial revolution, the workplace moved from small, often home-based shops to large, centrally located factories and offices. Villages gave way to towns, and towns to cities.

As we move into the 21st century, centralization is giving way again to smaller, decentralized units. It's no longer necessary in many types of work for all employees to be located in the same building—or even in the same city. Advanced technology has made this type of decentralization feasible and often more advantageous.

An increasing number of employees work in small branch offices that enable them to serve customers more effectively, and many work from their own homes, receiving assignments and returning finished work by way of computers, faxes, and express delivery services.

In this chapter, you'll learn how to anticipate and manage the challenges that will come about in the 21st century. We'll see team members operating from a location across town or across an ocean. We'll move toward small permanent staffs and expanded use of temps to meet immediate needs. We'll learn how a self-directed team may replace the traditional boss/subordinate concept and its impact on the role of the team leader.

Bye-Bye Cubicles, Hello Decentralization

You don't have to look in a crystal ball to see the future of business organization. All you have to do is observe what is taking place in progressive companies today.

The office of the 21st century will differ from the room full of little cubicles satirized in *Dilbert* cartoons. As more and more teams are used, the interaction among team members will be facilitated by having them work together in large modular spaces. Computers, reference material, fax machines, telephones, duplicators, and other equipment will be in easy reach of all members. Instead of calling meetings, team members can confer with each other casually and regularly. Some members may work at home some of the time, telecommuting or teleconferencing when needed. Work assignments will be distributed by computer to appropriate team members.

Interaction with other teams, other branches, and with customers, vendors, and others will be done primarily by e-mail, internal chat rooms, telephone, and *teleconferences.*

Teams will consist of a small core group, augmented when needed by extra personnel. These may be on-call workers (regular employees who only work when needed) people assigned by temp services, contract firm workers (employees of another firm whose services are purchased for a specific assignment), or from freelance, self-employed specialists retained for the assignment as independent contractors.

Team leaders in a decentralized environment face many new challenges. You must know how to do the following:

➤ Manage people when they aren't close by.

➤ Get to know team members when personal contact is limited.

Meanings & Gleanings

Decentralization shifts the focus of a business from one central facility to localized facilities where decisions are made and work is performed with minimum control from the central office.

Secret Weapons

When it's too difficult or expensive to bring people from a variety of locations to one place, try *teleconferencing.* In this process, participants assemble at teleconferencing centers in cities near where they work. Using TV and satellite techniques, they can see and speak to each other. Some large companies have their own teleconferencing facilities.

➤ Ensure that work gets done when your team members are scattered in several locations.

➤ Motivate your team, solve problems, resolve conflicts, and carry out all the functions of your job from a distance.

Managing Workers You Don't See Every Day

Working in a decentralized environment isn't a totally new concept. For years, sales managers have managed their sales staffs in locations far removed from the home office; dispatchers have managed truck drivers who are continually on the road; and chain store operators have managed stores in hundreds of locations. Study the way these people manage their employees. You can learn from them.

Jacqueline, the sales manager for a large cosmetics company, manages 20 sales areas in the United States and Canada, each employing from 10 to 15 sales representatives and support crews. She attributes her success in keeping her sales staff motivated and productive to five principles:

1. **All area managers and their staff members are treated as full members of the sales team—not as second-class citizens.** They're continually informed about all the same things that employees in the home office are told. The company shows them previews of advertising campaigns, sales brochures, and other materials before the materials are released and encourages their input.

   No matter where team members are located, they're kept informed of team and departmental goings-on. Jacqueline believes that a major factor in building team spirit is the day-to-day chitchat among team members about their interests and activities. Because employees miss out on this type of conversation when they work in different locations, the company sends to every salesperson a weekly chatty newsletter that includes tidbits about what's going on in its employees' lives.

2. **The team leader takes a personal interest in each team member.** Jacqueline telephones each of her area managers at least once a week just to chat about how things are going. If a sales rep does something special, she personally makes a congratulatory call. On an employee's birthday, she sends a card or an e-mail message, and on special occasions, such as weddings, births, or special anniversaries, she sends flowers or a snack basket to the team member's home.

3. **Meetings are held periodically so that members from various locations can regularly meet face to face.** To supplement the annual convention that all company salespeople attend, quarterly regional meetings are held. Sales reps at the meetings can meet reps from other regions in a more intimate environment than the convention provides. It gives them an opportunity to exchange ideas, get to know their colleagues as real people, and build up the team's *esprit de corps*.

317

Communication Breakdown

Employees in remote locations often feel left out of company business. Keep them informed of what's going on in the home office and in other regions. Let them share in celebrations and participate in successes.

4. **Sharing of ideas among members in all facilities is expedited.** The exchange of ideas isn't limited to meetings. Sales reps and area managers are encouraged to communicate with each other by phone, fax, and e-mail. They share with each other their experiences, sales approaches, and advice about handling problems.

5. **The team leader maintains personal contact with all members.** Jacqueline plans her regular office visits so that she can go out in the field with sales reps, hold motivational meetings, and discuss special problems. She makes occasional unannounced visits, just to say "hello" and let them know that she's personally interested in them.

These principles can be helpful not only with salespeople but also outside service technicians, branch-office staff members, and others who work in remote locations.

Introducing Telecommuting

The computer and modem (a device that enables your computer to share information with other computers via phone lines) have enabled companies to communicate in real time with anyone who also has a computer and modem. Documents, drawings, and statistical tables can be transmitted electronically to one person or to dozens of people simultaneously. This process has not only enabled companies to improve their decentralized operations but also to create the entirely new concept of *telecommuting*.

Secret Weapons

Make sure prospective telecommuters are fully aware of the negative as well as the positive aspects of working at home. Have the employee try it for a trial period before agreeing to a permanent arrangement.

Many people prefer working at home over having to fight traffic to and from their office. Some parents have turned to telecommuting to enable them to spend more time with their children and reduce day care expenses.

Companies have discovered that it's often advantageous to let employees telecommute: It frees up office space for other people and enables a company to use the services of experienced workers who may not be able to come to the office regularly. These workers include parents with young children, people who can't leave their homes because they care for elderly or ill relatives, and people with a temporary or permanent disability.

Not every type of job is suitable for telecommuting. Many jobs require constant interaction with others on the job or the use of expensive or complex equipment that cannot be provided for home use.

Here are some types of jobs, that *can* be done at home:

➤ Various types of clerical work

➤ Data entry

➤ Telemarketing

➤ Customer service

➤ Certain accounting functions

➤ Design and drafting

➤ Creative work such as writing advertising copy, writing technical manuals, artwork, and editing

With a little imagination, jobs that seem to be limited to the office often can be redesigned so that they can be done at home.

Making Telecommuters Part of Your Team

Dr. Frank Ashby, a consultant who has worked with many companies that use telecommuters, suggests that the key to success is a well-designed plan for orienting and training all telecommuters. This plan should be followed by ongoing interaction between the leader and the telecommuter.

Provide guidelines for dealing with the special problems of working at home. Many people who are accustomed to the routine of an office find that they flounder when they have to work without direct supervision.

Ashby recommends training in at least the areas of time management and priority setting. He recommends these guidelines for telecommuters:

➤ **Set specific hours that you plan to work— and stick to them.** Although some telecommuters are paid on an hourly basis and must keep time logs, most work in salaried jobs in which their work is measured not by hours worked but by their achievement of key results areas (see Chapter 21).

Some jobs require telecommuters to be available at the telephone or at the computer during normal business hours; in others, the specific hours worked aren't important as long as the work is done and the manager knows when the employee can be contacted.

➤ **Set up working hours when children are in school or napping.** If you have children who

Meanings & Gleanings

The process of *telecommuting* uses technology to enable people to perform their work at home or at a remote location from the central office by receiving assignments and submitting completed work through a computer equipped with a modem.

aren't in school, arrange working hours for times when you're less likely to be disturbed or when another adult is available to take care of them.

➤ **Set priorities so that you're always aware of deadlines and progress on each assignment.**

Managers should make telecommuters as much a part of the team as people who work side by side in the office, and should treat them accordingly:

➤ Keep telecommuters informed of all team activities, even those in which they're not directly involved.

➤ Have them come to the office for business meetings, training programs, and company or department social events.

➤ Invite them to participate in such extracurricular activities as bowling leagues, softball teams, and family picnics.

➤ Put them on the distribution list for all the same materials they would receive if they were in-house employees.

➤ Require that they visit the office regularly—not just for discussion of their own work but also for in-person discussions about team activities and to give them an opportunity to interact with other team members.

➤ Make yourself easily accessible by telephone, and return voice mail or other messages promptly. Many leaders call telecommuters periodically just to show a personal interest and to give them the opportunity to exchange ideas about overall activities—not just specific work assignments.

Prospective telecommuters should be made aware of the many potential problems of working at home. One home-based computer programmer complained that her friends and neighbors barged in for friendly chats or to ask her to accept deliveries, be available for service people, and even watch their children. She had to make clear to them that she was an at-home worker, not a lady of leisure. Being assertive cost her some "friends," but it was essential.

Another at-home worker soon found that the freedom of working at home, setting his own time schedule, and avoiding rush hour didn't make up for the socialization of the workplace. He missed the interaction of daily contact with colleagues, the gossip around the water cooler, and even the daily parrying with his boss. He chose to return to the office.

Manager's Minute

In addition to regular benefits such as health care and paid leave, dependent-care flexible spending accounts, flexibility in work scheduling, and casual business attire are the most widely offered fringe benefits to help people juggle work and life issues.

Outsourcing: Working with Independent Contractors

It's expedient for some companies to subcontract major aspects of their operations to companies better suited to deal with them. Subcontracting enables them to concentrate on what they do best and not be hindered by facets of their work that others can do more effectively.

One frequently *outsourced* company function is payroll. By subcontracting this nonproductive activity to specialists, companies save time, money, and aggravation. ADP, one of the largest computing firms in the United States, computes payroll for more than 200,000 companies.

Navistar International, a manufacturer of heavy equipment and trucks, subcontracted the management of its tire warehouse to Goodyear, which has more expertise in managing a tire warehouse. Goodyear's expertise resulted in major savings in inventory and storage costs.

A major midwestern university's attempt to enter the growing business seminar field became bogged down because, although it had the faculty and the facilities to provide excellent programs, it didn't have the expertise to market them to the business community. By subcontracting this activity to an established seminar organization, the university was able to build the program into a much needed profit center.

If your company is considering outsourcing a function over which you have jurisdiction, follow these suggestions to help ease the transition:

Meanings & Gleanings

Companies increasingly *outsource*, or subcontract to outside sources, work that previously had been done in-house. As companies become "leaner and meaner," they outsource activities that are peripheral to their main functions. Some examples are payroll, traffic, training, computer programming, advertising, and certain manufacturing activities.

321

➤ **Help choose the contractor.** As a knowledgeable person in your field, you should be familiar with companies that specialize in the areas involved. Volunteer to research available companies, interview the owners, or become the primary contact with prospects. When the contract goes into effect, you and the contractor will have already established a working relationship.

➤ **Use the soon-to-be displaced manager (if there is one) as the contractor.** When Holly was told that her market-research section was to be eliminated and the function outsourced, she was devastated. She had worked long and hard to attain her position. Her manager called her aside and said, "Holly, I've looked into some of the firms that are possible sources for our work, and none of them is as good as you. You have the experience and know-how, and, moreover, you're familiar with our products and could get to work on them with minimum disruption. You should set up your own market research firm. We'll be your first customer, and our work should give you a good start. You'll be free, of course, to seek other customers. It could be the break of a lifetime."

For Holly, the situation was the beginning of a great new career. For the company, it eased the transition because the long working relationship between Holly and her manager eliminated the starts and stops inherent in a new relationship.

➤ **When you begin a new working relationship with a contractor, take the time to get to know each other.** Visit the contractor's facility. Invite her to attend a staff meeting and discuss with your team how she operates and how they can work together to obtain the greatest benefit from the new system.

➤ **Clearly set up the manner in which you expect the contractor to interact with your team.** For example, rather than have a single end deadline for a large project, you may prefer to establish interim deadlines by which the contractor should complete particular portions of the job. If you want to receive weekly status reports or meet personally with the contractor on a predetermined schedule, spell that out up front.

➤ **Hold regular meetings.** Make it a regular practice to meet periodically with the members of the contractor's staff who work on your account. Your attention will make them feel that they're part of your team and solidify the relationship.

➤ **Handle problems quickly.** Deal immediately and diplomatically with any problems that develop between you so that your working relationship doesn't suffer.

➤ **Make the contractor's staff part of your team.** Invite the members of the contractor's staff who work on your account to company conventions, social functions, and in-house training sessions that relate to matters of mutual interest.

➤ **Review the contractor's work in the same way you evaluate an employee.** Cooperative contractors welcome honest performance evaluations so that they can meet their customers' needs and maintain a high level of customer satisfaction.

Job Sharing: One Job, Two People

Although not limited to women who have children at home, job sharing was initiated so that people who could not or did not wish to work full-time could work half-time. Two people share one job. For example, one worker works from 8 A.M. to noon and the other 1 to 5 P.M., or one person works Mondays and Wednesdays, the other Tuesdays and Thursdays and each works alternate Fridays. The salary for the job is divided between them and benefits are adjusted according to company policies. According to a survey by the Society for Human Resources Management (SHRM), 23 percent of companies surveyed in 1998 employed people in work-sharing positions.

The advantage is that an experienced worker is always on duty to perform the work. The downside is that there may be a loss of continuity, and as the perspective of each person may differ somewhat, a loss of consistency. Most firms that have instituted job sharing have reported favorably on its results.

Manager's Minute

The "flattening" of companies—eliminating layers of middle managers—has increasingly led companies to contract work to outsiders. Some companies have become, in a sense, "general contractors," in which their management consists of a cadre of specialists who set goals, develop concepts, and then assign work to and coordinate the activities of contractors.

Flextime: Coordinating a Team When Members Work Different Hours

A great many companies allow employees to select the time they start and end work. Some people may work from 8 to 4; others 9 to 5; still others 10 to 6. All staff is on duty during the greater part of the workday—from 10 A.M. to 4 P.M. This enables people to take care of personal matters such as getting kids off the school before leaving for work or being home after school or coordinating work schedules with a spouse. The SHRM survey noted that in 1998, 55 percent of the surveyed firms offered flex time, up from 42 percent in 1997.

Setting flexible hours is not always feasible. It won't work in situations where all workers are needed at the same time as in most manufacturing operations. It also creates problems when the early arrivers need information or material from people who are scheduled to come in later—holding up work. But in a great number of situations this can be worked out.

Team leaders whose members come in and leave at different times have special problems in coordinating their work. Team meetings, which in companies with traditional hours are usually held in early morning or late afternoon, must be scheduled for midday—not always a convenient time as it often interrupts work in progress. The leader has the added problem of communicating with staff members on matters arising when they are not on duty. Most serious is that team leaders don't work from 8 to 6. They are not around to lead, guide, and assist members whose schedules differ from their own.

To deal with this, as a team leader, you should:

➤ Establish clear-cut policies concerning matters that, based on experience, are likely to develop when you are not around.

➤ Give team members authority to make decisions that are needed in your absence.

➤ Be available by telephone at all times (here's where your cell phone comes in handy).

➤ Vary your shift (come in early some days, late others).

The Flexible Work Force: Use Staff Only When Needed

The trend toward smaller permanent staffs started in the 1980s and is becoming standard practice in large companies. Why pay wages, benefits, and perks to people who are only needed at peak periods? There are three major sources for obtaining such employees:

1. **On-call workers.** These are a list of employees who have been trained by the company in the requisite skills. They often are former employees who have been downsized or have retired. They are called in when the need arises. This is a common practice in seasonal businesses. The advantage is that you have a pool of skilled workers who are available and easily identified and contacted. The limitation, of course, is that good workers can often find more steady employment and are not there when needed.

2. **Contract workers.** There are firms whose chief business is to sell the services of their employees to other companies. For example, the engineering field abounds with "job shops," which perform engineering functions for companies who do not have or need a full-time engineering team. A construction company needs civil, mechanical, and electrical engineers to work on the design of a project—a four- or five-month job. They contract the assignment to a job shop that will either do the engineering at their own premises or send a team of engineers to work on the project at the offices of the construction company. When the job is finished, the engineers move on to another assignment.

In recent years companies have "leased" employees from a variety of contract shops for all kinds of jobs ranging from cleaning up after a flood or hurricane to filling rush orders to providing computer technology. The client companies save the time, trouble, and expense of recruiting personnel not only for jobs that are of short duration, but also sometimes for entire operations. Such firms have very few permanent staff members and lease all but their key managers.

3. **Temp services.** Unlike the contractors discussed above, temp services provide personnel to work at company premises usually for a short time. For example, to replace employees who are on sick leave or on vacation—an assignment that may last from one or two days to several months. Temps are hired to handle special projects or deal with rush orders.

Temps are not put on the payroll. The company pays the temp service a fee for each employee, and the temp service pays the workers. Although the fee is higher than the amount they would pay a regular employee, it is cost effective because the company pays no benefits to temps and eliminates the high cost of recruiting for a short duration job. Because temps are trained in office skills, the only training they need is to learn the specifics of the work assignment.

Manager's Minute

The U.S. Bureau of Labor Statistics reported the following changes in work arrangements between 1995 and 1997.

Total employed	123.2 million	126.7 million
Traditional arrangements	111.1 million	114.2 million
Independent contractors	8.31 million	8.46 million
On-call workers	1.97 million	2.0 million
Temp agency workers	1.18 million	1.3 million
Contract firm workers	652,000	809,000

Over the past few years there has been an increase in using temps in managerial and professional jobs. Companies have hired temporary managers to head up a company during a transitional period. For example, when the president of a small firm in Long Island, New York died last year, his heir apparent was his 25-year-old son. The Board of

Directors, realizing that the young man was not prepared to take over the job, hired an experienced manager from a temp service to run the business and train the son.

According to the National Association of Temporary and Staffing Services (NATSS), one of the fasting growing demands for temps has been in the professional segment (accounting, law, sales, and management).

Secret Weapons

As your role as team leader shifts from day-to-day manager to advisor and counselor, it opens new challenges for you. It's an opportunity to use your creativity in planning long-term assignments, taking on assignments that broaden your background, and becoming even more valuable to your organization.

Meanings & Gleanings

A *self-directed team* has no permanent team leader. Team members are self-managed. Some teams have permanent administrative leaders to handle paperwork, but members rotate as project leaders. Team members schedule work, hire and train new members, budget funds, and monitor their own performance.

Working with Self-Directed Teams

Some management gurus predict that the role of supervisors and managers will eventually change completely from leader to advisor. They believe that all work will be accomplished by *self-directed teams*: no boss, no team leader—just a team of dedicated people working to service their internal or external customers.

Utopian? Idealistic? Maybe. It's unlikely that this system will take place soon or ever be the standard business structure, but self-directed teams are already in place in certain companies.

As noted in Chapter 20, self-directed teams are part of the empowerment process. Self-management isn't the only way to empower people, but it is the end-all of true empowerment.

Making Self-Direction Work

Most people—leaders and members alike—need careful preparation for their new roles. Training in group dynamics is the first step. Managers and team leaders accustomed to making decisions and giving orders must be conditioned to look at their roles as that of advisor and counselor. Members accustomed to having decisions made for them must be trained in decision making and be oriented to accepting responsibility.

As a manager, keep in mind that you can't rush into making a major change in the way people work. Change should be made by evolution, not revolution. You cannot just put out a bulletin that says, "Effective this date, we work in self-directed teams." It takes time and conditioning for such a radical change to work its way into the system.

The team leader still has an important place in the early stages of self-direction. It's that person's responsibility to ensure that the group dynamics work, to assist members in problem-solving techniques, and to stay available to do what is necessary in the transition.

The team leader gradually becomes the team coordinator and shares leadership functions with team members. She devotes more time to coordinating with other teams and projects outside the immediate team.

When a self-directed team is finally in place, members do the day-to-day planning, operations, and decision making. They set goals, measure their own performance, and, if necessary and appropriate, discipline members. The former team leader becomes the team's advisor, providing technical support and acting as a consultant.

The Downside of Self-Direction

Self-directed teams have been hailed by some managers as the wave of the future. But these types of teams are not a panacea, and they have their limitations:

➤ Except for some very progressive organizations, the concept of self-directed teams is too radical for many companies to seriously consider. It involves changes in their thinking for which they are not ready and may take them years to understand and accept.

➤ Many team members find it unpleasant or difficult to evaluate a peer's performance and to recommend disciplinary action against other team members.

➤ As noted in the discussion of empowerment in Chapter 20, many people don't want to be empowered.

➤ Self-directed teams call for a highly motivated group of people who strive for peak performance from themselves and their co-workers. A large percentage of people are satisfied being "average" workers and aren't committed to putting out the necessary extra effort and energy.

Communication Breakdown

If your organization is moving toward self-directed teams, your role can change from leader to just another team member. There's nothing wrong with this situation if that's want you want, but it can also provide you with the opportunity to move up to an even higher position. If this is your goal, accept the change as a challenge.

➤ Current team leaders are sometimes reluctant to give up the power and authority of being a leader—even in more traditional working teams. Many fear not only that they'll lose power but also that their jobs will become superfluous.

The Least You Need to Know

➤ The workplace is changing from a centralized facility to groups of people working in distant locations or even from their homes.

➤ When team members are scattered in different locations, keep them informed of what's going on via newsletters, e-mail, telephone calls, and personal visits.

➤ To ensure that telecommuters feel that they're part of your team, follow up careful initial orientation and training with ongoing interaction between you and the telecommuters.

➤ Treat telecommuters the same way you treat other members of your team. Have them come to your office periodically for face-to-face discussions with you and other team members.

➤ Get to know your subcontractors' staff members. Make them a part of your team by keeping in close touch, visiting their facilities, and inviting them to yours.

➤ More and more of company personnel will not be traditional employees, but part-timers, job sharers, contract employees, or temps.

➤ Self-directed teams, in which the team leader becomes a coordinator and advisor, is one way people can be empowered.

Part 7
Doling Out Discipline

When you hear or see the word discipline, the first thing that usually pops into your mind is punishment. Look at that word again. Notice that by dropping just two letters, it turns into disciple, a synonym for "student." Both words are derived from the Latin word meaning "to learn." If you look at discipline, not as punishment, but as a means of learning, both you and your associates get much more out of it. You are the coach, and your associates are the learners.

Unfortunately, people don't always learn what they are taught. Despite your best efforts, some of your team members may not perform satisfactorily. If infractions still occur, even after you've clearly explained the rules, you must take steps to get things back on track.

Regardless of the cause, discipline begins when you work to correct the problem. When you've made every effort to help your associates learn and when all else fails, only then does discipline take the form of punishment.

This part of the book looks at the steps involved in progressive discipline and explores the dos and don'ts of punishment and termination.

Chapter 25

Spare the Rod and Spoil the Employee

In This Chapter

➤ The steps of progressive discipline

➤ How and when to reprimand

➤ Written warnings

➤ Probation and suspension

➤ Is there a better way to discipline?

Some companies have workers who have always met all the requirements of their jobs, followed all the company rules and regulations, and never had to be disciplined. They are robots, but even in technocrats' wildest dreams, robots will never totally replace humans. All except the most routine and highly structured work must be done by people, who from time to time don't meet expectations, are absent or come to work late, and violate company rules and must be corrected.

This chapter looks at the system of progressive discipline used by most organizations today and examines how it can be used effectively by team leaders. You'll learn when a reprimand is appropriate and how to reprimand a team member without causing resentment.

You'll learn when and how to "write up" an employee and when he should be placed on probation or suspended. This chapter also explores some alternative approaches to progressive discipline.

Keep in mind that the contents of this chapter are based on general practices that are used in many organizations. Your company's policies may differ. You may get some good ideas from this chapter that you can't use now, but you can suggest them to your company's management. Until your company incorporates these ideas into its policies, however, follow your company's current practices.

Meanings & Gleanings

Progressive discipline is a systematic approach to correcting rule infractions. A typical program has six steps, beginning with an informal warning. If the warning doesn't succeed, the following steps are taken, in order: disciplinary interview, written warning, probation, suspension, and termination (*if necessary*).

Progressive Discipline

In most organizations, it's important for every member of a team to be at his or her workstation at starting time. If one person comes to work late, it can hold up an entire team.

Suppose an employee was late three times in his first month on the job. You spoke to him about it, and for several months he kept his promise to be on time. He was late one day last week, and this morning he was late again. His reason for the tardiness is vague. Your informal chats with him about the matter haven't done any good, so now you're ready to apply *progressive discipline*.

The Reprimand: An Informal Warning

The chats you've had with the team member weren't part of the progressive discipline system; instead, they were a friendly reminder of his responsibility to your team.

The first official step in the progressive discipline system is often called the "oral," or "verbal," warning: You take the team member aside and remind him that the two of you have discussed his lateness and that, because he continues to come to work late, you must put him on notice. Inform him of the next steps you'll take if the behavior continues.

You may be exasperated about a team member's failure to keep a promise to be on time. It's normal to be annoyed if your team's work is delayed, but don't lose your cool. A typical conversation shows you what *not* to do:

You (angrily): How many times do I have to tell you that we need you here at 8 o'clock? You know that we have a deadline to meet today. Haven't you any sense of responsibility?

Employee (annoyed): I was only 10 minutes late. It's not my fault—I ran into a traffic problem.

You: If you had left home early enough, you wouldn't have had a traffic problem. The rest of us were here on time. You just don't have a sense of responsibility.

Employee: I have as much of a sense of responsibility as anyone.

You: If you're late again, I'll write you up.

Did this conversation solve anything? The objective of an informal warning is to alert team members that a problem needs correction. By using an angry tone and antagonistic attitude, you only rile the person and avoid solving the problem.

Let's replay that reprimand in a better way:

You: You know how important it is for you to be here when the workday begins. The entire team depends on all of us being on time.

Employee: I'm sorry. I ran into unusual traffic this morning.

You: We all face traffic in the morning. What can you do to make sure that you'll be on time in the future?

Employee: I've tried alternative routes, but it doesn't help. I guess I'll have to leave earlier every day so that, if I do run into traffic, I'll at least have a head start.

You: That sounds good to me. You're a valuable member of our team, and being on time will help all of us.

When you're preparing to reprimand someone, to ensure that you conduct the reprimand in the most effective manner, reread the guidelines for reprimanding below.

Communication Breakdown

Never reprimand people when you're angry, when they're angry, or in the presence of other people. Reprimands should be a private matter between two calm people working together to solve a problem.

Guidelines for Reprimanding

Time the reprimand properly. As soon as possible after the offense has been committed, call the employee aside and discuss the matter in private.

Never reprimand when you're angry. Wait until you have calmed down.

Emphasize the *what*, not the *who*. Base the reprimand on the action that was wrong, not on the person.

Begin by stating the problem and then ask a question. Don't begin with an accusation: "You're always late!" Say instead, "You know how important it is for all of us to be on the job promptly. What can you do to get here on time from now on?"

Listen! Attentive, open-minded listening is one of the most important factors of true leadership. Ask questions to elicit as much information about the situation as you can. Respond to the associate's comments, but don't convert the interview into a confrontation.

Encourage your team member to make suggestions for solving the problem. When a person participates in reaching a solution, there's a much greater chance that it will be accepted and accomplished.

Provide constructive criticism. Give your team member specific suggestions, when possible, about how to correct a situation.

Never use sarcasm. Sarcasm never corrects a situation; it only makes the other person feel inadequate and put upon.

End your reprimand on a positive note. Comment on some of the good things the person has accomplished so that he or she knows that you're not focusing only on the reason for this reprimand, but instead on total performance. Reassure the person that you look on him or her as a valuable member of your team.

They Always Have an Excuse

If you've been in management for any length of time, you've probably heard some wild excuses. No matter how silly, ridiculous, or improbable the excuse may be, listen—and listen carefully—for these reasons:

➤ Until you listen to the entire story, you cannot know whether it has validity. In most companies, there are acceptable reasons for not following a company rule or procedure. Under extenuating circumstances, it's sensible to be flexible when you enforce the rules.

➤ Even if an excuse is unacceptable, let your team member get it out of her system (a process called *catharsis*). When people have something on their mind, they won't listen to a word you say until they get their story out. Whether it's a team member's tardiness or a customer's complaint, let the person talk. Only after a person's mind is clear will he listen to you. Afterward, you can say, "I understand what you're saying, but the important thing is to be here on time."

Asking for a Plan of Action

When you deliver a verbal warning, throw the problem back to your team member. Rather than say, "This is what you should do," ask "What do you think you can do to correct this situation?" Get people to come up with their own plans of action.

In a simple situation such as tardiness, a plan of action is relatively easy to develop: "I'll leave my house 15 minutes earlier every day." In more complex situations, a plan may take longer to develop. You may suggest that the person think about the problem for a day or so and arrange a second meeting in which to present and discuss it.

Documenting a Reprimand

Even informal reprimands shouldn't be strictly oral. You should keep a record of it. Legal implications mandate that you document any action that could lead to serious disciplinary action.

Some team leaders document an informal warning by simply noting it on their calendars or entering it in a team log. Others write a detailed memo for their files. You should use the technique your company prefers.

Conducting a Disciplinary Interview

If an employee repeats an offense after receiving a verbal warning, the next step is the disciplinary interview.

This interview differs from a reprimand in that it is more formal. A verbal warning is usually a relatively brief session, often conducted in a quiet corner of the room. A disciplinary interview is longer and is conducted in an office or conference room.

A disciplinary interview should always be carefully prepared and result in a mutually agreed upon plan of action. Whereas a plan of action after a verbal warning is usually oral, the resulting plan in a disciplinary interview should be put in writing. It not only reminds both the leader and the team member of what has been agreed on but also serves as documentation.

To ensure that a disciplinary interview is carried out systematically, use the following discipline worksheet.

Secret Weapons

An alert and observant team leader can anticipate problems before they develop. Be alert for any deviations from standards before they become problems. By dealing with team members' rule infractions early on, you can usually avoid disciplinary procedures.

Discipline Worksheet

Part I (Complete before interview begins)

Team member: _____ Date: _____

Offense: _____
_____
_____

Policy and Procedures provision: _____

Date of occurrence: _____

Previous similar offenses: _____
_____

What I want to accomplish: _____
_____

Special considerations: _____
_____

Questions to ask at beginning of interview: _____
_____
_____

PART II (Keep in front of you during interview)

- Keep calm and collected.
- Listen actively.
- Emphasize the *what,* not the *who.*
- Give *team member* an opportunity to solve the problem.
- Get the whole story.
- Don't interrupt.
- Avoid sarcasm.

PART III (Fill out near end of interview)

Suggestions made by team member: _____
_____
_____

Agreed-on solution: _____
_____
_____

PART IV (Action taken: Fill in when interview is finished)

Documentation completed: _____
_____

Writing Up Warnings

The next step in progressive discipline is to give the offender a written warning—a letter or form that will be placed in her personnel file. Written warnings often are taken more seriously than the first two steps. Employees don't want negative reports in their personnel files, and even the possibility that they'll be "written up" serves as a deterrent to poor behavior.

If the written warning concerns poor performance, specify the performance standards and indicate in what way the employee's performance fell short of the standards. Also state what was done to help the employee meet the standards. This will protect you against potential claims that you made no effort to bring the performance up to standard.

If the warning concerns infraction of a company rule, specify the nature of the offense and what disciplinary steps were taken before writing the warning (see the following two sample letters).

Memo for Poor Conduct

From (team leader): _____ Date: _____

To: _____

On (date) _____ , we had a discussion concerning _____

_____

_____

At that time, you agreed to _____

_____

Because you have not complied with this agreement, you are being formally notified that if the above matter is not corrected by (date)_____ , additional disciplinary steps will be taken as specified in Section ____ of the Policies and Procedures manual.

Signed (team leader): _____

Team member's comments: _____

_____

_____

Signed (team member): _____

To protect your company from potential legal problems, check any form letters concerning discipline with your legal advisors before sending them to be printed.

Meanings & Gleanings

One way of providing a team member with another chance to improve performance or correct unsatisfactory behavior is to give the member a specified period of time (30 days, for example) to accomplish the change. If the improvement is not made during this period of *probation*, the next step in the progressive discipline is taken.

Although it's always advantageous from a legal standpoint to have employees sign *all* disciplinary documents, it becomes imperative when the warning itself is in writing.

You can't force anyone to sign anything. If an employee refuses to sign a disciplinary document, call in a witness—a person who isn't directly involved in the situation—and repeat your request. If he still refuses, have the witness attest to that response on the document.

To avoid misunderstandings, give copies of all disciplinary documents to the employee. In addition, you should send a copy to the human resources department to include in the person's personnel file.

The sample poor conduct letter (above) and poor performance letter (below) can help you prepare written warnings. Refer to them for ideas about how to phrase a written warning.

Memo for Poor Performance

From (team leader): _____ Date: _____

To (team member): _____

The performance standard for (specify job) _____ is (specify standard in quantity, quality, or other terms) _____
_____
_____

Your performance has not met these standards (give details): _____
_____
_____

To help you, I gave you ____ hours of special coaching. The areas covered include:
_____
_____

Signed (team leader): _____

Team member's comments: _____

Signed (team member): _____

Putting Employees on Probation

Until now all your attempts to correct a team member's performance or behavior have been positive, and you've provided advice and counsel. If nothing has worked, your next step is to put the team member on probation. Set a deadline for adjusting the situation.

What you're doing is giving your associate one more chance to shape up before you invoke some form of punishment. Most people take probation seriously—they know that you mean business.

The two primary reasons for progressive discipline are poor performance and poor conduct. If performance is a problem, probation is the last step before termination. If all the retraining, counseling, and coaching you give a team member fails, you can give the person one last chance to overcome the problem over a probationary period. If that doesn't help, additional disciplinary steps won't help. If you can transfer the person to a more suitable job, do so; if not, you have no other choice than to terminate him.

Company practices for administering probation vary considerably. They're governed by union contracts, company policy manuals, or sometimes unwritten (but previously followed) practices. Usually the notification of probation is in the form of a written statement, signed by the team leader or a higher ranking manager and acknowledged by the employee. The employee keeps one copy; the team leader gets another copy; and the human resources department keeps a copy in its files.

Probationary periods vary from as few as 10 days to the more customary 30 days and sometimes even longer. If an employee makes significant progress, lift the probation. If she repeats the offense after the probation is lifted, you can either reinstate the probation or invoke the next step.

When an offense violates company rules (tardiness, absenteeism, or other misconduct), proceed to the next step, which is usually suspension.

Suspension: The First Real Punishment

You're severely limited in the ways you can punish employees. Ever since flogging was abolished, only a few types of punishment can be legally administered. The most commonly used method, short of termination, is suspension without pay.

Although team leaders often have some leeway in determining the length of a suspension, most companies set specific suspension times depending on the seriousness of the offense.

The mechanics of issuing a suspension are similar to that of probation. Union contracts often

Secret Weapons

The downside of suspending a team member is that you lose that person's contribution to the team effort during the suspension period. Make every effort to keep the person employed by training and counseling so that suspension isn't necessary.

mandate consultation with a union representative before suspending an employee. Most companies aren't unionized and require approval for suspensions by both the manager to whom the team leader reports and the human resources department. Appropriate documentation specifying the reason for the suspension and the exact period of time involved should be made, signed by the appropriate manager, and acknowledged by the suspended employee.

If an employee returns from a suspension and continues to break the rules, your next step may be a longer suspension or even termination.

Termination: The Final Step

The chief purpose of progressive discipline is to give the offending employee an opportunity to change his or her behavior and become a productive, cooperative team member. Take stricter steps only after less strict steps have failed to solve the problem. The objective is to help the person succeed so that termination isn't necessary. If the employee fails to improve, however, the termination should take place.

The practical and legal facets of terminating employees are discussed in detail in Chapter 26.

Affirmative Discipline: A New Approach

Some companies have done away with punishment, based on this logic: Team members are adults, adults take responsibility for their own actions, and punishment is therefore childish.

Here's how affirmative discipline works:

1. When a person is hired, the team leader and the new team member thoroughly discuss company rules and policies. The new employee is asked to make a commitment to comply with the rules.

2. If a rule is violated, the team leader points out the infraction and reminds the person of the agreement to comply with the rules. Both parties sign a memo to document the meeting.

3. If a violation occurs again, a second conference is held. The team member is asked to sign a special affirmation statement to show that the company takes the rules seriously and expects all employees to do the same.

4. If a member violates a minor rule for the third time or a major rule even one time, the leader asks the team member whether he really wants to continue working for the company. If the answer is yes, the team member is asked to sign a document acknowledging the violation and indicating that he understands that additional violations will lead to termination.

5. In some organizations, the employee is then asked to take a day off—with pay—to consider seriously whether she can live up to the commitment. Why is it a paid day off? By paying an employee under these circumstances, the company is expressing confidence in the person and in the system: It puts its money where its mouth is, not by punishing them, but by treating them as adults.

Communication Breakdown

It's not a good idea to extend a probationary period. If a team member makes some progress by the end of the probationary period but his behavior still isn't up to par, you can extend the time period—but only once. Continuous probation is bad for morale and rarely solves the problem.

Companies that use affirmative discipline report that although terminations do occur occasionally, discipline problems significantly decrease.

In most organizations, senior management makes the decision to convert to an affirmative discipline system and ensures that it's applied throughout the company. With the increasing autonomy some companies grant to teams, the team itself may have the authority to implement affirmative discipline within the team.

Letting Team Members Monitor Their Team

When you have a highly motivated team, the need for discipline becomes superfluous. Each member of the team becomes a support person and a motivator to other members.

If a team member is slow in some aspect of her work, other team members can share their working shortcuts; if someone arrives at work late or frequently takes extra time at lunch, his colleagues can explain that it affects their activities. The team leader often doesn't have to reprimand or engage in formal disciplinary measures.

If everyone on a team is committed to meeting the team's goals and is given the tools to measure their own and the team's progress, they become self-controllers. The need for formal discipline fades into the background and is used only rarely, when all other means have been exhausted.

341

The Least You Need to Know

➤ Progressive discipline gives employees several opportunities to correct their behavior before any form of punishment is applied.

➤ When you reprimand a team member, stay cool, be constructive, and focus on the problem—not on the person.

➤ Disciplinary interviews should result in a mutually accepted plan of action to correct the situation.

➤ All disciplinary actions should be documented. ("If it ain't written down, it ain't never happened.")

➤ Probationary periods give team members another chance to improve performance or correct behavior.

➤ Affirmative discipline treats employees as adults: Counseling replaces threats, and commitment replaces punishment.

➤ Well-coordinated teams control their own performance and influence the behavior of every team member. Formal discipline usually becomes unnecessary.

Chapter 26

I THOUGHT IT WAS JUST A FIGURE OF SPEECH!

"You're Fired!"

In This Chapter

➤ Terminating someone after progressive discipline has failed

➤ Preparing for a termination meeting

➤ Terminating employees spontaneously

➤ Knowing what "employment at will" really means

It's never pleasant to fire people. Even if you're glad to get rid of someone, firing is a disagreeable task that most people do reluctantly. Yet sometimes your only course of action is to terminate an employee. A series of disciplinary steps usually leads to this final act, but occasionally circumstances warrant an unplanned discharge.

Terminating employees is a serious matter that always needs careful consideration. In most companies, before a supervisor or team leader can terminate anyone, approval must be obtained from both the person to whom the leader reports and the human resources department. This step is important to ensure that company policies and legal requirements are fully observed. This chapter examines the importance of this process.

The End of the Line in Progressive Discipline

Employees who have experienced the steps of progressive discipline (see Chapter 25) should never be surprised when they get fired. Presumably, at every step along the way they were told what the next step would be. When you suspend an employee—the next-to-the-last stage in the disciplinary process—you must make clear that, if he doesn't improve in the areas that are suggested, the next step is termination.

Communication Breakdown

Some people will sue for any reason. When you fire someone, you may have to defend your actions in court. Keep complete records and appropriate documentation for all steps that led to the termination. Make sure that what you do is in accordance with your company's policies. Or, if there's no written policy, study how similar situations were handled in the past.

Secret Weapons

If an employee raises his voice, lower yours. Most people respond to a raised voice by raising their own. By responding in a soft voice, you disarm the other person. It has a calming effect.

Careful: What You Say and How You Say It Are Important

Because the issue of firing employees is such a sensitive one, you must do it diplomatically and be fully aware of any legal implications. Ask your human resources department for advice about dealing with this situation.

Some team leaders get more upset about having to fire someone than the person who is being fired. Here are some suggestions to help you prepare:

➤ Review all documents so that you're fully aware of all the reasons and implications involved in the decision to terminate the team member.

➤ Review all that you know about the team member's personality:

What problems have you had with the person?

How did she respond to the preceding disciplinary steps?

How did you and the team member get along on the job?

How did he relate to other team members?

What personal problems does the person have that you're aware of?

➤ Review any problems you've had in firing other employees, and map out a plan to avoid those problems.

➤ Check your company's policy manual or discuss with the human resources department any company rules that apply.

➤ Relax before the meeting. Do whatever helps you clear your mind and calm your emotions. If you've done your job correctly, you've made every effort to help the team member succeed. The progressive discipline system has given the person several chances to change, so you don't have to feel guilty about the firing.

It's Show Time!

You've stalled as long as you can. Now you're ready to sit down with the employee and make clear that this is the end of the line.

Find a private place to conduct the meeting. Your office is an obvious spot, but it may not be the best one. A conference room is better because, if the fired employees breaks down or becomes belligerent, you can walk out.

Most people who are fired expect it and don't cause problems. They may beg for another chance, but this isn't the time to change your mind. Progressive discipline gives people several "other chances" before they reach this point. Don't let the termination meeting degenerate into a confrontation.

If the employee gives you a hard time, keep cool. Don't lose your temper or get into an argument.

It's a good idea to have another person in the room at a termination meeting. A person being fired may say or do inappropriate things. Also, you may become upset and say something that's best left unsaid. The presence of a third person keeps both you and the employee from losing your temper and from saying or doing something that can lead to additional complications.

The best "third person" in a termination meeting is a representative from the human resources department. If this person isn't available, call in another manager or team leader. If the employee belongs to a union, the union contract usually stipulates the presence of a union delegate.

Having a third person in the room when you terminate an employee also provides a witness if an employee later sues your company. Suppose that a former employee files an age discrimination suit several weeks after being fired for poor performance. She claims that during the termination meeting, you stated that the company needs younger people in order to meet production standards. Although the claim is false, you'll have to spend time, energy, and money to defend against it—and it's your word against the other person's.

Manager's Minute

Most people are fired at the end of the workday on Friday afternoon. Some companies prefer to terminate employees in the middle of the week, however, so that people have a chance to begin looking for a new job the next day and not brood about the firing over the weekend.

If you request that a third person attend termination meetings, former employees will be less likely to file false claims because they know that they'll be refuted by a witness.

In most organizations, when a termination meeting ends, the employee is sent to the human resources department for outprocessing, or handling the administrative details for completing the separation procedure. If your company assigns a team leader to handle this chore, follow the company's procedures carefully.

Use the termination checklist below to ensure that you take the necessary steps in terminating an employee.

Termination Checklist

Name of employee: _____ Date: _____

Part I: If discharged for poor performance, steps taken to improve performance:

Date   Action

_____

_____

_____

Comments: _____

_____

_____

If discharged for poor conduct, list progressive disciplinary steps taken:

Date   Action

_____ Informal warning

_____ Written warning

_____ Disciplinary interview

_____ Suspension

_____ Other (specify) _____

_____

Comments: _____

_____

_____

Part II

Have you reviewed all pertinent documents?   _____

Have you treated this case in the same way as similar cases in the past?   _____

Has this action been reviewed by your immediate superior?   _____

By human resources department?   _____

By legal department?   _____

Does employee have any claim pending against company?   _____

Any workers' compensation claims?   _____

Other (specify): _____

Part III: Termination interview

Conducted by: _____

Date: _____ Place: _____

Witness: _____

Comments: _____
_____
_____

Final actions: _____
_____

ID and keys returned? _____

Company property returned? _____

Final paycheck issued? _____

Additional comments: _____
_____
_____

Spontaneous Termination: When You Fire Someone Without Progressive Discipline

Are there times when you're so annoyed with people that you wish you could just be the old-school boss and tell them to get out? Of course, there are. That's why progressive discipline was instituted—so that supervisors don't let their emotions of the moment dictate their actions.

Occasionally, termination without warning is permitted. These occasions are rare and usually limited to a few serious infractions that are clearly delineated in company policies. Serious offenses include drinking on the job, fighting, stealing, and insubordination. Because these charges aren't always easy to prove, be very careful before you make the decision to fire someone without progressive discipline. You must have solid evidence that can stand up in court. Law books are loaded with cases in which people who, because of a rash firing decision, have sued former employers for unlawful discharge, defamation of character, false imprisonment, and whatever else their lawyers can dream up.

Insubordination, which is one of the most frequent causes of spontaneous termination, isn't always easy to prove. If an employee simply fails to carry out an order, it's not grounds for termination. Unless a failure to obey instructions can lead to serious consequences, it's better to use progressive discipline. On the other hand, if a team member becomes unruly in his refusal (if he hollers and screams or spits in your face, for example), spontaneous discharge may be appropriate.

Documenting a Spontaneous Discharge

When you fire someone after progressive discipline procedures fail, you have an entire series of documents to back you up. In spontaneous termination, however, you have no documents.

Immediately after a termination, write a detailed report describing the circumstances that led up to it. Get written statements from witnesses. If you can, get the employee to sign a statement presenting her side of the story. In the event that this discharge is challenged, having the terminated employee's immediate comments will protect you in case she presents a different version of what happened.

Meanings & Gleanings

When an employee quits because of intentional unfair treatment on the job, it is "constructed" by the courts to be equivalent to being fired and is referred to as *constructive discharge*.

You Can't Fire Me—I Quit!

Suppose, after all your efforts to help someone improve his performance, you tell him that you have to let him go. You explain that if he quits voluntarily, it will look better when he applies for another job. This option may sound sensible, but what happens if Mark applies for unemployment insurance and is told that he's not eligible because he quit?

If you give someone the option of resigning, be sure to inform the person about loss of unemployment insurance and any other negative factors.

Secret Weapons

As angry as you may be about the trouble an employee has caused or how nasty he may be, don't use the termination meeting to tell the person off. A termination is a business decision, not a personal one.

Now suppose that you think you'll be shrewd in getting rid of the person: "If I fire him, he'll give me problems. I'll just make his life so miserable that he'll quit." Over the next few weeks, you give him as many unpleasant assignments as you can. You time his returns from breaks and even how long he spends in the restroom. You chastise him for every minor violation of company rules, and, after a few weeks, he quits.

Don't be shocked when the person sues your company for unlawful discharge! When you tell the court, "I didn't fire him—he quit," the judge will respond "Not so. This is a *constructive discharge*—your treatment forced him to quit." You must then pay the person back wages, rehire him, or make a satisfactory financial settlement.

What "Employment At Will" Really Means

Unless you have a personal contract with your employer or are a member of a union, you and all your team members are "employees at will."

This concept has governed employment since colonial times. Bosses always had the right to fire employees, and employees could always quit. Only recently has this concept been challenged.

To understand *employment at will*, you first have to know a little about our legal system. Americans are subject to two kinds of law: legislated acts and common law. The former are the laws passed by Congress, the states, and local governments. Common law is based on accepted practices as interpreted by court decisions over the years.

The primary difference between the two types of law is that common law can be superseded or modified by legislation and can be changed in individual cases by mutual agreement between the parties involved. A violation of common law is not a criminal offense and is handled in a lawsuit as a civil action. Legislated statutes can be changed only by amendment, repeal, or court interpretation.

Employment at will, a common law principle, has been modified over the years by various statutes. For example, some laws prohibit a company from firing or refusing to hire someone for union activity, race, religion, national origin, gender, disability, and age. Your right under common law to hire or fire at will is, therefore, restricted in these circumstances.

Meanings & Gleanings

Employment at will is a legal concept under which an employee is hired and can be fired at the will of the employer. The employer has the right, unless restricted by law or contract, to refuse to hire an applicant or to terminate an employee for any reason or for no reason.

This principle also means that you can agree to waive employment at will by mutual consent. You can sign a contract with your company in which you agree not to quit and it agrees not to fire you for the duration of the contract. Or your company and a union can agree that no union member will be fired except under the terms of the contract. In both cases, the company has given up its right to employment at will.

Employment Rights When No Contract Exists

During the past several years, a number of cases have extended employees' rights that are not covered by specific legislation. Courts in several states have ruled that, although a company's policies and procedures manual isn't a formal contract, it can be considered to have the same effect as a contract.

In one case, a supervisor at a New York publishing firm was fired without having the benefit of progressive discipline measures. He sued on grounds that the policy manual

Communication Breakdown

You cannot waive a legislated right by signing a contract. An employee cannot agree to work for less than the minimum wage, for example.

Secret Weapons

To avoid legal problems, be sure to have all the facts before you fire someone. Investigate: Get witnesses, and get legal advice. Don't discuss the case with people who don't have a need to know.

called for progressive discipline before terminating an employee. In his supervisory capacity, he was required to follow the manual when he had to discharge one of his staff members. When he was fired, however, the company didn't follow the procedure. The company's contention was that the manual was intended only as a guide and not as a rigid procedure. The court ruled in favor of the employee. It said that, if a policy is published in a manual, employees can expect that it will be followed.

To avoid this type of problem, attorneys advise their clients to specify clearly in their company policy manuals that they are "at will" employers and to include a statement to that effect on their employment-application forms.

Oral Commitments

Suppose, during an interview, you told Stella that her job would be permanent after a six-month probationary period. A year later, your company downsizes, and Stella is laid off. She sues. She says, "I left my former job to take this one because the team leader assured me that it was a permanent job." You respond, "I made that comment in good faith. Our company had never had a layoff." Your reply won't be good enough—the court will award Stella a large settlement.

An Ounce of Prevention

To avoid these types of these complications, follow these guidelines:

➤ All managers and team leaders should be trained in procedures concerning termination and adhere to them.

➤ Team leaders or anyone who represents management should never make commitments concerning tenure or other employment conditions orally or in writing.

➤ Make written job offers only after consulting with legal specialists.

➤ Never use the term "permanent employee." *No one* is a permanent employee. If your company must differentiate between temporary and part-time staff members, refer to the full-time people as "regular employees."

➤ On all documents and records relating to employment conditions, state that the company has a policy of employment at will.

The Least You Need to Know

➤ Prepare for a termination meeting by studying all the pertinent documents, reviewing the team member's personal characteristics, and psyching yourself up for the meeting.

➤ Check with your human resources department to ensure that all policies are followed and laws complied with.

➤ Invite a third party to participate in and witness termination meetings.

➤ Use spontaneous termination only for extreme infractions.

➤ Other than for reasons prohibited by law or waived by contract, an employer can fire any employee for any reason or for no reason ("employment at will").

➤ Oral commitments to an employee about tenure or conditions of employment are as binding as written agreements.

Chapter 27

Separations, Layoffs, and Downsizing

In This Chapter

➤ Uncovering the real reasons people quit

➤ Temporary reductions in the workforce

➤ Downsizing: Bye–bye, job!

The days when a person joined a company after graduating from high school or college and stayed until retirement have long since passed. Most people now have several jobs during their working years. Sometimes it's a personal decision to leave a company, and sometimes it's involuntary—a company reduces its workforce, or an individual is discharged.

Every time an employee leaves a company, whether it's voluntary or involuntary, it costs the company a great deal of money. The investment involved in hiring, training, and supervising that person, in addition to the enormous administrative expenses that are incurred, are lost forever. The company loses production output until a replacement is hired and trained, and the interaction among team members is disrupted every time there's a change in the makeup of the group. Team leaders must make every effort to keep turnover down. This chapter explores those issues.

Learning Why Good People Quit

Suppose you've worked hard to build up a team member's skills and that, just when she has become effective, she quits. Then, another employee, who for several years has been one of your steadiest, most reliable workers, comes in one day and gives you his notice.

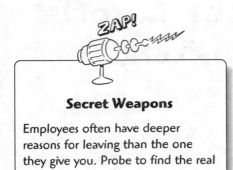

Secret Weapons

Employees often have deeper reasons for leaving than the one they give you. Probe to find the real reasons.

People may leave a job for any number of reasons. Sometimes it's personal: A spouse has to relocate for a job, or someone decides to return to school to pursue a different career. There's not much a team leader can do to reduce turnover based on personal factors.

Often, the reason is job-related. Employees may feel that they aren't making the progress they had hoped for, that their salary is too low, that working conditions are unsatisfactory, or that the job has become boring. In these cases, it's sometimes possible to reduce turnover by identifying recurring problems and correcting them so that other team members don't leave for the same reasons.

Conducting a Separation Interview

A *separation interview,* sometimes called an *exit interview,* is designed to help team leaders or supervisors determine the real reasons people leave a job and to obtain information about the company or the job that may have caused discontent.

One reason you may be able to get more information during a separation interview is that people often feel freer to open up when they have nothing to lose.

Usually separation interviews are conducted by the human resources department. But when teams work in locations that have no human resource representative, team leaders may be required to interview people who leave other teams in that facility.

Here are some guidelines for conducting an effective separation interview:

➤ To avoid getting superficial or even misleading reasons from a departing employee, don't ask, "Why are you leaving?" You can develop better information by asking good questions. Ask questions about the job itself:

What did you like most about the job? Least?

How do you feel about the progress you've made in this company?

How do you feel about compensation, benefits, and working conditions?

From the patterns of answers you get from people who are leaving your company, you can gain insight into facets of the job you hadn't realized. If you hear numerous reports of dissatisfaction in specific areas, take action to investigate them; if the reports are valid, correct the problem, or else turnover will continue to climb.

➤ Ask questions about supervision, such as, "How would you describe your team leader's style of leading the team, and how did you react to it?" and "What do you feel were your team leader's strengths and weaknesses?"

It's important to explore the area of employee-supervisor relations because it causes problems in many companies. Feedback from an exit interview makes team leaders aware of factors that may have caused problems so that they can take steps to correct them. They can also learn why they've been commended and be encouraged to reinforce those areas.

Communication Breakdown

An unbiased, objective separation interview shouldn't be conducted by the team leader or supervisor of the employee who is leaving. The interview should be conducted by a member of the human resources (HR) department, the leader of another team, or another management-level person.

➤ Ask questions that might give you insight into other problem areas: "If you could discuss with top management exactly how you feel about this company, what would you tell them?"

This open-ended question often elicits interesting responses. Let employees speak freely. Avoid leading questions, and encourage people to express their true feelings, attitudes, perceptions, fears, and hopes about your organization.

➤ If an employee has accepted a job with another company, ask, "What does your new job offer you that you're not getting here?" The answer may repeat some of the things you've already discussed, but it may also uncover some of the ways your company failed to meet this person's hopes, goals, or expectations.

Knowing What to Do When Employees Give Notice

Some supervisors and team leaders take an employee's resignation as a personal affront. "How could she do this to me?" Be aware that other team members are carefully monitoring the way you handle this situation, however. Take care to make the transition smooth.

The following suggestions help reduce the confusion that often results when a team member leaves your company:

➤ Don't blow up. I once worked for a manager who considered anyone who quit to be disloyal. If someone gave him the courtesy of two weeks' notice, he ordered the person to leave immediately. He then bad-mouthed the employee to everyone in the company. The result was that employees quit without giving notice, which caused serious production problems.

➤ Agree on a mutually satisfactory departure date. You may need time to readjust your plans.

➤ Request a status report on the team member's projects so that you can arrange for others to handle them. Develop a list of vendors, customers, or other people outside your department that the member interacts with so that you can notify them of the change.

➤ Contact your personnel department to arrange for either an internal transfer or hiring from outside.

➤ Let other team members know as soon as you're notified. Tell them how it will affect their work until someone else is hired.

Manager's Minute

No law requires employees to give notice when they leave a company. The customary two-week notice is a courtesy that gives team leaders the opportunity to plan for a smooth transition. If you feel that the continued presence of this person may be disruptive to the team, you don't have to accept the notice, and you can then arrange for immediate separation.

Furloughs: Short-Term Layoffs

Meanings & Gleanings

When companies don't have enough work to keep their work-force busy or when they want to reduce payroll to increase profits, workers are dismissed. These *layoffs* are sometimes temporary (until the workers are needed) and sometimes permanent.

If you work in an industry in which work is done seasonally (construction, certain clothing manufacturing, landscaping, and the automobile industry, for example), you're accustomed to temporary *layoffs* or *furloughs*. Workers in these fields expect to be laid off at certain times of the year and plan their lives accordingly. They're usually covered by unemployment insurance or, in some union contracts, additional payments. When the new season begins, most of them are rehired.

Some layoffs are unexpected, however, even though they're temporary. Business may slow down or a company may cut its payroll, for example. Laid-off workers have a reasonable chance of being rehired when business picks up, but they have no guarantee.

Although some people will wait for a recall, many choose to look for other jobs. This situation poses a problem for the company because many experienced workers won't be available when they're needed.

Alternatives to Layoffs

When team members know that a layoff is for a specified period and that the company has a history of calling back the entire team after a furlough, they're less likely to seek other jobs. If a layoff is indefinite but you know that you will be rehiring sooner or later, take steps to keep available as many people as you can so that, when the recall comes, your team will be intact and ready to function.

When you're part of a smooth running, highly productive team, a layoff can be devastating. The loss of some workers means that the surviving members will have to do more work to pick up the slack. Team interaction that had been developed over time is lost and must be rebuilt. Morale suffers, and productivity is most likely reduced. The best way to rebuild morale is to find alternatives to a layoff.

This list describes some ways companies have avoided layoffs:

➤ **Pay cuts.** The main reason for most layoffs is to reduce payroll. When companies institute a general pay reduction for all employees (including management), the entire workforce shares the burden.

It's easier to reduce the payroll in a unionized organization. Because a union speaks for its entire bargaining unit, it can negotiate this technique as a means of saving its members' jobs.

Where no union exists, a company can arbitrarily cut its payroll. No one wants to take a pay cut, of course, but some people aren't willing to suffer a small personal loss to save even a close colleague's job. Unless management can "sell" it to employees by appealing to their nobler motives, a pay cut causes more problems than it solves.

➤ **Work sharing.** All team members share the work that remains after jobs are eliminated. The standard work week is reduced by working fewer hours each day or fewer days each week; another alternative involves working full weeks, but fewer weeks each month. With this strategy, hourly pay remains the same, but reduced hours decrease the payroll.

Work sharing enables companies to keep skilled employees during slow periods and enables teams to stay together. Employees earn less total pay but retain their benefits. Some states have amended their unemployment-insurance laws so that employees can collect some unemployment benefits during work-sharing periods.

➤ **Early retirement.** One way to minimize the number of employees who are laid off during an indefinite layoff is by encouraging older workers to retire earlier than they had planned. Under the Age Discrimination in Employment Act (see

Chapter 11), companies cannot compel employees to retire. They can offer incentives, however, to make it worth their while. When more highly paid senior employees leave a company, the payroll is reduced significantly.

Usually, an entire team isn't laid off. Unless you have a union contract or rigid policy which mandates that layoffs happen on a seniority basis, keep your best team members—those who can form the cadre of a new team if some of the laid-off members don't return when they're recalled.

Communication Breakdown

As much as you may want to keep laid-off team members available for recall, don't mislead them with false hopes. It not only isn't fair to someone who may turn down another job but also can have legal repercussions. Former employees have sued companies because of implied promises to rehire that didn't materialize.

Secret Weapons

Even if you know that a laid-off team member has accepted another job, offer the person the opportunity to return to your team. He may not be satisfied with the new job and may prefer to rejoin your team.

Keep in touch with laid-off team members. Phone them, and send them the company newsletter. Let them know that you still consider them part of your team and that you're looking forward to the recall so that you can work together again.

Rehiring Furloughed Workers

Seniority in most companies is the basis of both layoffs and recalls. The most senior employees are the last to be let go and the first to be rehired. But this approach isn't always the most desirable one. If you have no contractual obligation to do so, it may be more advantageous to rehire people according to the skills you need as the work expands. Your immediate need might be for a specialist in one area, but the most senior furloughed member may have a different skill. In this way, you can rebuild your team most effectively.

Downsizing: The Permanent Layoff

As defined earlier, downsizing involves the elimination of a job. An entire facility may be closed, an entire unit or department eliminated, or an organization restructured by doing away with certain jobs or entire job categories.

The downsizing of major corporations over the past few years (see Chapter 19) has eliminated tens of thousands of jobs, causing disruptions not only in the lives of laid-off workers but also often to entire communities. This section explains how to cope with the fallout from downsizing cuts.

"WARN"—The Law on Downsizing

To ease the burden on laid-off workers, Congress passed the Worker Adjustment and Retraining Notification Act (WARN). This law applies to companies that have 100 or more employees when they have mass layoffs or plant closings. The law exempts companies with fewer than 100 employees. Companies that are covered aren't required to comply with the law when they lay off small numbers of workers. It affects only mass layoffs.

A *mass layoff* is a layoff or reduction in hours at a single site that affects 500 or more full-time employees or 50 or more if they constitute at least 33 percent of an active, full-time workforce. A *reduction in hours* means to cut hours worked by 50 percent or more each month for a six-month period or longer. A company must give notice to employees who will be laid off at least 60 days before their final day of work. There are some exceptions to this rule, so check with your legal department to determine how it affects you.

Manager's Minute

When a company closes a facility or lays off a large number of people, you may need certain employees for continuing production. Offer them financial incentives so that they'll stay to the end after they've been given notice. At this point, you need them more than they need you.

Dealing with Downsizing and the EEO Laws

Until relatively recently, members of some minority groups and women weren't usually hired or promoted to certain positions because of past company policies or community practices. During the past few years, many companies have made significant strides in bringing minorities and women into the workforce.

If seniority is the policy followed during downsizing, minorities and women—who often have relatively low seniority—are often the first to have to leave. This practice can have an adverse effect on a company's affirmative action endeavors.

The Civil Rights Act of 1964 specifically exempts companies that have established a seniority system for layoffs and rehiring from being charged with discrimination if seniority is the basis for their actions. There is, however, an exception: If a member of a protected group can show that she personally experienced discrimination that resulted in lower seniority than if there had been no discrimination, that person may claim protection.

Suppose a woman was rejected for a job as a traveling auditor in 1980 because that company didn't hire women in that category and that she applied again in 1985 and was hired. If she is laid off later because of her lack of seniority, she can sue, claiming that, if not for that discriminatory policy, she would have had higher seniority. Each case is decided on its own merits.

Secret Weapons

When a team member leaves, reexamine the job description and specifications. A person performing a job often molds it to conform to his special interests or talents. You may not have the same view of the job, however, and this is your chance to readjust the job description.

Providing Continuing Benefits

Under the federal law known as COBRA (Consolidated Omnibus Budget Reconciliation Act), employees of companies with 20 or more employees are entitled to maintain their health insurance coverage for 18 months after they leave a company (disabled people can maintain it for 29 months). The company isn't expected to pay their premiums, however. Former employees who enroll in COBRA must pay the full premium at the same rate the company had been paying (usually considerably less than if they had to purchase individual insurance) plus a small administrative charge. COBRA also provides for continuing health insurance coverage for survivors of employees who die.

Processing Out Laid-Off Employees

The administrative details of the separation processing is usually done by the human resources department. In smaller companies or at branch facilities that have no HR department, a team leader usually handles the process.

Inform the people who are to be laid off at an appropriate time. If your company is covered by WARN, you must provide written notice 60 days in advance. If it's not covered by WARN, there's no required time, but it's only fair to give adequate notice about when they will be laid off. For temporary layoffs, two weeks is typical; for permanent layoffs, 30 days.

At the time of the separation, follow the guidelines below. Using a checklist will ensure that everything is covered.

➤ Discuss the continuation of benefits under COBRA, as discussed earlier in this chapter.

➤ Discuss severance pay. No law requires severance pay, but some union contracts do mandate it. Many companies voluntarily give severance pay to laid-off workers. The amount varies from company to company and often within a company by job category. Check your company policy.

➤ If appropriate, discuss the callback procedure.

➤ If an employee isn't receiving a final paycheck at the same time he is leaving the company, specify when it's expected.

➤ If provisions have been made to help laid-off employees seek other jobs, refer the person to whomever is responsible for that function.

➤ Retrieve company property: keys, credit cards, ID cards, tools, company computers used at home, computer log-on IDs, or computer passwords, for example.

➤ If an employee has incurred expenses for the company, such as travel and entertainment that have not yet been reimbursed, arrange for prompt attention to this matter.

➤ Answer any questions the employee has.

➤ Arrange for the employee to clean out her desk, office, or locker.

➤ Arrange for forwarding of any mail and messages that are received at the company after the employee leaves.

➤ Express your good wishes.

The Least You Need to Know

➤ By conducting good separation interviews, you can learn the real reasons that people leave a company and then take the appropriate preventive measures to reduce turnover.

➤ When a team member resigns, ease the transition by getting a status report about what she has been working on. Reassign that work until a successor is in place.

➤ Try to find alternatives to layoffs, such as work sharing, shorter hours, or general pay cuts.

➤ Keep in touch with temporarily laid-off team members to ensure the likelihood that they'll return when needed.

➤ If your company is covered by the WARN law, it must give 60 days notice when it closes a facility or lays off a large number of employees.

➤ COBRA mandates that laid-off employees be allowed to continue their medical insurance coverage for a specified period if they pay their own premiums.

Meanings and Gleanings Glossary

affirmative action   A written plan to commit to hiring women and minorities in proportion to their representation in the community where the firm is located. Required of companies that have government contracts in excess of $50,000 and more than 50 employees.

affirmative discipline   A technique in which employees, instead of being punished, are counseled and asked to make commitments to comply with company rules.

Age Discrimination in Employment Act (ADEA)   As amended, prohibits discrimination against individuals 40 years of age or older. Some state laws cover all persons over the age of 18.

Americans with Disabilities Act (ADA)   Prohibits discrimination against people who are physically or mentally challenged.

aptitude test   A test designed to determine the potential of candidates in specific areas, such as mechanical ability, clerical skills, or sales potential. The tests are helpful for screening inexperienced people to determine whether they have an aptitude for the type of work in which a company plans to train them. Most aptitude tests can be administered and scored by following a simple instruction sheet.

arbitration   A process in which two parties present their sides of a problem and an arbitrator decides how the problem should be resolved. *See also* **mediation**.

behavioral science   The study of how and why people behave the way they do.

benchmarking   A process of seeking organizations that have achieved success in an area and learning about their techniques and methods.

body language   A method people use to communicate—not only by what they say but also by their gestures, facial expressions, and movements.

bona fide occupational qualifications (BFOQ)   Positions for which a company is permitted to specify only a man or only a woman for a job. There must be clear-cut reasons, however, for why a person of only that gender can perform the job.

brainstorming   A technique for generating ideas in which participants are encouraged to voice any idea, no matter how "dumb" or useless it may be. By allowing participants to think freely and express ideas without fear of criticism, they can stretch their minds and make suggestions that may seem worthless but that may trigger an idea that has value in the mind of another participant.

buzzword   A bit of jargon—a phrase or term—that comes to be in popular use throughout society for a short period of time.

case study   A description of a real or simulated situation presented to trainees for analysis, discussion, and solution; used in graduate schools, seminars, and training programs to enable trainees to work on the types of problems they're most likely to meet on the job. Case studies are often drawn from the experiences of real companies.

channel of communication   The path information takes through the organization. If you want to give information to (or get it from) a person in another department, you first go to your boss, who goes to the supervisor of the other department, who, in turn, goes to the person with the information, who gets it and conveys it back through the same channels. By the time you get the information, it may have been distorted by a variety of interpretations.

charisma   The special charm some people have that secures for them the support and allegiance of other people.

Civil Rights Act of 1964   Title VII, as amended, prohibits discrimination in employment on the basis of race, color, sex, religion, and national origin.

coasters   Long-term employees (not likely to be fired because of their tenure) who have gone as far as they can and "coast along" until their retirement.

COBRA   An acronym for the Consolidated Omnibus Budget Reconciliation Act, in which employees of companies with 20 or more employees are entitled to maintain their health insurance coverage for 18 months after they leave the company (29 months for people who are disabled at the time they leave). The company isn't expected to pay their premiums. Former employees must pay the full premium at the same rate the company had been paying (usually considerably less than if they had to purchase individual insurance) plus a small administrative charge.

communication   The process by which information, ideas, and concepts are transmitted between persons and groups.

constructive discharge   When an employee quits because of purposeful unfair treatment on the job, it is "constructed" by the courts to be an involuntary termination.

control point   A point in a project at which you stop, examine what has been completed, and correct any errors that have been made (before they blow up into catastrophes).

counseling   A means of helping troubled associates overcome barriers to good performance. With careful listening, open discussion, and sound advice, a counselor helps identify problems, clarify misunderstandings, and plan solutions.

cross training   A method of training team members to perform the jobs of other people on the team so that every member is capable of doing all aspects of the team's work.

decentralization   When the focus of a business is shifted from one central facility where all decisions are made and most of the work is done to localized facilities where, within guidelines, decisions are made and work is performed autonomously.

delegation   A process that enables you to position the right work at the right responsibility level, helping both you and the team members you delegate to expand your skills and contributions, while ensuring that all work gets done in a timely manner by the right person with the right experience or interest in the right topic.

documentation   A written description of all disciplinary actions taken by a company to protect it in case of legal actions. ("If it ain't written down, it ain't never happened.")

downsize   To lay off employees, primarily when business is slow, so that a company can reduce costs. Downsizing differs from traditional layoffs in that total job categories are eliminated—people who held these jobs have little chance of being rehired *See also* **layoff.**

employee assistance program (EAP)   A company-sponsored counseling service. Many companies have instituted these types of programs to help their employees deal with personal problems that interfere with productivity. The counselors aren't company employees; they're outside experts who are retained on an as-needed basis.

employee stock-ownership program (ESOP)   A program in which a major portion of a company's stock is given or sold to employees so that they actually own the company.

employment at will   A legal concept under which an employee is hired and can be fired at the will of the employer. Unless restricted by law or contract, the employer has the right to refuse to hire an applicant or to terminate an employee for any reason or for no reason at all.

empowerment   Sharing your managerial power with the people over whom you have that power.

Equal Pay Act of 1963   An act which requires that the gender of an employee not be considered in determining salary (equal pay for equal work).

goals/objectives   Interchangeable terms to describe an organization's or individual's desired long-run results.

going rate   An amount paid to employees to keep them from leaving a company.

365

grievance   A formal complaint, usually based on the violation of a union contract or formal company policy.

gripe   An informal complaint about working conditions or other aspects of an employee/company relationship.

halo effect   The assumption that, because of one outstanding characteristic, all of an applicant's characteristics are outstanding (that person then "wears a halo"). The opposite is the *pitchfork effect,* or the symbol of the devil: You assume that, because one trait is so poor, the person is entirely bad.

hot button   The one thing in a person's makeup that really gets him excited—positively or negatively. (To really reach someone, find that person's hot button.)

"I" meeting   An idea-generating meeting at which each participant presents at least one idea for solving the problem being considered.

intelligence test   Like the IQ test administered in schools, this test measures the ability to learn. It varies from brief, simple exercises that can be administered by people with little training to highly sophisticated tests that must be administered by a person with a Ph.D. in psychology.

job analysis   The process of determining the duties, functions, and responsibilities of a job (the *job description)* and the requirements for the successful performance of a job (the *job specifications*).

job bank   A computerized list of the capabilities of all employees in an organization.

job description   A listing of the duties, responsibilities, and results a job requires.

job enrichment   Redesigning jobs to provide diversity, challenge, and commitment (and to alleviate boredom).

job-instruction training (JIT)   A systematic approach to training that has four steps: preparation, presentation, performance, and follow-up.

job posting   A listing on company bulletin boards of the specifications for an available position. Any employee who is interested can apply. After preliminary screening by the human resources department, employees who meet the basic requirements are interviewed.

job specifications   The requirements an applicant should possess to successfully perform a job.

joint leader/associate evaluations   Using the same evaluation format, associates evaluate their own performance. The leader also evaluates the performance. The final report results from a collaborative discussion between leader and associate.

just-in-time delivery   Rather than store large inventories of supplies, companies today arrange with suppliers to deliver supplies as needed. The project manager or team leader must interface with the suppliers to schedule and ensure that supplies are delivered at the exact time they're needed.

KITA   *A kick in the* you-know-what.

KRA (key results area)   An aspect of a job in which employees must concentrate time and attention to ensure that they achieve the goals for that job.

lateral thinking   Looking at a problem from different angles that may give new insights into its solutions (instead of approaching it by logical thinking).

layoff   Termination of employees permanently or for a specific period of time due to lack of work or restructuring of an organization.

leadership   The art of guiding people in a manner that commands their respect, confidence, and wholehearted cooperation.

M.O. (method, or mode, of operation)   The patterns of behavior a person habitually follows in performing work.

management   The process of achieving specific results by effectively using an organization's available resources (money, materials, equipment, information, and employees).

mediation   A process in which two parties present their sides and a mediator works with them to reach a mutually satisfactory solution. *See also* **arbitration.**

mentor   A team member assigned to act as counselor, trainer, and "big brother" or "big sister" to a new member.

motivators   Factors that stimulate a person to expend more energy, effort, and enthusiasm in a job. *See also* **satisfiers.**

negative personality   A person's outlook in which any suggestion is taken as a personal affront, any new assignment is accepted with reluctance, and relations with coworkers and leaders are usually considered confrontational.

network   To make contacts with managers in other companies to whom you can turn for suggestions and ideas.

objective   *See* **goals.**

open book management   A management style in which employees are considered full partners in the operation of a business. One characteristic of this management style is that employees have a direct stake in their company's success (if the business is profitable, they share in the profits; if not, there are no profits to share). Another characteristic is that every employee has access to numbers that are critical to tracking the company's performance and is given the training and tools to understand them.

opportunity   The combination of being in the right place at the right time and having the ability and desire to take advantage of it.

outsourcing   Contracting to outside sources any work that previously had been done in-house. As companies become "leaner and meaner," they outsource activities that can be done more effectively by outside specialists. Some examples are payroll, traffic, training, computer programming, advertising, and certain manufacturing activities.

367

ownership   A feeling that you're a full partner in the development and implementation of a project, committed to its successful achievement.

performance standards   The results expected from persons performing a job. For performance standards to be meaningful, every person doing that job should know and accept these standards.

performance test   A test that measures how well candidates can do the job for which they apply (for example, operating a lathe, entering data into a computer, writing advertising copy, or proofreading manuscripts). When job performance cannot be tested directly, a company may use written or oral tests about job knowledge.

personality test   A test designed to identify personality characteristics that varies from *Readers Digest*-type quickie questionnaires to highly sophisticated psychological evaluations.

piece work   A system of compensation in which earnings are based solely on the number of units produced.

pitchfork effect   *See* **halo effect.**

platinum rule   "Do unto others as they would have you do unto them."

prioritize   To rank tasks, by determining their degree of importance, to accomplish your goals on the job or in your life and in taking action accordingly—putting first things first.

profession   An occupation requiring special training or advanced study in a specialized field. Physicians, lawyers, psychologists, and engineers all have to take advanced education and pass examinations to qualify for certification in their professions.

progressive discipline   A systematic approach to correcting infractions of rules. A typical program has six steps, the first of which is an informal warning. If this step isn't successful, it's followed by (as necessary) a disciplinary interview, a written warning, probation, suspension, and, possibly, termination.

project manager   A team leader assigned to head up a specific project, such as the design and manufacture of an electronic system or the development and marketing of a new product.

quality circles   Groups of workers who voluntarily meet on a regular basis to discuss ideas about improving the quality of a product or service they produce.

real time   What's going on here and now. The actual time in which a process occurs (for example, a computer can report real-time data or information about the status of a situation as of the time it's provided).

recruit   To seek candidates to be considered for employment, usually done by personnel or human resources departments.

reengineer   To radically restructure the design of business processes (not just tinker with methods and procedures). When companies reengineer their processes, its managers must rethink everything they're doing in order to take advantage of the changes that will be made.

religious practices   Practices that include, according to the EEOC, not only traditional religious beliefs but also moral and ethical beliefs and any beliefs an individual holds "with the strength of a traditional religious view."

results oriented evaluation system   A system in which performance expectations are agreed on at the beginning of a period and measured at the end of that period. At that time, new goals are developed, which are to be measured at the end of the next period.

role playing   A variation of case studies in which participants act out the parts of the characters involved. Used chiefly in studying problems in which interaction between characters is a major aspect.

satisfiers   Also called maintenance factors; the factors—including working conditions, money, and benefits—employees must get from a job in order to expend even minimum effort in performing their work. After employees are satisfied with these factors, however, just giving them more of the same factor doesn't motivate them to work harder. *See* **motivators.**

selection   A process of screening applicants to determine their suitability for a position. Preliminary screening is usually done by the human resources department; subsequent screening is done by supervisors or team leaders.

self-esteem   The way you feel about yourself. If you think of yourself as a success, you will be a success; if you think of yourself as second-rate, you will always be second-rate—unless you change your self-perception. And it *can* be done.

self-directed team   A team with no permanent team leader; team members are self-managed. Some teams have permanent administrative leaders to deal with the paperwork, but members rotate as project leaders. Team members schedule work, hire and train new members, budget funds, and monitor their own performance.

sexual harassment   Any unwelcome sexual advances or requests for sexual favors, or any conduct of a sexual nature when an employer makes submission to sexual advances a term or condition of employment, either initially or later on; or when submission or rejection is used as a basis of working conditions, including promotion, salary adjustment, assignment of work, and termination, or has the effect of interfering with an individual's work or creating a hostile or intimidating work environment.

simulcast   To bring together the audio and video so that they interact and intensify the message that's being communicated.

single use plan   A plan developed for a specific nonrecurring situation; for example, introducing a new product, moving to a new location, or opening a new facility.

SOP (standard operating procedure)   A set of standard practices in which company plans and policies are detailed (sometimes called "the company bible").

spontaneous termination   A situation in which an employee is discharged without progressive discipline, usually precipitated by an egregious violation of company rules such as fighting, drunkenness, or gross insubordination. *See* **progressive discipline.**

stress or distress   A chronic state of anxiety caused by unremitting pressures of job, personal, or societal problems.

synergy   Two or more people or units working together so that the contributions of each enhances the results by more than the individual contribution by itself. "The whole is greater than the sum of its parts," or 2 + 2 may equal more than 4.

team   A group of people who collaborate and interact synergistically in working toward a common goal.

telecommuting   Technology that enables a person to perform work at home or at a location remote from a central office by receiving assignments and submitting completed work via computer.

total quality management   A management system in which the focus of an entire company is placed on producing high-quality products or services. It involves statistical processes, training in both the technical and intangible aspects of quality management, and the commitment of all levels of employees to work toward continuous improvement.

training manuals   Handbooks for teaching routine tasks; they make the training process easy for both trainer and trainees and can always be referred to when an employee is in doubt about what to do.

trait system of performance evaluation   A system in which employees are rated on a series of traits, such as quantity and quality of work, attendance, and initiative. Ratings are usually measured on a scale from poor to superior.

upward communication   The flow of ideas, suggestions, and comments from people in lower echelons of the organization to those in decision-making positions.

work sharing   An alternative to layoffs in which all team members share the work that remains after some jobs are eliminated. The standard work week is reduced by working fewer hours each day or fewer days each week. Another alternative is working full weeks, but fewer weeks each month. The hourly pay remains the same, but because of reduced hours, the payroll is decreased.

WARN (Worker Adjustment and Retraining Notification Act)   A law that applies to companies that have 100 or more employees when a mass layoff or plant closing occurs. Notice must be given to those employees at least 60 days before their final day of work. There are some exceptions to this rule, so check with your legal department to determine how it affects you.

Publications Dealing With Managing People

The field of management is dynamic. Companies experiment with new approaches. New laws and new interpretations of old laws are promulgated by state and federal government agencies. The ups and downs of the economy change the ways organizations deal with their employees.

Managers, team leaders, and others who deal with people problems must keep up with what's going on. The best way to be on the cutting edge of change is to read regularly several of the magazines that cover these matters.

Nearly every industry and profession has periodicals devoted to its field—and most of these magazines have occasional articles on management techniques and interpersonal relations. Such periodicals are excellent sources of information.

Here is a list of some of the better publications that either specialize in the art of management or have significant coverage of it.

Across the Board
The Conference Board
845 Third Avenue
New York, NY 10022
Phone: 212-339-0345
Fax: 212-980-7014
Web site: www.conference-board.org

Business Week
1221 Avenue of the Americas
New York, NY 10020
Phone: 800-635-1200
Fax: 609-426-5434
Web site: www.businessweek.com

Forbes
60 Fifth Avenue
New York, NY 10011
Phone: 800-888-9896
Fax: 212-206-5118
Web site: www.forbes.com

Fortune
Time & Life Building
Rockefeller Center
New York, NY 10020
Phone: 800-621-8000
Fax: 212-522-7682
Web site: www.fortune.com

Harvard Business Review
60 Harvard Way
Boston, MA 02163
Phone: 800-274-3214
Fax: 617-475-9933
Web site: www.hbsp.harvard.edu

HR Magazine
Society for Human Resources
Management
1800 Duke Street
Alexandria, VA 22314
Phone: 703-548-3440
Fax: 703-836-0367
Web site: www.shrm.org

Management Review
American Management Association
Box 319
Saranac Lake, NY 12983
Phone: 800-262-9699
Fax: 518-891-3653
Web site: www.amanet.org

Nations Business
711 Third Avenue
New York, NY 10017
Phone: 212-692-2215
E-mail: editor@nbmag.com

Training
50 S. 9th Street
Minneapolis, MN 55402
Phone: 612-333-0471
Fax: 612-333-6526
Web site: www.trainingsupersite.com

Training and Development
American Society for Training and
Development
1640 King Street
Alexandria, VA 22314
Phone: 703-683-8100
Fax: 703-683-9203
Web site: www.astd.org

Workforce
245 Fischer Avenue
Costa Mesa, CA 92626
Phone: 714-751-1883
Fax: 714-751-4106
Web site: www.workforce.com

Working Woman
135 W. 50th Street
New York, NY 10020
Phone: 800-234-9765
Fax: 212-445-6186
E-mail: wwmagazine@aol.com

Associations Dealing with Human Resource Matters

Professional societies in your industry are excellent sources of information. Membership in one or more of these groups can give you access to the latest developments in your field, experiences of other members in dealing with problems similar to yours, opportunities at meetings and conventions to meet your peers in other organizations, and often, resource material from other companies' libraries or archives.

Here is a list of associations that may be of value to you.

American Association of Industrial Management (AAIM)
293 Bridge Street
Springfield, MA 01103
Phone: 413-737-8766
Fax: 413-737-9724

> An association of managers of manufacturing organizations. Provides publications and special reports.

American Management Association (AMA)
1601 Broadway
New York, NY 10019
Phone: 212-586-8100
Fax: 212-903-8168
Web site: www.amanet.org

> Membership is by company. Provides seminars, publications, and library facilities on all aspects of management.

American Society for Training & Development (ASTD)
1640 King Street
Alexandria, VA 22313
Phone: 703-683-8100
Fax: 703-683-8103
Web site: www.astd.org

> Dedicated to professionalism in training and development of personnel. Local chapters throughout United States. Annual national convention. Publications include magazine, special reports, and books.

Employee Assistance Society of North America (EASNA)
PO Box 634
New Hope, PA 18938
Phone: 215-891-9538
Fax: 215-891-9538
E-mail: 72722.465@compuserve.com

> Source to locate individuals and organizations that provide various types of employee assistance programs.

International Foundation of Employee Benefit Plans (IFEBP)
18700 West Bluemound Road
Bloomfield, WI 53008
Phone: 414-786-7100
Fax: 414-786-8670
E-mail: pr@ifebp.org

> Excellent source of information on employee benefits. Accredits benefits specialists.

National Association of Personnel Services (NAPS)
3133 Mt. Vernon Avenue
Alexandria, VA 22305
Phone: 703-684-0180
Fax: 703-684-0071
E-mail: naps@dc.infi.net

> Source of information about private employment agencies.

National Association of Temporary and Staffing Services (NATSS)
119 S. St. Asaph Street
Alexandria, VA 22314
Phone: 703-549-6287
Fax: 703-549-4808
E-mail: natss@natss.com

Provides information on temporary personnel agencies.

Society for Advancement of Management (SAM)
630 Ocean Drive
Corpus Christi, TX 78412
Phone: 540-342-5563
Fax: 512-994-2725

Provides publications and conferences on various aspects of management.

Society for Human Resources Management (SHRM)
1800 Duke Street
Alexandria, VA 22314
Phone: 703-548-3440
Fax: 703-836-0367
E-mail: shrm@shrm.org

Members are human resource specialists in all types of companies and organizations. Provides publications, special reports, and books. Local chapters throughout the United States conduct monthly meetings. National convention annually.

Women in Management
30 North Michigan Avenue
Chicago, IL 60602
Phone: 312-263-3636
Fax: 312-372-8738

Dedicated to special problems of women in management positions.

Index

U-V